To

Alice, Arthur and John

TRANSFERABLE PERSONAL SKILLS

A Student Guide

DAVID W G HIND
SENIOR LECTURER IN MARKETING & TOURISM MANAGEMENT
NEWCASTLE UPON TYNE POLYTECHNIC

Design by Flora Pearson of Computer Design, Durham
Illustrations by Richard Draper

Published in Great Britain by Business Education Publishers Limited, Leighton House, 10 Grange Crescent, Sunderland, Tyne and Wear SR2 7BN

Tel: 091 567 4963

ISBN 0-907679-22-6

First published 1989

Reprinted 1990

Printed in Great Britain by Athenaeum Press Limited, Unit 3, Mill Lane Industrial Estate, Newcastle upon Tyne.

Tel: 091 273 7737

PREFACE

The term 'transferable personal skill' is new. Defining a transferable personal skill is quite easy - it is a skill personal to the individual that can be used in many different situations. A few years ago, before the term was introduced, such skills were often quoted as being communication skills, interpersonal skills or social skills. Recently, however, it has been felt that there are other personal skills that the individual needs to master in addition to these.

The feeling now is that individuals need to be competent at problem solving; decision taking; working with, and leading others; expressing their ideas numerically, in written and oral forms of presentation; and handling interpersonal encounters such as negotiation sessions or interviews. The demand for individuals to become competent in these areas has come primarily from employers.

Surveys have been conducted to establish what employers think about the young people they recruit from colleges. A major and frequently noted finding is that the employers are disappointed with their new recruits' abilities to articulate their ideas, to work effectively with others, to solve problems and to use their initiative. The employers in their recruitment and selection processes now place great store on the applicants' competence with regard to these skills.

In response to these demands from employers, the education sector is now paying great attention to the whole area of transferable personal skills training. The educational validating bodies such as BTEC, CNAA and the universities, as well as government bodies like the Training Agency, are actively encouraging universities, polytechnics and colleges to integrate transferable personal skills training into all their courses.

It is the aim of the education sector to ensure that all young people embarking on their careers have the skills that are sought by employers. While employers' needs for specific areas of subject knowledge vary over time, their demand for young people with competent transferable personal skills will never decline.

At a time when the demand is growing for young people to display competent transferable personal skills, what books are available on the subject? There have been many texts published on communication skills, interpersonal skills, social skills, negotiating, leadership, presentation skills - and all the other skills sought by employers. However, each text tends to concentrate on only one or two of the personal skills, and might adopt a theoretical stance rather than a practical one. This results in a book that is lengthy and necessitates much reading before an understanding is gained of how such skills can be applied in practice. Currently, there are few books that draw together all the skills that have been identified by employers and the educational validating bodies, into a coherent text that is totally practical in nature.

It is with this in mind that this book has been written. The author in writing the text has tried to make it as 'reader-friendly' as possible. The learner's viewpoint has been firmly considered - what type of book do learners need in order to help them to develop further their transferable personal skills? The assumption that has been made is that learners need a text that is straight-to-the-point; is written in a non-academic way (skills learning is highly practical); that divides each skill into its constituent parts; and provides a series of checklists that can be referred to time and again, to indicate what is good practice with each of the skills that is covered. Thus, a prime purpose of this book is to act as the learner's reference text that can be read whenever a particular transferable personal skill has to be used.

If the reader wishes to investigate the theoretical aspects underpinning transferable personal skills there are many scholarly, refereed books available. However, if the reader wishes to find out how to apply such skills in practise then this text will be of value.

Having set out the purpose of this book, and its style of presentation, who should read it? The book has been written to include a wide variety of different transferable personal skills - those required by employers and the educational validating bodies, and additional ones that inevitably will be of much benefit to the individual learner. The skills covered are highly transferable to different situations and can be used by many different people.

Thus, this book itself is highly transferable. The content discussed means that the readership profile is wide. Students at polytechnics and universities will find that skills training features more prominently in their learning and will benefit from using this book. People in employment wishing to develop further their personal skills will find the points discussed of value to them. Individuals following a self-development programme in skills training will learn from reading this text. Teachers and trainers who wish to improve the transferable personal skills of their students will be able to use this text as a reference source to inform them what constitutes a competent level of skills performance. Indeed, all those who are interested in transferable skills development will gain from studying the guidelines discussed in the following chapters.

The content of this book has been gained from the author's experience as a Senior Lecturer in Marketing and Tourism Management at Newcastle-upon-Tyne Polytechnic. A central part of his teaching has been to develop further the transferable personal skills of the students he has been teaching. As a result of carrying out research into skills development much has been learned about the subject. The content of this book is also based on established principles for the implementation of the various skills - thus it draws on 'common knowledge'.

This book, therefore, is written by a practitioner of skills training, rather than by an academic interested in the theoretical and philosophical issues involved in the subject. It has been written by a practitioner whose prime concern is to improve the skills performance of his students in practical settings rather than to equip them to be able to debate the subject in abstract essay questions.

The author acknowledges that much of what is written is not new, but accepted norms of behaviour. What is novel is the drawing together of all the skills into one book and presenting the content in a totally practical manner.

THE AUTHOR

David Hind is a Senior Lecturer in Marketing and Tourism Management at Newcastle-upon-Tyne Polytechnic. His career has been spent entirely in the Service Sector.

Initially he worked for the National Westminster Bank where his responsibilities included organising training courses for new recruits and he spent much of this time developing their personal skills. Following this, David moved into the Travel and Tourism Industry working for specialist adventure tour operators in W. Europe, N. America and S.E. Asia. These experiences confirmed to him the need for all employees to develop competent transferable personal skills.

Since entering education a major part of David's teaching, research, and publication has centred around transferable personal skills training.

ACKNOWLEDGEMENTS

In writing this book I would like to express my gratitude to all those colleagues and friends who have provided constructive comments on the content and format of the text. I would also like to thank Peter Hughes, Paul Callaghan and John Ellison who edited the book, Richard Draper who provided the illustrations and Flora Pearson who designed the cover.

DWGH

Newcastle-upon-Tyne
1988

CONTENTS

Chapter One

INTRODUCING TRANSFERABLE PERSONAL SKILLS

Chapter One

INTRODUCING TRANSFERABLE PERSONAL SKILLS

WHAT ARE TRANSFERABLE PERSONAL SKILLS?

Transferable personal skills (TPS) are a set of social behaviours and skills that you can learn to help you interact with other people in a variety of different situations. These social behaviours and skills are personal to you, although they do not necessarily come naturally, and once mastered can be applied in a variety of different situations, hence they are transferable.

What constitutes a TPS is more difficult to decide as many different types of skill can be identified. In recent years, such skills were thought to focus primarily around communication, interpersonal, or social skills. It was felt that individuals ought to be effective oral communicators, or competent inter-relators with other people. The thrust now, though, is for a wider range of skills to be identified, skills which will be of use in many different situations.

The skills discussed in this book include not only the traditional ones of communication, interpersonal and social skills, but also learning and study skills, body language skills, and numeracy skills. The high order, complex TPS of working with, and leading other people, problem solving, decision making and critical thinking are covered as are skills in information gathering and consultancy. Special applications of a variety of skills are drawn together in chapters on making a presentation, being interviewed, and taking part in sales or negotiation sessions.

The reason for including such TPS in this book is that these are felt to be the core skills that you will need to master to assist with your career development. All individuals have to be able to communicate with others in a variety of different styles. Oral communication occurs through informal conversation as well as by formal presentation. Business letters and reports have to be written, as do curriculum vitae and application forms. When you are called for an interview you must know how to behave in order to be successful. All individuals are involved with selling and negotiating situations - whether it be 'selling' themselves at interviews or negotiating with colleagues as to who will complete a certain task. In order to influence others assertive skills are required.

Thus, TPS extend beyond those skills important to ourselves as individuals, and encompass how we interact and work with other people. Much work is undertaken in groups so group skills need to be developed. Just as it is important for individuals to be able to work harmoniously as group members it is also important for them to be able to analyse problems and to take decisions.

You can improve your problem solving and decision making by following systematic procedures. Information is frequently required to assist the thinking processes involved with problem solving and decision making, and you need to be aware of how to gather valid and reliable information. When undertaking projects for other people, such as gathering information, in which you act as a consultant, a credible working relationship has to be established with the client. Being aware of consultancy skills will help you in this process.

Encompassing all of the abovementioned skills are learning and study skills. TPS are not developed overnight but over a considerable period of time. To be able to learn from each new business and social encounter and to be able to structure a self-development programme you must be aware of how learning and studying can be made more effective.

WHY ARE TRANSFERABLE PERSONAL SKILLS IMPORTANT?

The demand for individuals to master successfully a wide portfolio of TPS is a relatively new trend that is now being fully supported from both the public and private sectors. It has come from a number of different sources: employers, educational validating bodies, and government.

In April 1986 The Sunday Times published the results of a survey conducted by Peter Wilby. The purpose of the research was to establish the level of satisfaction of employers with the young people they recruited from colleges. In total some 450 employers completed the questionnaire. The findings from the research make interesting reading.

While the employers were generally satisfied with the subject knowledge of their new recruits, they explicitly stated that they were dissatisfied with the TPS of the young people. The employers were of the opinion that their young recruits were inarticulate, tongue-tied, showed little initiative, and were unable to work effectively with other people. A conclusion that came from the research was that young people, in order to be successful in the career market place, would need to develop competent and effective TPS.

This view is further supported when reference is made to career vacancies advertised in the press. Some career advertisements are very explicit when detailing the profile of the likely candidate for the post:

> "You are determined and energetic. You have a high level of numeracy, literacy and presentation skills. And you're very flexible...capable of working

effectively as part of a team or when interfacing with management and colleagues at all levels. You have the ability...proven or latent...to manage people now or in the not-too-distant future, and make things happen."

PA Personnel Services, 1987

Such an advertisement leaves no doubt as to the TPS that the successful applicant will need to display. Indeed, it could be asserted that employers are now attaching more importance to young recruits' TPS than they do to their subject knowledge or technical abilities.

Marks and Spencer, when selecting recruits for its Management Training Programme, is just as interested in selecting individuals who display management aptitude, as well as academic achievement. The selectors look for leadership skills, sensitivity towards other people, decisiveness, and flexibility. British Aerospace, who recruit large numbers of engineers and computer scientists, also look for evidence of the ability to lead, to initiate new ideas, to communicate, and to solve problems when appraising new employees. Unilever is not only interested in recruiting intelligent employees, but looks for people who are able to analyse problems rapidly and accurately, who can work in groups, are able to communicate with other people and to influence them. Indeed, these abilities appear on the 'shopping list' of many major employers from all industrial sectors - engineering, manufacturing, mining, as well as the service sector.

From the above discussion it is apparent that the career market place is now changing from being dominated solely by the bright, academically gifted person, to being the domain of the person who has management aptitude, displayed in their TPS, in addition to intellectual abilities.

In response to the demands of employers, the educational validating bodies are paying much attention to the whole area of TPS training. TPS development is now featuring prominently on Business & Technical Education Council courses (BTEC), on courses validated by the Council for National Academic Awards (CNAA), as well as by the universities. BTEC have produced a set of common skills that its courses must adopt. BTEC expects the TPS of students to be developed through all the units being studied, and that these skills will be assessed and contribute towards each student's overall grade.

Thus, young people currently studying courses of further and higher education are being required to develop their TPS and to use their academic environment as a practice ground for developing abilities that will be appropriate for their future careers. In their assignments students are no longer assessed only on their subject knowledge or technical abilities but also on their TPS. To be successful at attaining high grades in this area students need to be aware of what a competent level of performance is for each TPS that is being assessed. The chapters in this book will provide such an insight.

This thrust in curriculum development is being supported by the government which in a White Paper published on 1 April 1987, stated that:

> "...education must also ensure, for instance, the further development of skills in communication and numeracy and the fostering of positive attitudes to enterprise and work generally."

In 1987 it was announced that £100 million would be made available by the Manpower Services Commission (MSC) to fund the integration of enterprise initiatives into courses of education. 'Enterprise' is defined by the MSC as the creation and response to opportunities, the generation of ideas and seeing them through, and accepting responsibility and accountability. The MSC (now the Training Commission) sees enterprise as applying to all human endeavour, in public and voluntary service as well as in industry and commerce. A major component of enterprise skills are TPS. Thus, individuals who seek to become entrepreneurs will need to be influencers and persuaders, as well as information gatherers, problem solvers and decision takers. By developing abilities in these areas entrepreneurial skills will be enhanced.

There is clearly, therefore, an external justification for you to develop your TPS. Additionally, such development will benefit you personally. TPS training involves much self-evaluation - analysing and judging your own abilities. This process will inevitably result in your getting to know yourself better. When this has been achieved you will be able to plan your future - which career will be most suited to your skills, which should be avoided. The self-evaluation process will also probably identify any characteristics that might hinder your inter-relationships with other people. When such traits have been identified, steps can be taken to overcome them, making you more 'personable' or sociable.

The training programme will involve much practice and rehearsal of new behaviours and skills. As time progresses and these new behaviours become part of your portfolio of TPS, your self-confidence and self-assurance will improve. Situations that once were felt to be daunting, such as interviews or formal presentations, now become enjoyable experiences in which you are happy to display your abilities to other people. For some people these specific personal benefits of TPS training are more important than the wider career implications, especially for the more introverted individual who shies away from social encounters.

The discussion in this section indicates that it is most important for you to develop competent TPS. From an employment perspective, employers will be looking more closely at the personal skills of applicants when deciding who to recruit for a career vacancy. To prepare young people for their careers, the educational institutions are now including TPS training into many more courses, and formally assessing the abilities of their students, the grades from which will contribute to the students' overall qualification. Thus, the value of mastering a wide portfolio of TPS cannot be understated.

WHO SHOULD DEVELOP COMPETENT TRANSFERABLE PERSONAL SKILLS?

Anyone who wants to improve their career prospects will need to master effective TPS. Students on all courses of further and higher education will need to develop their TPS to help them achieve their full career potential. People looking for employment will have much to gain by being able to offer such abilities to prospective employers and people already in employment will gain by building on their TPS strengths and overcoming their weaknesses. People who simply wish to become more self-confident, or wish to be able to influence other people more effectively will gain by improving their TPS and following the guidelines that are provided in this book.

The points discussed in this book are highly transferable and will be of value to all who are concerned with improving their interpersonal effectiveness, or that of their students.

HOW ARE TRANSFERABLE PERSONAL SKILLS DEVELOPED?

TPS are not developed overnight. In fact the TPS learning process is an arduous, life long process with each new business and social encounter offering you the opportunity to develop further your TPS. Learning occurs in a variety of ways.

Trial and error of new skills and behaviours will indicate to you which TPS are effective in different situations. Reflection on these skills and behaviours will assist the learning process. In addition to learning by trial and error, formal training will also be of value.

Stru .tured learning in a classroom environment will be important, especially if more active learning strategies such as role-playing exercises are used. These allow you to practise new behaviours in a 'safe' and controlled setting, before they are tried out in the real world. Demonstrations, which you can later model, enable good practice to be followed at the outset. Texts, such as this, have a part to play as they can analyse the constituent components of various TPS and act as a permanent reference source.

In developing TPS each learning strategy mentioned above has to be considered. The challenge for you is to adopt a frame of mind which welcomes each learning strategy and views the development of TPS as a process that necessitates using the more active types of learning. A key element when developing new skills is that of practice. Only through active participation in the learning programme will you be able to practise, and hence further develop your abilities.

The nature of TPS training is potentially threatening to all learners as much embarrassment and offence could be caused when analysing the behaviour of each participant. Thus, to be successful, the learning has to be implemented in a sensitive way. Both learner and tutor must appreciate this. If an authoritarian approach is adopted by the tutor then the learners will feel reluctant to participate. Sensitivity must be shown to the feelings of all the participants - a TPS in its own right.

Chapter Two discusses in more detail how learning occurs. What is important to understand is that you can learn new skills and behaviours. As part of his teaching, the author always incorporates an element of TPS training into the learning activities of his students (see Hind, 1988). Research was conducted to evaluate the effectiveness of this training, the results

---

Hind, D.W.G, 1988 'Evaluating an Interpersonal Skills Training Programme', Business Education, Vol 9, No1.

of which were conclusive. Ninety six per cent of the students who completed a recent TPS training programme indicated that they felt that their personal skills had improved as a result of it. All the skills that were included in the programme showed a marked improvement as the programme developed. In addition to improving their skills, 98% of the students found the programme to be enjoyable, and 94% believed the 'quality' of the course had been enhanced because of it.

As a learner, you must appreciate that TPS training will not be easy. You will have to learn to evaluate your own TPS, where both your strengths and weaknesses are identified. For some learners this might mean self-confrontation, because for the first time in their lives they will see themselves as others do. This is all part of the TPS learning process as it is only when you see yourself as other people do that you can start to modify your behaviour so that more effective personal relationships and skills are established.

How, then, can this book help you in the TPS learning process?

THE PURPOSE OF TRANSFERABLE PERSONAL SKILLS TRAINING

All learning is concerned with changing behaviour, and TPS training is no different. The purpose of the training, though, is not to change your personality, but to allow you to become more competent at using a variety of TPS. As a result of the training, however, the learner may become a more 'personable' individual, more self confident or less anxious when thrust into unfamiliar situations.

The implications of this are important. TPS training is not designed to force you into conforming to rigid, stereotyped patterns of behaviour. Although guidelines can be given as to what a competent TPS is, it is not possible to suggest universal behaviours that can be used in each business or social encounter you will face. This is because each encounter will be different, and each person will bring different abilities to the situation. At its best, TPS training will broaden your range of behaviour and increase your awareness of the variety of transferable personal skills available.

Thus, a primary purpose of this book is to make you more aware of the TPS that have been identified by employers and educational validating bodies as being important to young people. As has been stated previously, if you master a variety of TPS you will be better placed to succeed in the career market place.

The following chapters look at TPS that have been identified as being important. Each TPS is outlined and then divided into its constituent parts. Checklists are used to draw your attention to the key components of each skill that is considered. This provides a practical reference guide to the constituent elements of each TPS. By this means, you will have close to hand points to be borne in mind when using any of the skills.

This book has been written to be used in two main ways. Firstly, it will be a useful complementary text to a formal period of TPS training that is developed by a tutor. When a particular personal skill is being covered in the programme, you can refer to the relevant chapter in this book to gain a knowledge and understanding of the constituent components of the skill under consideration. All the core skills that form the basis of many different types of TPS training programmes will be found in this book.

Secondly, this book will allow you to structure your own TPS self-development programme. For example, before an interview is attended, the checklists provided will inform you of the preparation stages you should go through in order to succeed at the interview. To learn from the behaviours used during the interview a post-evaluation process is outlined. Likewise, when a formal oral presentation is to be made, similar guidelines are provided.

In writing this book your needs as a learner have been borne firmly in mind. A major emphasis has been placed upon ensuring that all points made have a practical relevance. To achieve this, each chapter includes a series of checklists that you can follow when implementing a particular skill. By adopting this style it is hoped that the text is as practical as possible (TPS are only developed by practising them time and again). As a result of this approach little attention is paid to the underpinning theories that suggest why a particular skill should be used in a certain way in order to achieve a competent performance. There are other books that cover these areas of TPS development. It is felt that what is important for the reader of this book is to know and understand how a TPS should be, and can be, used in practical situations.

Please note that to avoid the implication that TPS relate to a single sex, the terms he and she are used in alternate chapters to refer to both males and females. In this way we hope to avoid the potential difficulty of sexual stereotyping.

Chapter Two

LEARNING AND STUDY SKILLS

Chapter Two

LEARNING AND STUDY SKILLS

You cannot develop transferable personal skills overnight. In fact it is a life-long process, and each time you meet a new situation in your business or social life it will provide you with the opportunity to try out new behaviours, to reflect on them and to evaluate them. If you are to manage this self-development programme successfully, you need to be aware of how you learn. You will also need study skills to help you learn both in the classroom and from private study in your own time. In this chapter we will examine learning and study skills which should help you with your own self-development. Indeed, learning and studying are TPS in their own right as once you have developed such skills they can be used in a wide variety of different settings.

LEARNING

Learning is the gaining over time of skills, knowledge, experience or attitudes. Learning is the process of changing your behaviour so that you will be able to do something that you were unable to do before the learning took place. When you have learnt something, you should be able to see and measure your change in behaviour and this will allow you and your tutors to decide how successful you have been in the learning process.

Learning takes place in a sequence involving three inter-related stages. These are shown below in a learning model.

The Learning Model

EXPERIENCE
of new behaviour and situations

LEARNING
of new behaviours
and situations

REFLECTION
of new behaviours
and situations
by self and peer
evaluation

Your existing experience of different situations in which you have found yourself, and the behaviour of different people which you have seen, form the building blocks for your new learning. From such experiences and observations you can reflect on your own abilities and identify your TPS strengths and weaknesses. Once you have done this, you can develop new forms of behaviour that will allow you to overcome your weaknesses and improve your strengths. In the chapters of this book we shall look at each of these three stages, particularly as they relate to TPS.

There are a number of different types of learning but for the purpose of this book we shall consider four main types:

1. Learning to do something
2. Learning to memorise something
3. Learning to understand something
4. Learning a skill

We shall look at each of these in turn.

1. LEARNING TO DO SOMETHING

You will face many situations which involve you in learning to do something, whether it is to give an oral presentation, write a report, or to interview an applicant for a job. Whatever the situation there is a simple process involving three steps you can apply:

(i)   determine the purpose of what you are trying to learn
(ii) identify the procedures involved
(iii) practise the task

(i) Determine the purpose

When learning to do something you must have a clear understanding of the purpose of what you are trying to achieve. You need to understand why you are giving the oral presentation, or the reason for writing the report, or why the interview is taking place.

In the same way, you need to identify the reasons for trying to develop your transferable personal skills. You can justify it on the grounds that employers now demand a high level of competence in such skills. Employers seek to recruit articulate people who can communicate, who are numerate, and have the ability to work in groups and to solve problems. If you do not possess such skills then you may find it much more difficult to progress in your career.

Therefore it is important that you recognise why you are developing these skills. If you do not, then you might lack motivation towards the TPS training programme. If this is the case, you will tend to lose concentration, pay little attention to any advice and information that is given to you, and so reduce the amount of progress that you will make.

(ii) Identify the procedures involved

When you have become clear about why you are learning to do something, you should then identify any procedures that need to be followed in order to complete the task successfully. In a number of situations there are norms or guidelines that you have to follow. For example, when you write a business letter there are conventions that should be followed if you want your letter to be laid out and presented in a professional way so that it will create a favourable impression on the person receiving it.

You should understand these procedures. If there are no norms or guidelines, you will have to use your own judgement to decide the most appropriate procedures to follow.

(iii) Practise the task

You will learn to do something successfully only by practising it. Once you have identified the procedures for completing the task, the next stage in the learning process is to practise, following any guidelines that are provided. This part of the cycle is important. You should try to follow all the guidelines correctly and accurately. You have to establish good habits for completing the task at the outset, as it will be difficult to correct bad habits at a later stage.

You will probably find that you have to learn the activities involved in completing the task at a relatively slow pace, practising each individual component until you have mastered it, and frequently refering to the norms or guidelines. As you successfully learn and memorise new tasks you can move on to more complex ones. With practice, your speed in completing the task will increase, and you will not need to refer to the guidelines so frequently.

One of the most commonly used methods of learning to do something is by a tutor giving a demonstration of how to complete a task successfully:

The Demonstration of a Task

Often one of the best ways of learning how to do something is to watch someone else doing it. The tutor can demonstrate how a particular task should be completed. For example, the tutor might show you the skills involved in interviewing an applicant for a post, or demonstrate how to use the voice effectively when giving an oral presentation. You will learn from such demonstrations only if you watch and listen to the tutor very carefully:

* Note the body language that is used by the tutor - for example, her hand gestures, her posture, her facial expressions, her eye contact and her appearance and dress.

* Listen carefully to how she uses her voice. When does she use different speeds of speech, and why? How frequently does she vary the tone of her voice, and to what effect?

* What types of speech does she use?. For example does she use witticisms or humour? How much jargon does she use? How does she introduce and conclude the speech?

* Does she use special equipment? For example, watch how she switches on and focuses the overhead projector. Which disk drive on the personal computer does she use?

* During the demonstration if you do not understand any activities that she demonstrates then you should ask questions until you do understand what is being done, and why it is being done.

* You should try to identify and understand the key points in the demonstration. For example, the tutor should draw your attention to the three stages of an oral presentation - the introduction, the development of the argument and the conclusion - and show how linking sentences can be used to add coherence to these stages.

* You should make additional notes to help you to memorise the sequence of events, and you should file these notes for future reference.

When the tutor has demonstrated the activity, you should practise it as soon as possible after the demonstration. You should use any equipment or aids that are required to undertake the activity. You should concentrate on doing the key activities slowly until you have achieved a certain level of competence and you are beginning to undertake the sequences in the process almost automatically without having to refer to your notes or other guidelines.

Written instructions for a task

Another way of learning to do something is by following written instructions. In some situations all that you will have are written instructions on how to complete the tasks involved. For instance when you buy a home computer, it is unlikely that a trainer will be included in the purchase price, only a written manual. The person who wrote the manual has hopefully paid considerable attention to making sure that it is easily understood. In reading such instructions, however, you need to follow certain guidelines:

* Read through the entire document, or at least an entire section, before putting into practice the instructions. Become familiar with all sections in the manual.

* Read through the manual or section again, as it is unlikely that you will understand all the points on the first reading.

* Start at the beginning of the manual, or the relevant section, and read slowly through the instructions, implementing exactly all the directions that are given. If problems arise then start again. Do not hurry the process, but work at a controlled pace.

If you follow these guidelines (providing the instructions have been reasonably well written) then you should complete all the necessary tasks successfully. If you make a mistake then do not worry as this should also be seen as part of the learning process. Sometimes it is the process of making mistakes which turns out to be the most memorable learning experience. If you do make an error, you should analyse it to find out what the problem is, and why it occurred. You should then repeat the correct way of completing the task until you have mastered it.

2. LEARNING TO MEMORISE SOMETHING

Much learning requires you to memorise something, whether it be sequences in a process, data, or the content of an oral presentation. Memorising something is the process of acquiring information, retaining it in your brain, and then being able to recall it at a later time. There are three components of your memory:

> (i) the sensory information storage system
> (ii) the short-term memory store
> (iii) the long-term memory store

(i) The sensory information storage system

This stage of the memory process involves you in receiving information from the environment through your senses. This may involve reading instructions from a manual, watching a demonstration given by the tutor, listening to an audio-tape, or touching, tasting or smelling something.

Sensory information is transmitted to your brain via your nervous system, but most of it is only retained for a matter of minutes before it is forgotten.

(ii) The short-term memory store

Some of the sensory information that your brain receives, however, is transferred to your short-term memory, especially sensory information that is already familiar to you. Here, you interpret the sensory information into a more meaningful form. It can then be recalled immediately, and combined with other knowledge, perceptions or ideas that you already have stored in your memory, helping you to understand what your senses are experiencing. The capacity of your short-term memory, though, is relatively small.

(iii) The long-term memory store

Your long-term memory has a greater capacity than your short-term memory and can recall information that has been accumulated over quite a long period of time. Thus, it is the most important part of the memory, and also the most complex.

You should aim to commit all the information that you consider to be important and relevant to your long-term memory so that you can recall it and use it at a later time. Information you have retained in your long-term memory can be used for many different purposes, such as recalling facts, helping to solve problems, and critical thinking. When you are learning something new, you do this best if information is transferred into your long-term memory store building upon your previous knowledge and understanding.

You can use a number of techniques to help store information in your long-term memory. The first stage in the process is to translate the information into a form that you can remember more easily. Association techniques are useful:

* Group similar pieces of information together. For example, it costs the same to fly from London to Bangkok as it does to fly from London to Delhi, Los Angeles, San Francisco or Nairobi.

* Pair information or things together - it costs the same to fly from London to Bangkok, Delhi, Los Angeles, San Francisco and Nairobi, and also takes the same flying time.

* You could make up a story linking these pieces of information together -Thai Airways fly from Bangkok to Delhi, then to Nairobi, before arriving in London en route to the west coast of America.

* You could try to visualise the information to be remembered - Bangkok visualised by its temples and palaces, Delhi by its rickshaws, Nairobi by African safaris, London by Buckingham Palace, Los Angeles by Hollywood and San Francisco by the Golden Gate bridge.

Once you have translated the information you wish to remember into a more memorable form, you should write it down, then read it out loud, and then read it through again, each time trying to commit more of the information to your long-term memory.

If you have to learn a great deal of information, you should break it down into discrete parts which are then the focus of your attention, with the repetition process continuing until you are able to recall all the information without having to refer to your notes. You can help this rote learning process, by using a number of special aids:

* Using rhymes to remember information - "thirty days hath September, April, June and November...".

* Using the first letter of key words to remember them - mnemonics, for example the marketing mix is referred to as the 4 P's - the product, promotion, price and place.

* Using word associations to differentiate between words which are pronounced the same but spelt differently for example associate stationary with a parked car and stationery with a pile of papers.

The easiest way to remember new things is to connect them with what you already know. This requires conscious efforts to link in the new material to your long-term memory. One way of doing this is to make notes of links with existing knowledge as you gain new information.

You will not help yourself to memorise things if you are mentally or physically tired. A tired mind will be unable to assimilate new information. You will stand a better chance of remembering information that you gain while your mind is fresh. You should avoid prolonged periods memorising information, especially those in excess of 2 hours. You should take breaks every 30 minutes when you should do something else - make a cup of coffee, or stretch your legs. This will help to refresh your mind and assist your memory process.

When you have completed the memorising period, you should immediately review what you have been studying. This should involve a quick re-read of any notes that you have made, listing again the main points. This should keep your level of recall high for the next 24 hours. The following day you should undertake a second review. This time it should be a quick review of the previous day's learning to reinforce the memory process, committing the information gained to your long-term memory. At the end of the week, you should review all the material you have learnt in totality, so that you can identify and understand the relationships between the various pieces of information. You should condense further any notes that you have made, but retain the originals for future reference.

After a month has elapsed you should follow the review process again, reading through your condensed notes and seeing how much of the original material you can remember. If you have any problems in recalling the information you should refer back to the original notes and re-read the relevant section until you have committed it to memory.

3. LEARNING TO UNDERSTAND SOMETHING

When you understand something you are able to explain it. Understanding something means comprehending it, whether it is a statement, an object, a concept or a principle. When you are learning to do something, it is important to understand the procedures in the process and then to practise them until they have been mastered. Memorising information involves being competent at using a variety of techniques that can assist with its recall. Learning to understand something is different. You will find rote learning (repetitive learning) of little use here and there is little scope for practice as understanding something involves mental processes as opposed to physical ones. How then, can something be understood? The starting point is to ask questions.

(i) Questions

You should ask questions of yourself as well as of other people. When you are listening to an explanation given by a tutor, or when you read instructions, you should ask yourself what are you listening to, or hearing, and what it means to you. For example after a talk on the nature of 'marketing' you should answer the question:

"What does marketing mean to me?"

At the same time you should be relating the new information to what you already know, and considering its implications. If you cannot answer the questions that you are asking yourself, then you should try and seek the answers from other people such as your tutors.

You need to ask open questions that demand more than a 'yes' or 'no' answer. You should try and develop a hierarchy of questions that follow the sequence:

"What", "Where", "When", "Who", and "How"

Sequencing questions in this way will allow you to take the answer and build the information upon the previous answer given. Your answers to these questions will provide information that will describe what is taking place, and will help further your understanding of the situation under consideration:

"What information do I need to solve the problem?"
"Where is this information to be found?"
"When should I obtain this information?"
"Who will be able to provide it for me?"
"How should I gather the information?"

If you are trying to find an explanation to something concentrate on questions beginning with "Why":

"Why has this problem developed?"
"Why can't you help me?"

You should ask questions until you understand the situation. This may well require some persistence on your part. If the answers that you are getting are not helping you to understand what you wish to know, then re-phrase the questions until you get a better answer. If persistent questioning still does not provide you with a clearer picture of the situation, however, try making comparisons with similar situations.

(ii) Comparisons

Look at similar situations and circumstances to see if there are any relationships or patterns which might help you to explain what you are trying to find out. By comparing situations and dividing each into its constituent parts, you can achieve a better understanding of what you are studying. For example, if you are trying to understand what constitutes an effective oral presentation, you might find it useful to analyse the oral presentation of an accomplished public speaker and identify the factors that account for her success. When you have done this you will find that it is possible to develop a checklist of factors that you can use to compare and contrast the oral presentation skills of others. The checklist might look something like this.

The accomplished public speaker will use:

a) different tones of voice;
b) different speeds of speech;
c) inflection in the voice;
d) facial expressions to support her verbal message which will be pleasing to the audience;

e) gestures that are supportive and complementary to the message, rather than distracting and repetitive;

f) a posture which displays an air of self-respect and self-confidence.

The unaccomplished public speaker will exhibit characteristics that are the opposite of these.

(iii) Solving problems

We shall discuss the topic of problem solving in greater depth in Chapter Twelve but for the purpose of this section, you need to appreciate that the process of solving problems can help when you are trying to understand something. Solving problems involves transferring knowledge and understanding that you already have stored in your long-term memory to new situations.

By using your current level of knowledge and understanding and applying it to the new situation you might be able to come up with alternative solutions for solving the problem. You can then evaluate these solutions to see which is most appropriate for solving the problem.

To be a successful problem solver you must use your intellectual skills and pose questions that will help you to shed light on the problem you are considering. If you can solve the problem you are in a much better position to understand why it occurred in the first place, and how it can be overcome if it arises again in the future.

When you think you understand a problem, a good test of your understanding will be your ability to explain it to others. If you can do this accurately and without causing confusion you will have demonstrated your understanding.

Learning skills

So far we have discussed how you can learn facts and concepts, and how you can gain a clearer understanding of a given situation. All of these learning approaches are important when you are learning new skills, but there are other aspects to skills development.

All skills, no matter what they are can be learnt. Skills are learnt by dividing the skill into its constituent parts and then rebuilding these parts into the coherent whole. You have to organise and co-ordinate the constituent parts before you can master the skill as a whole. You have to learn lower order skills, or basic skills, before you can progress to the high order ones.

Human beings have the ability to learn a great variety of different skills. From birth onwards, you learn new skills with each new social encounter. As you progress through life and enjoy a challenging career, you have to master fresh skills. The three stage Learning Model that we used to introduce this section will form the building frame for skills development. You can help your learning process, though, by being aware of how to learn from certain teaching strategies that might form part of the TPS training programme. 'Active' teaching strategies such as role-playing exercises might be designed by your tutor, with the exercises being video-recorded. We shall now consider how you can learn most effectively from these strategies.

Role-play exercises

A role-play exercise is a situation in which you act out, or perform certain skills and behaviours, in a simulated situation. Each learner is given a certain role to perform and you are free to develop your role as you wish, or according to guidelines that are provided.

Role-play exercises are valuable learning strategies in that they allow you to practise new skills in a controlled, safe setting, before they are used in the real environment.

However, to learn from role-play exercises you should bear in mind the following guidelines:

* You should commit yourself whole-heartedly to the exercise and adopt the role that is required. If you lack commitment then you will not contribute fully and you will not learn as much, and you may hold back other people.

* You should prepare thoroughly beforehand as this will allow you to gain an understanding of the role you have to play, and the behaviours you will have to adopt. Indeed, if you rehearse the role which you have to perform before participating in the role-playing this will increase your confidence.

* If you find this kind of learning strategy 'threatening', you should remember that you are acting out a role, and so you should adopt a frame of mind that recognises this. Indeed, you might find it easier to divorce yourself totally from your own personality and character, and 'step firmly into the shoes' of the role that you have to perform.

You are bound to feel a certain amount of apprehension before a role-playing exercise. This is a positive sign as it shows that you are concerned about what is to take place and it will help to ensure that you contribute to the best of your ability. If you feel complacent towards the exercise then you might not contribute as effectively.

No doubt you will be nervous during the early stages of the role-playing exercise, but as it progresses and your confidence builds, you should become more relaxed. Experience shows that once the initial nervous period has passed, most learners relax and enjoy performing their roles.

Role-playing is not an end in itself. While it is highly beneficial to be able to practise new skills in a controlled and safe setting, you will learn more if there is feedback after the session. A most effective way of providing such feedback is by video-recording the exercise.

BEING VIDEOED

You will find that video recording role-playing exercises should greatly improve your learning of skills because the recordings provide 'live' feedback of how you have performed and how others see you. Video recordings can highlight some aspects of your behaviour of which you were previously unaware. Just as role-playing exercises might feel threatening to you, so too might being videoed. Thus, to help you overcome any trepidation about it try and follow these procedures:

Before the recording:

* Prepare thoroughly for the exercise which is to be videoed. Rehearse your role and the behaviour you will adopt beforehand.

* If possible rehearse in the room which is to be used for the recording and have a complete run-through of the exercise, with the video-cameras recording this rehearsal. This will familiarise you with the environment and the equipment, and any props that are to be used.

* If a video-recording of the rehearsal is made, watch a play-back of it immediately afterwards. Ideally this should be in private, rather than with the other learners taking part. This will allow you to come to terms with seeing yourself on the screen and also give you an impression of how others see you.

* Identify any distracting mannerisms you might have, such as pulling at your hair, or scratching your nose, as these may detract from the behaviour that you are trying to practise in the exercise.

The actual recording:

* The night before the recording, run through again all the behaviour you will employ in the exercise, making sure that you are not using any distracting mannerisms.

* Arrive for the recording in good time so that you can calm your nerves and gather your thoughts and so focus on the exercise ahead.

* When the exercise commences, concentrate 100% on the role you have to perform. Ignore the cameras, microphones, and lights.

* Look at the other learners participating in the exercise, do not look at the cameras, or touch any of the microphones - these are very sensitive and will pick up the slightest sound.

* Do not be distracted by people entering the room, or other disturbances - 'the show must go on'.

* Do not detract from the serious side of the exercise by giggling. If you cannot control yourself, then quietly leave the recording studio, otherwise everyone else will be distracted.

* Pay careful attention to your dress and grooming. You should wear clothes that will enhance your appearance, and groom yourself in such a way that is pleasing to look at.

* If possible view the tape immediately after the exercise. This will familiarise you with the behaviours you have used and allow you to make more constructive use of the feedback sessions.

The feedback session

You should learn a lot during the feedback session. This session will be most successful if you follow certain guidelines:

* Be totally honest when discussing your behaviour with your peers and the tutor. First identify those aspects of your behaviour that have been successful and say why they are strengths. Then identify those aspects of your behaviour where there is room for improvement and suggest how you can modify them.

* At all times be positive. There will be some skills in which you will be proficient - acknowledge these. At the same time accept that there will be room for improvement in other areas.

* Always focus attention on the skill rather than the person. When providing feedback to other learners never make the comments personal to them, rather refer to the way in which the skill was performed.

* Be objective and constructive when giving feedback to your fellow learners- suggest ways in which their behaviour could be improved.

* When accepting feedback from others, do not take it as a personal criticism. You should not always try to justify your behaviour, or argue with those providing the feedback - listen to their comments, digest them, and acknowledge the validity of what is being said.

If you remember the above points when taking part in video-recorded exercises then you should be more successful in the way you learn skills. All that is required is for you to acknowledge that there is room for improvement and to commit yourself to taking active steps to overcome your weaknesses and turn them into strengths. Without this commitment, you will not improve your TPS.

The learning process is complex. You need to appreciate that there are many different types of learning. In this chapter we have considered only four. These, however, have wide transferability and are highly pertinent to TPS training. From the discussion so far it is evident that many different approaches are involved in the learning process. You need to be aware of which approaches are most appropriate for you, and for the type of learning that you are seeking to achieve.

A demonstration by a tutor is useful in that you can see a model of correct behaviour provided by the tutor, which you can then imitate. Complex tasks can be divided into discrete stages that can then be demonstrated before you practise and repeat them until you have mastered them. With demonstrations, the tutor is also available to answer any questions that you might have.

If you are trying to learn using written instructions, you have a permanent reference guide which you can refer to time and again, until you have mastered the correct behaviour. Unfortunately, written instructions are not able to answer questions.

In addition to learning by demonstration and written instructions, another common means you could use is trial and error. When you experiment with a new form of behaviour, you should get some form of feedback as to how successful it is. Sometimes it is by making errors that you gain the greatest amount of learning. Once you have mastered a new form of behaviour and have repeated it frequently, you should develop a greater level of competence. Remember that "practice makes perfect".

TEACHING RESOURCES WHICH HELP IN THE LEARNING PROCESS

To help you in the learning process, your tutor may use a number of different teaching resources. To gain the most from such resources it is important for you to recognise how and why each is being used. These learning resources should motivate and arouse your interest so that you are keen to learn and concentrate on the learning process. If the resources are well prepared and interesting to use they should also help with the retention process and help you to recall information. Carefully designed resources will also enable you to make full use of your time, and help you to apply your learning to real situations in the future. Your tutor might use a great variety of learning resources such as:

* Information handouts - these summarise the main points to be learnt and provide you with background reference material.

* Worksheets - can help to structure the learning process, or can be used to help with the retention and recall of information. With these you are expected to write on the worksheet, filling in missing words, labelling diagrams, correcting errors or filling in the results of an experiment.

* Case studies - these might simulate a real situation and involve you applying your intellectual skills to solve problems. Different approaches can be used for tackling case studies ranging from individual work to group analysis.

* Role-playing exercises - as we have already seen these enable you to practise new behaviours in controlled settings allowing you to make errors which can then be overcome before you face similar situations in the real world.

* Video tapes - again, as we have already noted, these provide recordings of your skills being applied in practice and enable you to evaluate how well you can use the TPS in question.

We have not been able to cover every type of learning resource in the above examples. Instead we have tried to show that there are a number of learning resources that you can use to develop further your TPS. As technological advances occur a greater variety of learning resources become available. The proliferation of computer simulations that can be used for learning is one such example, providing you with a different learning experience. However, as well as using the range of learning resources available, to be able to learn most efficiently, you need to develop study skills.

STUDY SKILLS

You need to develop study skills because much of your learning takes place on an individual basis, perhaps as part of your self-development programme. To make the most of the learning resources that are available, you must be aware of how to take notes from verbal or written messages, you must be able to read efficiently, and you need to be able to structure the learning process. In this section we shall examine each of these areas.

DEVELOPING STUDY TECHNIQUE

You must develop your own technique for studying. You must appreciate that to complete your studies you will have to devote some of your leisure time to learning and studying.

Making time available

You will have to make time available for structured learning. No doubt you will have other commitments - family, friends, hobbies and other pressures. Not only will you have to accommodate these, but you will also have to find time to study . The key is to establish a balance between each demand on your time. You should not devote all of your time and energy to learning at the expense of your other interests and activities. If you did this, you would not end up as a 'well-rounded' individual, but as someone who has no other interests apart from study.

Time management, therefore, is crucial. Decide on those times of the day which for you are the most conducive to studying, and then schedule your other interests around them. Initially, you should try out different times, until you have established a routine which allows you to find time for studying alongside the other demands on your time. A key ingredient contributing to the success of any learning programme is self-discipline. If you are unable to motivate yourself to undertake regular study periods then you will find that your learning suffers. You require a strong determination to succeed. To reinforce this determination, you need to understand how you will benefit by successfully completing the learning programme.

Finding the right place

A further important factor in effective study is to find the right place in which to work. Certain types of learning, for example memorising information, require a quiet environment free from distractions. For most individuals a room at home which is quiet and respected by other members of the family as a study room, will be the best study setting. You must have space available for any necessary books or equipment, and a table and chair for writing. You should try and keep noise distractions to a minimum, even to the extent of not listening to the radio, or watching TV. Distractions such as these might make you feel relaxed, but they reduce your concentration and impede the learning process.

When you have found a time and place for studying, they should not be wasted. The approach that you adopt during your study periods will inevitably affect the final outcome.

STUDY SKILLS

Studying is a TPS which you can develop and improve. Some individuals appear naturally studious. They are content to spend hours on end learning. For others, studying requires effort - other interests have to be ignored, distractions removed, and full concentration given to the learning process. To help in this process you should draw up a study timetable. This involves the following steps:

* Set a personal objective that you want to attain as a result of undertaking the learning programme. This might relate to the grade you wish to achieve, or the skills you want to acquire.

* Then, decide how many hours a week you will need to reach that objective. To determine how much study it will require might require consultation with another learner who has experienced the same programme, or with the tutor.

* Allocate these hours to different days of the week, ensuring you achieve a balance during the week, and with other interests - remember not to spend too long on any one session e.g. set aside 2 hours on Monday afternoon and 1 hour on Monday evening; 2 hours on Tuesday evening; 2 hours on Wednesday afternoon etc.

* Start to schedule the work and topics you have to cover over a period of weeks to make sure that they can be learnt in the time available.

* Prepare a formal study timetable for the duration of the learning programme. On the timetable set target dates for completing certain topics or assignments.

* Make sure that the timetable allows for periods of relaxation in and around the study periods. Have at least 1 day free from study each week, and also a few longer breaks of a couple of days, or a week, at times during the learning programme.

* Try to adhere to the timetable and try not to fall behind. If this occurs then you might have to make sacrifices elsewhere in your sphere of interests - for example you might have to miss out on a visit to the cinema. Keep a continuous check on the progress you have made to-date so that you do not fall behind.

* If pressures from studying build up, do not panic - it will be inevitable. Discuss the pressure with fellow learners or the tutor. Calm down and take an objective view of the work you have to cover in the time available. Indeed, write a new timetable, but take seriously the commitment of completing the study programme. Remember, never let your studies 'get on top of you' always 'keep on top of them'.

One characteristic of studying that affects all learners is the tendency to accumulate a great wealth of written material during a programme of study - books, handouts, photo-copies of articles, newspaper and magazine cuttings and notes. If you are not careful all of this information can become highly disorganised, or even lost. It is vital, therefore, that you devise a system for filing and organising all of the material that is collated, so that you can find relevant notes quickly.

We can give you a few suggestions for organising the accumulated material:

* Collate all material as soon as possible. Collation is the process of ordering information and fitting new information into existing structures.

* Keep all material that you collect in ring binders, box files, or pocket files. Label all files or use different coloured files for different topics or subjects. As you collate new material put it immediately into a file for safe storage.

* Number and index all material that is collated. A common method is to use a card index where each piece of material is given a separate card on which is written the title of the material, a brief synopsis of its content, its page number, the author, where it was obtained and its publication date. The separate cards should then be kept in a box under alphabetical or numerical order, acting as a speedy reference guide for you.

If you have access to a personal computer or word processor, then you can use these in a similar way for storing and retrieving information. An important point to bear in mind is that you must be quite discriminating when collecting information. You should question the relevance of all information before it is stored, otherwise you may have a tendency to accumulate too much. At regular intervals you should review the material that you have collected and remove that which is irrelevant to your needs.

A systematic approach to allocating time for study and the storing of information will help your learning process.

Reading skills

Learning often requires you to read a great deal of written material. Many people are concerned as whether or not they will be able to read all that the tutor recommends. You can reduce such a concern by developing competent reading skills. You should try to make your reading more rapid by developing the technique of speed reading. This does not mean reading the text as quickly as possible and ignoring its content. When reading for learning purposes, it is essential that you grasp the meaning of the material and understand the ideas that are presented. Therefore, it is important not to become obsessed just with the speed of reading. You should not sacrifice understanding simply to get to the end of a passage. Despite these cautionary words, it is possible for you to increase the speed of your reading and its effectiveness. However, this requires effort and practice on your part. You will have to adopt a new attitude to reading and learn new techniques of reading.

A NEW APPROACH TO READING

When learning to read at school, children are encouraged to read aloud. As your reading skills develop, there is no longer a need to pronounce each word verbally, and you are able to read in silence. However, many people continue to say each word in their head. This is known as subvocalisation. It is possible though, to read without doing this. Your brain is quite capable of understanding the written word without the need for constant pronunciation. Words are merely symbols for expressing the writer's thoughts. For example, consider the analogy of two friends waving to each other in the street. It is not necessary for either to say consciously "there's my friend waving to me" as each knows that the wave is a sign of greeting and friendship. An effective reader does the same with words. A group of words have a collective meaning and it is this meaning which you need to know, rather than each individual word in the phrase.

Developing such a skill is not always easy. You should try and look for the meaning of phrases rather than attempt to pronounce each word in your head. As the speed of your reading increases you will find that you are not pronouncing each word. The true sign of success will be when you can not only read quickly, but also understand what has been read.

So, this is a new approach to reading that you could adopt if you have to read and understand a great deal of written material. Techniques can be followed that enable you to master such an approach.

TECHNIQUES FOR INCREASING THE SPEED OF READING

As you are reading this sentence, your eyes are moving across the page until the end of each line is reached. Then your eyes will be switched back to the beginning of the next line and the process repeated. Your eyes move in a manner similar to that given below:

Line 1 As you are reading this sentence your eyes are moving

Line 2 across the page until the end of each line is

Line 3 reached. Then your eyes will be switched back to

Line 4 the beginning of the next line and the process...

In fact, your eyes move more than this, although you might be only barely aware of it. The eyes of a slow reader will fix on each word in a sentence in turn, before jumping to fix on the next word. Reading a sentence involves a series of fix-jump-fix-jump eye actions. To accelerate your reading, you should attempt to use fewer fixations (the technical term for the process). This demands fixing on every other word, or every third word, or, better still, only the significant words. By so doing, you spend less time reading the sentence, yet your understanding is just as good.

Another way in which your eyes move is to flick hither and thither across the page. This not only wastes time, but also spoils your concentration. Although this movement seems involuntary, you can curb it by following the course of written text with a pen or ruler.

Subvocalisation (mental pronunciation) slows reading. The longer the word, the longer you need to pronounce it, and the greater the time of the fixation. Whilst it can be helpful to subvocalise unfamiliar words, or when reading text to be learnt by rote, subvocalisation is not helpful when speed reading for understanding. By making a conscious effort to read faster, you can avoid subvocalisation.

Different words in a sentence perform different tasks. Only a proportion of the words carry the underlying meaning of the sentence. The other words provide the structure and give less important information. For speed reading, you only need to fix on the words which carry the meaning. Consider the following sentence:

'Playing squash is my favourite sporting activity on a Saturday.'

Six words carry the meaning: 'Playing squash...favourite sporting activity...Saturday'. The other four words: 'is my...on a' are likely to be implicit from the context. Sometimes a sentence will have few or no words which carry meaning germane to the text, in which case you can skim the sentence without fixations. Words which carry meaning are termed 'key words' and are usually nouns and verbs. An understanding of English grammar helps the eyes to find the key words in a sentence.

Other factors also influence your reading ability - mental and physical factors. Some people like to read their study notes in bed, prior to falling asleep. Bed, though, is not the best place for studying. Your mind and body tend to relax in bed and concentration wanes. Your comprehension of what is read will be weak, and you will find that you are unable to read quickly.

Your comprehension of what is read will be increased if you make notes of the content of the text. This focuses your mind on the content of the material being covered, and provides a permanent reminder and reference source of the major points raised in the text.

Effective reading, therefore, requires you to cover the text quickly, yet at a pace that enables you to comprehend what is being communicated. However, not everything can be read at a quick pace. Some parts of the text will inevitably be more difficult and more fixations will be needed. You must also understand the style of writing that the author is using.

Some authors will summarise the key points to be made in an introductory section, before expanding upon them in later paragraphs. You might find it advantageous to read the introductory section slowly, before reading quickly through the explanatory paragraphs. Unfortunately, there are no hard and fast rules that indicate which are the crucial paragraphs - you will have to use your own judgement.

In addition to quick reading you should also become adept at skimming. Here you miss out many words in the text, greatly reducing the comprehension of the message. Skimming is of use when you are trying to gain the broad content of a text, or when considering whether or not to read an article. When skimming the following points should be observed:

* Read all of the first paragraph of the text/article at normal speed. It frequently contains an overview.

* Also read the second paragraph as this might contain further insight into the content of the text/article.

* Read the last paragraph of the text/article as this frequently contains a summary or the main conclusions arrived at.

* Now decide whether the text/article is worth reading in full. If it is, run your eyes down the centre of each page at a fast pace picking out the key words on either side.

By adopting the above approaches to reading you will find that you are able to cover more material in the study time available.

Taking notes

In addition to developing reading skills, you must also be competent at taking notes. Taking notes when reading or listening is a very positive way of ensuring that you receive and understand the content of the message. The action of selecting and writing down the key points and ideas of the tutor or author concentrates the mind. Notes are also very useful for review and revision purposes giving you a synopsis of the area under consideration. However, you have to take care to ensure that note-taking does not get in the way of learning.

A problem that might arise is that you simply copy the material that is presented to you word for word from the printed page, or from the tutor, into your filing system. This, no doubt, will give the impression that you are working hard, but are you learning? The process of copying is a mere mechanical action. Your hands and eyes may be working, but your brain is not. It is the activity of selection and discrimination that forces you to think, and hence to learn.

Note-taking methods

People take notes in different ways. These can range from the neat, well laid out page after page, to the odd word underlined or written in the margin. The form of notes you take will depend on your own learning style and what you are trying to achieve. You could take such voluminous notes that when you come to re-read them it is hardly quicker than re-reading the original material. Alternatively, a few words or ideas noted many weeks earlier may give you insufficient depth to be of any real value.

The purpose of taking notes is to use them as a memory jogger at a later date. To be successful at this, the notes that you make should be linked to your existing knowledge and understanding. Thus, when you make notes, they should be linked into other areas which are familiar to you. To do this, you should not simply copy words directly from the text or the tutor, but should add in your own words, phrases and comments so that the notes are personalised to your own understanding of the topic under consideration.

Another approach to adopt is that of making 'rough notes' of a text or an exposition given by a tutor, when reading or hearing it, and then immediately afterwards transposing the notes into a form that is more meaningful. You should now devise your own headings and sub-headings and re-write your 'rough notes'.

Different material will require a different approach. The more complex the material being considered, the more detailed your notes should be. At other times, with other topics, you will find that the material is easily understood allowing you to make simpler and shorter notes. From our discussion so far, we can identify a number of guidelines:

* Notes should not simply be direct copies of other material; they need to be written in a manner meaningful to you and in your own words.

* Do not make notes about everything - be discriminating and selective. Pick out the key concepts, principles and facts.

* Add in connected knowledge or examples from existing knowledge and understanding - this helps with the memorising of the new material.

* Adjust the depth of the notes to the level and complexity of the material being considered.

Apart from making written notes you can adopt other methods such as using diagrams or flow charts:

The Note Diagram

Learning skills

Time & place

STUDY

Study technique

Writing skills   Reading

Notes

Note diagrams organise information and show connections between topics. They begin with the main subject in the centre of the page with sub-topics branching out from it. Only key words are included in the diagram to relate the ideas and branches together. Note diagrams have a number of advantages over conventional written notes:

* The notes provide a complete overview of the topic under consideration, using one sheet of paper. You are thus able to see the connections and relationships between topics.

* As only key words are used, there will be space for you to include additional, brief, explanatory notes at a later stage, should the need arise.

* During revision the chart can be used as a test of memory, seeing if you can add flesh to the bones of the diagram.

* The diagram can be used to link concepts together, thus assisting your comprehension of the topic under consideration.

When taking notes from the spoken word, you should bear additional guidelines in mind:

* Concentrate carefully on the spoken words of the speaker but don't write down everything. Ignore all distractions such as others talking, or thoughts of other activities. Look at the communicator when she is talking.

* Structure the notes according to the stages of the presentation - identify the 'introduction,' the 'development of the argument', and the 'conclusion', and give headings to each of these in the notes.

* Listen for signals from the communicator which indicate the important points e.g. the stressing of certain words, the repetition of phrases - note these down.

* Within each of the sections of the presentation indicate sub-headings and number them. Then write down the key words or phrases that apply to each sub-heading. Don't write down unnecessary words - in review sessions they will be a waste of study time.

* Write legibly and allow plenty of space - this enables additional points to be noted if the speaker backtracks and elaborates further.

* Write on loose-leaf paper that can be filed in a binder for safe keeping.

* After making the notes read through them to make sure that they make sense. Highlight the key points by using a highlight marker, or by underlining.

* If any references have to be read and noted, read them immediately after the presentation, and combine any notes that are made with those taken from the presentation. However, clearly indicate the source of any additional material that is referred to in the notes, as the source might have to be referred to again at a later date.

Being a skilled note-taker is an important TPS that is not only useful when learning, but will also be called into action when you attend meetings, negotiate with other people, or interview an applicant for a post.

Writing skills

In addition to being competent at note-taking, you must also develop effective writing skills. You must be able to express your own ideas and demonstrate that you have learnt and understood the material you have been studying. In some instances you will have to give an oral presentation, while in others you will have to produce a written document. Both of these areas will be discussed in more detail in subsequent chapters. The purpose of this section is to suggest a few points that you should remember when producing any form of written communication.

Prepare the ideas

It is a rare individual who can, without preparatory thought, write a balanced and well structured document. If you are producing written work, it will be made up of a number of different ideas and points. These will be floating around in your mind. So, before starting writing, jot down the main points to be covered in the order in which they are to be made. You could use a note diagram to indicate the structure of the message and highlight the key points to be made. As the structure is being planned you should be thinking of how the points will be made and of the phraseology to be used. These should be jotted down as well.

You should then read through the points that you have noted and arrange them into a logical sequence. Any points that now do not seem relevant should be discarded. Finally, you should produce a plan of the actual format of the document. This will be the framework that you will use for the written communication.

Choosing an appropriate style and structure

Now that you have developed a framework you can put pen to paper. You have to make a decision, though, about the style of writing to use (style refers to the phraseology and structure). If a particular format has been requested, then you should adhere to it. Reports are formally structured with headings and sub-headings, and use straight-forward non-emotive language. (Report writing style is considered further in Chapter Four.) Essays, though, necessitate a different style. Essays can use all manner of writing conventions in order to entertain the reader.

Referencing the text

When writing reports, essays or other written documents it is frequently necessary to refer to the works of other writers, whether it be to present their ideas, or to support the views that are put forward. Whenever you have to refer to the works of others, either directly by quotation, or indirectly by referring to someone else's ideas, then you should acknowledge them.

This is important for a number of reasons. Firstly, it is crucial that the original author is given credit for her ideas. If credit is not given then you could be accused of plagiarism - borrowing somebody else's ideas and works. In addition, everything that an individual writes down is protected by copyright - even a simple hand written note is protected by copyright. However, if you make reference to the source of such copyright material in the body of the text, and a full bibliography is provided, then the copyright material can be used to a certain extent. Indeed, by providing a bibliography you help the reader of the written document to investigate further the topic under consideration. A final reason for referencing the text is that it adds academic credibility to your document. The credibility of your document will be enhanced if you show that you have read widely around the subject under consideration. You will provide evidence of this by a bibliography.

There are two main methods that can be used for referencing a text:

> (i) the 'Harvard System'

> (ii) the 'Numeric System'.

(i) The Harvard System

This system involves the insertion of the surname of the reference's author into the text whenever mention is made of her work, together with the date that the work was published. Note that there is no need to include the author's christian name, or initials:

> The research indicated that accountancy was still perceived ".....as a bland profession whose members were all of a muchness,..." Eliahoo, (1985). The respondents.....

Where you do not use a direct quotation, the text should read as follows:

A number of models have been developed to explain the role of communications, see Strong, (1925); Lavidge and Steiner, (1961); and Rogers (1962). Lavidge and Steiner, (1961), developed a 'Hierarchy-of-Effects' Model. This model shows...

If you make reference to more than one document written by a particular author, these will be distinguished from each other by their different dates. However, if the documents were published in the same year then you should use a lettering system in addition to the year:

(1988a), (1988b), (1988c)

If two authors wrote a document you should use both surnames in the reference. However, with more than two authors, only the first surname should be used, followed by 'et al' to signify that there were others:

Knott et al, (1987)

If no author's name is given, for example with some reports, then you should cite the department that wrote the report, along with the publication date.

The purpose of the bibliography is to list all the references that you have used. The bibliography comes at the end of the document, and provides full details of each reference in alphabetical order of authors' surnames.

Books should be referenced as follows:

Author's surname and initials, date of publication, full title, edition (if more than one), publisher's name:

Knott G, Waites N, Callaghan P, and Ellison J, 1987, Computer Studies for BTEC National, Business Education Publishers Ltd

If the book contains a number of chapters written by different authors, and is edited by someone else then the reference will be:

Author and title of chapter, year of publication followed by the editor's name and title of book, edition (if more than one), publisher's name and date of publication, page numbers of chapter referred to.

Periodical articles (including those from magazines and newspapers):

Author, year of publication, title of article, title of periodical (underlined), volume number, part number, full date of publication, page numbers of article:

Hind D W G, 1988, Evaluating an Interpersonal Skills Training Programme, <u>Business Education</u>, Volume 9, Number 1, 1988, p55 - 64

Reports or government publications should be referenced by:

Originating body (e.g. department), date, title, edition, publisher, series title (if any), identifying code mark (if any):

Mintel, April 1988, Leisure Intelligence, Mintel, Travel Agents.

When theses or dissertations are referred to the reference will include:

Author, date of acceptance, title, followed by "Thesis submitted for...(qualification)", name of institution:

King G, 1988, The Marketing of Northumbria and Norway as Tourist Destinations, dissertation submitted for BA (Hons) Business Studies degree, Newcastle upon Tyne Polytechnic.

Where you make reference to publications that have previously been cited, you should use the words 'op cit'. The term 'ibid' is used when the reference that is referred to is identical to the immediately preceding one.

When writing the bibliography you should provide plenty of space between each reference to allow for easy reading.

(ii) The Numeric System

The key difference between the Harvard System of referencing and the Numeric System is that the latter does not include the publication's date in the body of the text. Rather, sequential numbers are used after the author's surname, which are then indexed in numeric order in the bibliography:

> The research indicated that accountancy was still perceived "... as a bland profession whose members were all of a muchness,..." Eliahoo (1). The respondents.....

BIBLIOGRAPHY

1 Eliahoo R, 1985, Scoopers of the City, The Guardian, 12 August 1985, p11

2 Hind D W G, 1986, Communications Strategies and the Accountancy Profession: An Empirical Study, The Service Industries Journal, Volume 6, Number 3, November 1986, p309 - 321

3 Gibbs A, 1984, Attitudes to Accountants, The Accountant, 25 October 1984, p3

Apart from the way in which the references are cited in the text, and recorded in the bibliography, all the other points discussed above remain the same. When writing a document, you should adopt a consistent approach to the referencing of the text - use one system, do not mix them in the same document.

Editing and revising the written document

There is an enormous temptation on completing a piece of written work to put it down and not read it again before it is handed over to the interested recipient. You should resist this on every occasion, no matter how insignificant the document.

When you have finished the written document you should put it aside for 24 hours and then re-read it when your mind is fresh. You should try to identify and correct all errors of grammar or fact. You should always adopt a conscientious and ruthless approach to the editing process. The reader will gain an impression of you from the document, and it is important to create a favourable impression. Indeed, it might be that you have to re-write whole sections of the document before you submit it.

As with all TPS, your writing skills will improve with practice over time. If you think you have a limited vocabulary then you could increase your word usage by keeping a glossary of words and phrases that will add variety to your writing style. If your grammar is weak then read the finished document aloud as it is often easier to recognise grammatical errors when you hear them.

The objective of this chapter has been to introduce you to learning and study skills. As much of the emphasis of TPS training lies with them, it will be important for you to be able to manage your own self-development. Learning and study skills lie at the heart of this process. In planning a self-development programme, it will be vital to accept that TPS are not learnt overnight. Thus, you should pace the programme so that you do not try and learn too many new behaviours too quickly. You should set yourself realistic targets for skills improvement and then develop a timetable that will allow these targets to be met. The learning methods discussed in this chapter will enable you to learn on your own, but do not forget that you can gain much valuable learning from sharing experiences with others.

Chapter Three

VERBAL COMMUNICATION SKILLS

Chapter Three

VERBAL COMMUNICATION SKILLS

It is extremely important for you to be able to converse with others and to present ideas and opinions verbally. Everyday you will be communicating informally with other people in general conversation and sometimes you will be required to communicate in a way which is much more formal, for instance when you have to give a planned and prepared presentation. This chapter will examine the first of these, informal communication, and in Chapter Eight we will look at the skills you should use in a more formal setting. In this chapter we consider the elements of speech which you can employ, how you can use your voice to communicate more effectively and how you can initiate, maintain and end conversations. We shall also look at the use of some special verbal communication skills which you should use in meetings, when giving instructions and in other circumstances.

SPEECH

You use speech to communicate ideas and opinions as well as your emotions and inner most feelings. You communicate each of these by using a variety of elements of speech that you can control and use to good effect. Such elements include:

        (i)   The tone of voice
        (ii) The emphasis used in speech
        (iii) The content of speech
        (iv) The use of figurative language
        (v)   The use of humour in speech
        (vi) The speed of speech you use
        (vii) The pronunciation used
        (viii)The pitch of your voice
        (ix) The use of inferred speech

We shall now consider the importance of each of these and the way you can use them to improve your verbal communication.

(i) THE TONE OF VOICE

When you speak to other people, it is important to maintain their interest and attention. The tone of voice you use, whether it is spontaneous or planned, can help or hinder this. Your tone of voice also signals emotions and feelings, such as anger or joy for example, and supports the content of what you are saying. Often it is the tone of voice that you use which actually signals the true meaning of your message. Consider the following question:

" What are you doing?"

If you were to pose this question in a harsh tone of voice then you will sound as though you are telling someone off. It is an admonishing statement, almost one of rebuke. Whereas if you speak with a soft tone of voice it becomes a caring question. Try saying the question out loud using different tones of voice and attempt to imply different meanings to it.

When you are in conversation you may need to consider carefully the tone of voice you use not only to add clearer meaning to the words themselves, but also to add variety to the speech and so help your listener maintain attention and interest. If you stick to a mono-tone voice you will soon cause your listener to lose concentration and so make your communication much less effective.

(ii) THE EMPHASIS USED IN SPEECH

By putting greater stress on certain words in a sentence you can alter the meaning of the sentence:

"**What** are you doing?"
"What **are** you doing?"
"What are **you** doing?"
"What are you **doing**?"

Try asking this question out loud and each time put the emphasis on the word which has been set in bold type. In the first of these questions you focus the attention of the listener on the action that is being undertaken. The second implies an element of disbelief on your part as to what is being done. In the third question you emphasise the person that is doing it, implying that he or she is somehow at fault or in error. In the final example you again question the action which is going on. Now try each of the questions again continuing to emphasise the word in bold type but attempt to vary the tone of your voice to imply concern, anger, amazement or any number of different feelings.

Similarly by saying a particular word in a certain way, such as by stressing particular consonants or vowels, or emphasising particular syllables, you can give a different meaning to the message.

People who are skilled communicators often use emphasis in speech to considerable effect not only to help the listener to understand the message but also to indicate hidden meanings which otherwise might not have been apparent. Politicians and lawyers are adept at this and often it is only when a speech is heard rather than read that you understand its true meaning.

(iii) THE CONTENT OF SPEECH

The actual words you use are clearly crucial if you wish to achieve effective communication. You should always try to use words which are appropriate to the 'reading age' of the listener. The words used in national newspapers are good examples of this. The Sun uses vocabulary which assumes that its readers need not have a 'reading age' greater than ten years old. In other words, the average ten year old child should have such a vocabulary and be able to read the paper. Obviously much of the vocabulary of the Guardian would be beyond the grasp of the average ten year old. It is important to bear in mind similar considerations when you are in conversation. You must assess your listener and make a suitable choice of words. Your listener should be able to understand fully the meaning of the words that you use. A common criticism of poor teachers is that they use vocabulary that is above the heads of their students. The use of jargon and technical language are prime examples of this and you should only use such terms if your listener is familiar with them or they are fully explained when they are used. It is a fallacy to think that you are being clever by using words that your listener is not familiar with. Your choice of words should be such that they clearly paint a picture in your listener's mind of your intended message and leave no room for ambiguity or confusion.

(iv) THE USE OF FIGURATIVE LANGUAGE

At all times you should try to make the content of your message interesting to listen to, so you avoid boring your listeners. You can achieve this in a number of different ways including the use of figurative language. By figurative language, we mean the use of such things as metaphors, similes and hyperboles. We shall try and explain each of these terms using examples.

> A **metaphor** is used to infer a resemblance between things or situations that are not really associated, for example if you were to describe a ferocious man as a 'tiger'.

> A **simile** is a figurative comparison which uses terms such as 'like' or 'as'. You could describe an ill-tempered colleague as a bear with a sore head.

> **Hyperbole** is the use of intended over-exaggeration. You may describe a person as being 'so fit he could swim the English Channel with both hands tied behind his back'. Obviously nobody is capable of such a feat yet by using such an expression you convey clearly the message that the person you are talking about is certainly in a good physical condition.

By using each of these you will make your conversation more interesting but do take care to ensure that there is no doubt in your listener's mind that the over-exaggeration, for example, is intended. Another important advantage you may gain by using figurative speech is that if you use it creatively, the message may well be remembered for a longer period of time.

It is extremely important, however, to make certain that your listeners are not offended by any of the associations that you might refer to in metaphors, similes or hyperboles, and that the use of the figurative language does not dominate your speaking to the extent that the intended content of your message is diluted and lost. In today's society you must recognise that you should not make remarks which can be taken as being racist or sexist. Not only are such remarks offensive, they can often result in your listener disregarding the rest of what is being said or regarding it as having little value. People who make racist or sexist comments now tend to be held in poor regard by the rest of society.

(v) THE USE OF HUMOUR IN SPEECH

People who are funny or humorous often maintain their listener's attention and interest to a much greater degree. But you must recognise that for many people trying to be funny is very difficult. You may not be naturally funny. It is very easy to lose your credibility and be regarded as a bore if your attempts at humour are not funny and do not amuse the listener. Jokes and funny stories need to be well told. You will no doubt know someone who persists in telling jokes and yet always manages to forget the punch line.

Many people can be extremely funny without telling jokes or stories. We often describe them as being witty. Again there are great dangers in trying to be witty if your listeners do not appreciate your humour or your attempts at wit fall flat. A witty remark about your friend's dress can easily be misinterpreted as an insult. The key to being witty is to judge the tone of the conversation and the relationship you have with your listeners. You must think quickly and respond to their remarks. In normal conversation you will not be able to rehearse witty comments but if you keep your mind alert, opportunities to bring a smile to your listener's face will often arise.

In chapter eight we will look at the way different forms of humour can be planned in advance and rehersed if you have to give a formal presentation.

(vi) THE SPEED OF SPEECH YOU USE

You can help to maintain the attention of a listener by the use of different speeds of speech. If you listen to skilful communicators you will notice that they often increase the speed of their speech to create anticipation with their audience, building up momentum before an important point, and then allowing a few seconds of silence to enable the message to sink in and the listener to reflect upon it.

If you pause while you are talking you may indicate a sense of deliberateness and thought. Using pauses can further help you to emphasise important elements, and allow you to gather your thoughts for the next stage of the communication. You must ensure, though, that you do not simply fill the silent pauses with distracting verbal mannerisms such as 'umms' and 'aahhs'. These will simply irritate your listener and detract from what you are trying to say.

(vii) PRONUNCIATION

It is important to try and pronounce the words you use correctly. If you constantly mispronounce words it will damage your credibility especially when your listener expects you to be fully conversant with the topic under consideration. Mispronunciations will also quickly distract your listeners from what you are saying and will reduce their attention.

It is often difficult to know how to pronounce words when you have only read them. If this is the case and you are unsure of the correct pronunciation of a particular word you can always refer to a dictionary. However, even then it is not always easy to end up with the correct pronunciation. The best way to learn how to pronounce new words is to listen, particularly to the radio and television. Newsreaders and presenters generally get most pronunciations right.

(viii) THE PITCH OF YOUR VOICE

The pitch of your voice is a combination of the tone that you use and the loudness of the sound that you make. You can create considerable emphasis on what you are saying by raising and lowering the pitch. Skilful communicators vary the pitch of their voices considerably, but in a conversational way as opposed to a theatrical manner. There is a need to be careful, for if you put too much variation in the pitch of your voice, this can be a further distraction for your listener.

What you require in your speech is a comfortable variation of harsh and soft tones, and of loudness and softness. Speaking loudly is not the sole key to gaining the attention of your listener despite the fact that many British people abroad seem to believe that this is the best way of getting through to foreigners. What you need to have is a voice that is pleasing to listen to. This can be developed by using different tones, varying speeds of speech, and a range of pitches. This can be developed through practice. A good example of the use of pitch in the voice is Mrs. Thatcher who is able to control the pitch of her voice in most circumstances. It is only when she gets angry or agitated that she sometimes loses this control and her voice rises in pitch and becomes rather shrill. Since becoming Prime Minister she has practised her tone and pitch so that there is a noticeable difference in the way she speaks in the late 1980s to the way she spoke in the 1970s - a clear example of TPS training.

(ix) THE USE OF INFERRED SPEECH

Another element of speech you can use to communicate your feelings and attitudes is that of 'inferred speech'. Here, the actual meaning of the words you use is not as important as their implied meaning. For example a manager might say to his deputy:

> "I see you're working flexi-hours again John"

This is not simply a matter of fact but a statement from the manager to his deputy that he has noticed a different pattern to the deputy's working day. The deputy is made aware that his manager has noticed this change and depending upon the way in which the message is communicated will be able to determine whether the manager approves or disapproves of it.

In other circumstances you may wish to use inferred speech to signify friendliness to others. Travellers on the same train can show friendliness by engaging in apparently pointless conversations, such as talking about the weather. The state of the weather is not as important as the travellers instigating a conversation. By talking about the weather the travellers are saying to each other:

> "Yes, I am interested in talking with you."

You will find this element of speech useful for relationship building and it frequently precedes more pertinent topics of conversation.

SPEECH DISTRACTIONS

While inferred speech is important you should always be careful not to over use it and if possible to avoid the repeated use of distracting speech mannerisms such as:

> "That's right," "O.K," "I mean," "You know," or "Well then"

You will find that if you repeatedly use such terms in speech it does become irritating to your listeners and might even lead them to mimic your speech mannerisms. If a person constantly uses distracting speech mannerisms such as this it is often a sign of nervousness and lack of confidence. You should try to identify such mannerism in your own speech and if they are present concentrate on avoiding them when you are in conversation.

We hop that you can recognise from what has been said in the previous sections that there are various ways in which you can make what you are trying to say more interesting to listen to, and more easily remembered. While talking comes naturally you must realise that you are not only transmitting a message but also signalling your attitudes and feelings. Indeed, by varying your speech you can radically change your listener's interpretation of what is being said. Therefore the varied use of speech is a skill that you need to master for informal conversations as well as formal presentations.

DIFFERENT TYPES OF VERBAL COMMUNICATION

As well as practising to improve the effectiveness of your speech, it is also important that you recognise that there are different types of verbal communication, each of which requires a differing approach in your communication style.

CONVERSATIONS

The most common form of communication which you will take part in is a conversation. It is something you will do everyday of your life. However, to be a successful conversationalist you require certain skills and we will now consider some of these.

LISTENING SKILLS

Listening is an important element in any successful conversation. The word conversation implies communication between people and if you do not listen to what the other person is saying then the communication process will break down. Therefore you need to pay attention to what is being said and try to follow the conversation. If there are a group of people taking part in a conversation, there is always a chance that your mind will drift and you will lose track of what is being said. If you do not want other people to do the same thing there are a number of approaches you can adopt to encourage people to listen to what you are trying to say. You can ask them questions, or seek their views and opinions on what you are saying.

If people are listening they tend to show this both in their verbal and non-verbal behaviour. They will nod their heads, lean forward or perhaps say "Yes, I see" or "That's true" or "I disagree with that". Conversely, if your listeners do not look at you but at some other object, or stare out of the window, or yawn, (or worst of all fall asleep!) then they are giving quite explicit signs that they are not listening.

You can learn to be a good listener. Here are a few simple guidelines:

* Always 'listen' with your eyes as well as your ears. By looking at the speaker you hear not only the words which are being spoken but will also be able to recognise the non-verbal signs which the speaker is giving. Often such non-verbal signs reinforce the verbal message and help you to understand the true meaning that the speaker is trying to give.

* Ask questions. If anything is unclear you should ask for it to be clarified, or if you disagree with what is being said then politely make the point.

If you are doing the talking you will find that your listeners will soon lose their concentration if:

* They think they have heard what you are saying before. Many old people begin to lose their short term memory and repeat the same stories again and again and it is important that you do not start such a habit. Therefore think about what you are saying. Do not repeat yourself if you can help it.

* The subject matter is too technical. Listening to a complex topic can be difficult and the listener might 'switch off'. You have to realise this and make your message easier to understand and support what you are saying with appropriate body language.

TALKING

Conversations obviously rely upon talking and while some people are more talkative than others, it is important that if the conversation is to be a success everyone must join in. A good conversationalist does not allow the conversation to be dominated by one or two individuals, so try and bring those who are more reluctant to talk into the conversation.

If you are shy you may need to develop conversational skills through practice with people who feel more confident in a conversational setting but who are not too dominating.

GAINING CONVERSATIONAL PRACTICE

(i) Starting conversations

Conversations can often start with factual information being exchanged, or general statements being made, for example:

> "Sales have increased by 20% over the last six months".

This sort of information can then be followed by statements giving details of how this was achieved. You may find that a conversation then moves on to discussions and expressions of feelings, attitudes and opinions about what is being described, thus:

> "I think much of this success has been due to the TPS training programme our sales staff has been through".

You can of course get other people to join in the conversation by asking them a question. This may be helped by using open questions rather than closed ones:

> "What do you think the increase in sales could be attributed to?"

demands more than simply a 'yes' or 'no' response. Try to avoid closed questions such as:

> "Do you think that the increase in sales could be the result of our TPS training programme?"

Indeed, you should recognise that asking questions is another common method of opening conversations as is making comments about the environment or the situation, greeting others, or exchanging personal details and comments:

Questions: "Why do you think there has been a fall in the quality of our supplier's product?"

"Why have sales exceeded the budgeted figure this year?"

Comments: "The productivity of the workforce has never been better."

"Absenteeism is always high after a public holiday."

Greetings: "Hello, how are you? Tell me what your research findings are"

Exchanging details: "Good morning. My name is Blake, Peter Blake from Sacks & Co. May I ask you a few simple questions?"

(ii) Maintaining the conversation

Once you have opened a conversation you need to keep it going. You will find that most of the conversations you have normally develop through a sequence of questions, answers, comments and opinions. You might discuss the topic under consideration in detail, or pass over it lightly. Try and keep the conversation open so that the other people involved feel that they can contribute. People are also less likely to contribute if they feel their opinions are going to be ignored or rejected. You should try to keep the conversation going by linking the various topics under consideration and by widening the scope of the conversation:

> "Talking about TPS training for sales people, I must admit that I went on a TPS course once and I feel it benefited my social life as well as my job."

Hopefully other people in the conversation will respond by keeping the conversation going. This statement could be followed by an open question from one of the listeners:

> "That's interesting, how do you think TPS training has helped your social life?"

Good conversational practice usually allows everyone to take turns in talking and listening and you must let the other person say their piece without too many interruptions.

(iii) Concluding a Conversation

At some stage the conversation will have run its course and you will need to conclude it in a reasonable way. Some conversations come to a natural end when nobody has anything else to add to the topic under consideration. Alternatively you may find it necessary to wind up the conversation in a suitable way. Normally people start to give out certain types of signal to show that they are ready to pack up. Note such signals as the person who is sitting forward in his chair, ready to stand up, or the one who repeatedly checks the time.

When the conversation is drawing to a close it is often the time to arrange to meet again:

> "So I'll see you again at the same time, in the same place, next week."

Just as you develop your own style of opening a conversation, so you develop your own style of closing one. Some people tend to be too abrupt, giving the impression that they cannot wait for the conversation to end. Others do not seem able to break away, which can be equally annoying if you have something else to do but do not want to be thought rude by breaking off too soon. Try and conclude on a positive note and in a friendly manner. If you fail to do so then establishing future conversations might be more difficult.

TELEPHONE CONVERSATIONS

Much of what we have said above applies to telephone conversations, whether they are for business or social reasons. A particular difficulty with a telephone conversation is that you are unable to read the body language of the person with whom you are talking. In particular, by not being able to see the gestures and facial expressions of the other party, you lose a certain amount of insight into what the other person is trying to convey.

Telephone conversations also make it more difficult to use humour, as frequently it is your facial expressions that suggest that you are being humorous. You need to develop a good telephone technique if you are to use it well.

If you are making a call try and think through in advance what you want to say so that you will not be ambiguous in the message you are trying to give. It is often useful to make a few notes to which you can refer while making the call. If it is a business call keep it short and to the point. Pay attention to the tone and pitch of your voice. You should speak more slowly than when you communicate face-to-face. This allows both you and the person you are speaking with to make any notes that may be necessary, and helps the other person to understand the message the first time without it having to be repeated.

If you are answering a call try not to let it ring for a long time before answering it. Be polite and give a pleasant greeting to the caller. Each caller should be made to feel that he or she is important and that the call is welcomed:

>"Edwards & Co Accountants. Good morning. How can I help you?"

or

>"Thank you for calling Edwards & Co Accountants. How can I help you?"

Establish the caller's name and position as soon as possible:

>"Who should I say wishes to speak to our Tax Accountant?"

At all stages keep the caller informed of the progress of his or her call:

>"I'm sorry, but Mrs. Evans, our Tax Accountant, is engaged at the moment. Can I take your number and ask her to call you back?"

If you take a message for someone else make sure that it is passed on as soon as possible so that the necessary action can be taken. Again when you are concluding the call, be polite:

>"Thank you for calling Mr. Edwards. I will make sure that Mrs. Evans returns your call as soon as she is free."

If you do not have a polite telephone manner, the caller will gain an unfavourable impression of you and your organisation. Its a good idea to keep a supply of message paper by the phone, and a pen that works, so that you can take legible notes.

MEETINGS

Meetings take many different forms, ranging from company annual general meetings to meetings of the local parent teacher's association committee. Meetings can be classified as being formal meetings, committee meetings, or command meetings.

Formal meetings and committee meetings have the common objective of arriving at a group decision on the topic under consideration. These meetings are controlled by the chairperson (the chair) who has to follow certain procedures for the conduct of the meeting. Command meetings are used to communicate information and tend to be called by group leaders. While the views of the group may be consulted, the group leader has the responsibility for taking any decisions, and is free to determine the procedures adopted at the meeting. At formal and committee meetings there is joint responsibility for any decisions that are taken, frequently requiring a majority vote before the motion (the proposal) is accepted. Once the decision has been taken, irrespective of the type of meeting, all parties must accept it.

Organising meetings

You should organise all meetings in a similar manner:

* Notice should be given to all people (in this chapter we will refer to them as delegates) expected to attend the meeting well in advance, allowing them to keep the day and time free from other commitments.

* The agenda for the meeting (the topics to be covered in a pre-determined order) should be circulated to all delegates to enable them to gather their thoughts on the topics to be discussed, and to prepare any papers or handouts. Examples of a notice for a meeting and an agenda are given in Chapter Five where we also discuss the preparation of minutes.

* Any papers or handouts that are to be referred to in the meeting should be circulated in advance to allow all delegates to become familiar with them, saving time during the meeting.

You should follow any constitutional procedures regarding the organisation of the meeting. For example, some meetings require a certain period of notice to be given for those attending, and articles of association and the Companies Act prescribe certain formalities.

Running the meeting

To ensure that the meeting is conducted in a formal manner you need to follow certain guidelines:

A chairperson must be appointed to control the meeting and steer the discussion through the points on the agenda.

A secretary needs to record the points that are discussed and agreed in the minutes of the meeting. The minutes should be a true record of the discussion that takes place. After the meeting copies of the minutes should be forwarded to all those attending, being their permanent record of it. (Minutes are considered in Chapter Five.)

All delegates should follow the procedures of the meeting that specify their participation and should contribute in an orderly and courteous manner.

Communicating at meetings

If you are participating at a meeting you will need to use the full range of your oral communication skills. You need to bear a number of considerations in mind:

* The purpose of many meetings is to come to a decision. Therefore, all delegates to the meeting should have an equal opportunity to contribute to the discussion. If one or two delegates are dominating the meeting then they should be restrained by the chairperson.

* Discussions can become heated. To reach rational and logical decisions, however, it is important that delegates should remain calm and refrain from using emotive language.

* If differing views are expressed, adopt a flexible approach to reach agreement.

* You must listen carefully. The meeting could involve detailed debate and to keep track of the debate you will have to listen carefully to what is being said. Making notes of the discussion will be useful for this.

* You should prepare for the meeting. If you need to undertake background research, do it prior to the day of the meeting. If there are papers produced for the meeting make sure you have considered them in advance rather than trying to skim through them while the meeting is in progress.

* Speak only when you have a valid point to make. Time will be constrained, so spurious comments will reduce the effectiveness of the meeting.

* If at the conclusion of formal and committee meetings no consensus of opinion is reached, a vote should be taken (according to the constitution of the meeting) so that a decision can be reached.

Chairing a meeting

If you are asked to chair a formal or committee meeting you have a special role to play in that typically you must adopt an impartial stance, unless the delegates are equally divided as to the decision to be taken, in which case you will normally have the casting vote. Much of the success of the meeting will lie with your management of it. To ensure the success of the meeting, you should observe the following points:

* Always speak clearly and concisely so that all of those at the meeting can hear you. Use some of the oral communication skills mentioned earlier in this chapter.

* Set clear objectives for the meeting which should be reinforced with the delegates in the opening introduction that you give as chairperson.

* Strictly follow the agenda with no digression from the topics under consideration. If the discussion that takes place is too superficial you should, as chairperson stimulate a more in-depth discussion or guide the meeting back to the topic under consideration.

* Control the meeting. Restrain the more vociferous people at the meeting and encourage the less communicative to participate.

* Try not to dominate the discussion. Your role as chairperson is to steer the discussion through the topics on the agenda.

* Listen carefully to the points being discussed, noting down the key arguments, summarising them and agreeing them with the delegates.

* You should be courteous at all times. Thank delegates for their contributions, and try to ensure that they remain courteous in their ssion.

* Carefully manage the time to allow all the points on the agenda to be covered. Indeed, you should give careful thought to the number of points on the agenda to prevent too many being listed for the discussion time available.

* When the items on the agenda have been fully discussed you should conclude the meeting by arriving at a decision that meets the objective that was initially set. If the delegates are unanimous in their decision then there will be no need for a vote. If there is disagreement, however, you will need to take a vote, and if the vote is evenly divided between those for and against the motion, you, as the chairperson, will have the casting vote.

* At the conclusion of the meeting, you should set a date for the next one, and thank the delegates for their attendance and contributions.

* A true record of the meeting should be noted in the minutes, which should be agreed by the delegates at the beginning of the next meeting.

Command meetings tend to be less formal than those considered above and frequently do not involve the taking of minutes. To be successful, however, many of the guidelines listed here do need to be observed, especially those relating to the chairperson's management of the meeting and the delegates' contributions.

COMMUNICATING INFORMATION

You will frequently use speech to give information to others, information that may be factual, technical or personal. You need to give special thought to this if the information is important. Do not try to give too much information verbally as you might 'overload' the listener. To be successful at communicating information you should identify the main points of the message and then concentrate on making sure that the listener fully understands these. This can be achieved in a number of ways.

Repeat data or technical points to help the listener to appreciate what is being said. Emphasise the data by slowing the speed of your delivery. Allow for pauses after important points have been made and stress these by deepening the pitch of your voice. This will help the listener to assimilate the message.

Take care not to present too much information verbally. If the information you wish to get over is complex, it may be better to present it in a written form as well or to use some form of visual display such as graphs, tables, and pie charts. You can verbally draw the listener's attention to the key points of the information and to highlight their implications:

> "Twenty five per cent of our sales come from the Northern Region. This table provides further detail. What this means is that..........."

If you do use tables, graphs or charts to communicate information give your listener time to read them before making the next point.

GIVING INSTRUCTIONS

If you have a position of authority you will probably have to give instructions to others. Instructions are often central to the operation of a group. Problems will arise though, if the instructions you give are not communicated clearly. Obviously, you need to bear in mind all the previous points about verbal communication but you should take special note of the following:

* Use language that will be understood by the listener to prevent any confusion arising.

* The instructions you give must be extremely explicit, leaving no room for misinterpretation if you use ambiguous terms.

* Make sure that the person to whom you are giving instructions has fully understood them by asking him or her to repeat them.

Apart from considering the content of the instruction, though you should also consider how it is to be given. You will create good team relations and respect if you give instructions in a courteous and polite manner. If you become irritable and aggressive when giving instructions you will not encourage loyalty, and also make it more likely that the instruction will be misinterpreted. Indeed, to prevent the possibility of such a misinterpretation, try to reinforce a verbal instruction in writing.

Verbal communication skills are important components of TPS and if you master them it will allow you to exchange knowledge, ideas, feelings and the whole range of emotions effectively. By becoming competent at communicating orally you will be better placed to gain from and enjoy interpersonal relationships with others. While it is important to be able to communicate verbally it is also important you are able to use body language, as body language is, at times, more meaningful than the spoken word. Chapter Four will examine the topic of Body Language.

Chapter Four

BODY LANGUAGE

Chapter Four

BODY LANGUAGE

We all use body language when we communicate with others. It is unavoidable. Even when you are not speaking, you are sending messages to others by your physical appearance, your gaze, your posture, your gestures and your facial expressions. You are not always aware, however, that you are sending such messages, partly because the person you are talking to might not be skilled in interpreting the meaning of body language and does not, therefore, respond to it.

Being able to use body language to communicate, and being skilled in reading it is therefore an important part of interpersonal communication. Body language indicates your moods and feelings and those of your listener. If you can recognise such messages you will be able to modify your delivery and adjust what you are trying to say. Indeed, it is particularly important to understand body language because it can often demonstrate more about the person you are talking to than the words that are being spoken. If you understand body language you will be able to recognise whether there is any difference between the meaning of the words which a person is speaking and her unexpressed opinion of you.

To develop an understanding of body language you must have a perceptual sensitivity, in other words the ability to observe and analyse another person's behaviour. This is especially important in a number of situations such as interviewing, negotiating and selling. If you do not fully understand body language, or you misinterpret the messages which it conveys then it is very easy to reach the wrong conclusion about what is happening and what is being said.

Body language, therefore, plays an important role in communication. It can replace words, it can emphasise what is being said, it can act as a stimulant to the conversation (for instance when a person nods her head in encouragement), and it can show whether there is any contradiction between what is being said and what is being thought. If you want to use your own body language successfully, and to read that of others, you should recognise what makes up body language.

THE CONSTITUENTS OF BODY LANGUAGE

There are seven main individual elements of body language:

> (i)   Facial Expressions
> (ii) Gaze
> (iii) Posture

(iv) Gestures
(v) Proximity
(vi) Touch
(vii) Appearance

(i) FACIAL EXPRESSIONS

Facial expressions are the most important aspect of body language. Your face is highly visible, it is mobile and flexible, and is capable of indicating your innermost feelings to other people. For example, your face can communicate your likes and dislikes; after eating horrible tasting food all that is required is a 'squirming', frowning face to show you have disliked the meal - despite the fact that you feel obliged to complement your host's cooking. In contrast, your broadly smiling face displays your joy at a rival's misfortune - even if you are expressing your deepest sympathy. Despair and frustration are evidenced by a deeply furrowed forehead - a clear indication to the lecturer that your assignment tasks are causing a problem. Emotions are often displayed in facial expressions even when you would prefer to hide them, as the face can be a spontaneous communicator of messages.

Most people tend to have similar facial expressions reflecting their feelings and so provide you with good feedback in face-to-face communication. You should be careful to examine facial expressions closely. When you communicate you should try to ensure that your facial expressions reflect what you are saying and are not contradictory for this can easily reveal uncertainty in the message that you are trying to convey. If you are a skilful communicator you will use your facial expressions to good effect.

(ii) GAZE

When you communicate face-to-face with others you will normally have eye-to-eye contact. This can signal a great deal about what is being felt by you and the person you are talking to. A strong gaze shows that you are being attentive and concentrating on what the other person is saying. If you become embarrassed you sometimes try to hide your embarrassment by breaking eye contact and looking elsewhere.

Breaking eye contact might also show that you are hiding something, or have made an error about which you are ashamed. Alternatively, a lack of eye contact may indicate that you dislike the other person and that you wish to withdraw from the conversation.

On the other hand if you do establish strong eye contact this usually indicates that there is a strong desire to communicate both on your part and that of the person you are talking to. In addition, by giving strong eye contact you can invite others to speak, by giving a prolonged stare with a slight nod of the head to act as a cue. To some extent its a cultural expectation that when people communicate with each other, they look at each other. If you tend to shift your eyes around when speaking, and never directly look the other person in the face, this tends not to inspire trust.

Gaze, therefore, is an important component of your body language. Your emotions and attitudes are portrayed via eye contact as well as other traits such as honesty. You have to maintain careful control of your eyes in dealing with other people. Just as shifty eyes need to be avoided so too should hard, piercing stares that might be a sign of aggression. What you should have is eye contact that looks at the other people to whom you are speaking, but this can be broken with the occasional blink and the occasional look away to make them feel more comfortable. When you talk to other people consider the eye contact they establish with you and the feeling it brings. Does the person make you feel at ease or uncomfortable? Can you tell whether they want to talk to you or merely feel they must?

(iii) POSTURE

How you move your body, how you stand or sit and the position of your limbs all reflect your attitudes and feelings about yourself and towards others. You can display a warmth and liking for someone by leaning towards them, or by sitting with your legs slightly apart, arms unfolded. You clearly display your dislike for someone, however, by turning away, or facing them with folded arms, or tightly crossed legs. Of course such signals might also be caused by other factors, for example the person might be feeling upset and this may come across as a dislike for you despite the fact that you are not the cause of their distress. If you like another person, or are in agreement about a particular topic or subject, it is likely that your body movements and posture will have similar patterns. When interpreting a person's posture, as when interpreting all aspects of body language you must take into account other signs and signals coming from the person.

A person's status can often be reinforced by their posture. If you adopt an elevated, domineering position, you may make others feel subservient while if you have an erect posture this can indicate a sense of pride and self-discipline. If you always stand with slouched shoulders and arched back this may be interpreted as being slovenly. People often express a feeling of anger by a tense or rigid posture such as the tightening of muscles, clenching the fist, or stamping the foot. A person who walks in a slow, cowered and defensive manner could be thought of as being timid, as opposed to the confident, purposeful walk of a more self-assured person. Your impressions of others and the impression they will gain of you will be influenced by posture and gait. It is also an indication of your personal dynamism and self-confidence.

You can use posture and body movements as useful punctuation marks during an oral presentation or a conversation. By shifting the posture of your body, or moving to another part of the room, you signal that a particular point has been completed and that another is about to be made. Such a pause created by changing posture can help your listeners follow the structure and development of the oral communication. Compare the teaching styles of some of your lecturers. Do they sit on the desk at the front, pace the floor or stay in a chair behind their desk? Try and assess whether their posture and body movements reflect their personalities and the way in which they teach and you learn.

Your posture, therefore, if you use it appropriately, is a strong support to any verbal message you wish to put across and is a component of body language that you need to control and use effectively.

The Smile of Friendliness

The Frown of Sorrow

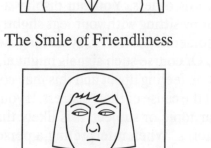

The Shifty Eye Gaze of Dishonesty

The Strong Eye Gaze of Trust

The Slovenly Posture

The Erect Posture of Pride

The Friendly Handshake

The Hostile Gesture

(iv) GESTURES

In certain circumstances you can use a gesture to replace the need for words. Indeed, it might be that your only way of communicating is by gestures, especially if you are trying to communicate with someone who does not speak English.

You can use gestures in a passive, informative sense as well as in an aggressive manner. A wave of the hand indicates that you have noted the presence of another person, whereas a heavily clenched fist beating down on a table shows that you are anxious, if not angry. Sometimes gestures are instantaneous such as stroking your own hair or scratching your face and these can demonstrate that you are uneasy or concerned about what is taking place.

It is quite often the subconscious gestures, of which you are unaware, that reveal a great deal about your innermost thoughts. Reading and interpreting these unintended gestures can provide a greater understanding of the communication that is taking place. If you are a person who continually fidgets, or who when talking always gesticulates, you could give the impression that you have a nervous disposition.

You should be aware of your own gestures, especially those that might be distracting to other people, so that you can take action to control them. Likewise, you also need to develop a repertoire of appropriate gestures so that you can use them to supplement the other verbal and body language messages that you give.

As with posture, you can use gestures to punctuate what you are saying. Gestures can emphasise and reinforce your verbal messages. It is important to master a variety of gestures, so that you do not over-use one which becomes monotonous or distracting. If you feel uncomfortable at using planned and controlled gestures there can be no substitute for rehearsal and practice. Just as it is important to rehearse and practise a presentation before you give it, so too is it important to practise gestures so that their use becomes second nature and spontaneous, rather than being forced and awkward.

(v) PROXIMITY

You can recognise how people feel about each other by how physically close they are to each other. You can communicate your status, your level of intimacy with another person and how much you like each other by the proximity with which you talk. If you like someone you tend to enjoy close proximity where other body language is used to demonstrate mutual fondness. People of a higher status tend to keep a more formal distance from those in subordinate roles.

Friends tend to adopt a closer presence to each other than work colleagues. Often if you are dealing with work colleagues and with people you are meeting for the first time you will maintain a physical barrier of distance between yourself and the other person until such time as you find you like each other and the physical barriers can be reduced.

What you are talking about also influences your degree of proximity with other people. If you are making a formal presentation there is normally a physical distance between you and your audience while more intimate exchanges take place at close quarters. Often you will find that only when the barriers to communication, such as physical distance are reduced, will you be able to communicate with other people more effectively.

Distance is not the only barrier to communication. If you speak from behind a desk this can sometimes be seen as being authoritarian, setting up a formal atmosphere, whereas speaking to someone when you are sitting beside them is more informal, making the other person feel at ease. In certain circumstances you may wish to maintain a physical barrier between yourself and the person you are talking to. A manager reprimanding a subordinate can reinforce her authority by sitting behind her desk. A female secretary might feel threatened if her male manager sits close to her while dictating a letter. She might think he is trying to 'chat her up'. In such cases you may feel that a physical barrier is appropriate.

On occasions you will find it is best if no physical barriers exist. If a friend has just received some distressing news then perhaps he or she would appreciate the reassurance and comfort of being hugged. If you trust someone at work you might find it easier to communicate if there are no physical barriers between you, preferring to talk sitting next to each other on a sofa, rather than from opposite sides of a desk.

(vi) TOUCH

How people touch one another is an important element of body language. The number of times you touch someone and the type of touch you use will depend on how well you know and like, each other. Touch is important in building relationships with others. Touch can break through some of the psychological barriers between people, and says to others that they are liked. In addition, touches, such as a pat on the back or shoulders indicates encouragement and emotional support.

Formal touches are important when you meet someone for the first time. If you give a firm, strong handshake this will indicate self-confidence, while a limp, weak handshake reveals timidity. Parting touches, once again the formal handshake, allow you to end on a positive note and say goodbye.

You must be careful when it comes to touching others, because some people might be naturally reserved and less open to such body language. While a brief handshake or pat on the back is acceptable to most people a prolonged and aggressive handshake, or over-intimate touch with a newly made acquaintance may make the other person feel uncomfortable, even threatened, and distrusting of the relationship with you.

(vii) PERSONAL APPEARANCE

Your self-image is reflected through your appearance, dress and grooming - whether you have neat well-cut hair, or straggly unkempt hair, whether the clothes that you wear are appropriate for the occasion or inappropriate. Your personal appearance often creates an initial impression that sometimes is very difficult to change. Your personal appearance is of importance when you consider body language because it is an aspect over which you have considerable control. Although very little can be done about the shape, features and size of our bodies, much can be done about what we wear.

The clothes you wear should be appropriate for the occasion. When you are dealing with others it is important that you should consider how you will appear. It is important to recognise when casual clothes are acceptable and when they are not. If you only like to wear jeans, then it is probably not a good idea to apply to work in a bank. Obviously if you are going for an interview for a job you should wear clothes that are appropriate. Attractive dress can play an important part in influencing others, particularly at formal functions such as interviews. Frequently, perceived attractiveness in dress increases your impact on the listener and might give you an advantage over a less well-dressed person. Many people also feel that neat formal dress indicates a sense of self-discipline, self-respect and conformity.

As your personal appearance can be partly controlled, it constitutes an element of your body language and helps to create a favourable, or unfavourable, impression of you, so think carefully about what you wear and how you look and try to adjust your appearance to match the circumstances you are going to be in.

INTERPRETING BODY LANGUAGE

All of the elements of your body language that we have discussed in the previous section combine to present an image to other people. Equally you must recognise the signals that others are giving through their body language. This section will attempt to help you decode the messages more clearly. Under each heading we will give examples of behaviour which indicate the way people feel. Please note that no single characteristic which we quote is conclusive evidence of the way a person is thinking. However the examples we give are just some of the more common signs people show under these circumstances.

People who are willing to listen

People are willing to listen to you when they:

* Rub their hands together
* Lean forward when standing
* Sit with their body forward
* Rest their chin on the palm of their hands.
* Look directly at you
* Nod in agreement with what is being said
* Interject with supportive comments such as 'Yes I see' or 'That's right'

People who are showing friendliness

People show they want to be friendly when they:

* Smile
* Use strong eye contact
* Have a static body and posture
* Stand or sit with open, unfolded arms and legs, facing you
* Use non-threatening gestures such as handshakes, pats on the back or arms
* Initiate and maintain conversation
* Use humour in their speech
* Are polite and courteous to you

People who are anxious to interrupt

People who wish to interrupt you:

* Place their hand on your arm
* Fidget with their ear or raise their hand
* Look directly and intently at you
* Shift their posture when sitting
* Move when standing
* Talk to their neighbour

People who feel frustrated or rejected

When people are feeling frustration or rejection they:

* Use aggressive, downward hand gestures
* Pummel their hands together, or hit the table or desk top
* Tighten their clothing
* Raise the tone of their voice
* Become red in the face and blush
* Withdraw from verbal communication

People who feel threatened

When people feel threatened by you and are being defensive they:

* Tightly fold their arms, or cross their legs
* Frown at you
* Withdraw their eye contact
* Become verbally aggressive - raising their tone of voice or shouting
* Stand their ground

People who feel superior

People who feel superior to you may:

> * Lean back in their chair, or sit with their legs over the chair arm
> * Grasp both lapels to their jacket, and raise their heads
> * Use gestures that point at others, for example an index finger or pen
> * Look at the ceiling when talking
> * Make sure that their body position is above that of others such as standing when other people are sitting or sitting in a chair that is higher off the ground
> * Ignore the comments of others

People who do not wish to communicate

People who do not wish to communicate with you signal this by:

> * Ignoring completely other people - not looking at them or responding to questions with one word answers
> * Looking down, placing their hands on their foreheads
> * Erecting barriers to communication such as placing their feet on the desk or table
> * Use frowning or scowling facial expressions

You should take care not to over-generalise as each individual will adapt her use of body language according to cultural and social norms and her own personality and experiences.

Chapter Five

WRITTEN COMMUNICATION SKILLS

WRITTEN COMMUNICATION SKILLS

Apart from communicating by using the spoken word and body language you will also have to use the written word. All organisations generate considerable amounts of printed information in the form of handouts, memos, letters and reports. It is therefore important that you are able to demonstrate your written communication skills.

A number of common points apply to all forms of written communication:

* The style of writing should be grammatically correct

* The written document, whether typed or handwritten, should be neatly and legibly presented and in a consistent style

* You should carefully check and correct the written document before despatching it, ensuring correct spelling and terminology.

These points are general guidelines, but you do need to bear them in mind to ensure the quality of your written documents. You may have to produce many different forms of business communication. Being able to write such documents effectively is a TPS. We will now consider a number of specific types of written communication.

THE WRITTEN WORD

HANDOUTS

Handouts have a number of purposes, but are most commonly used in support of oral communications. They can remind the audience of the important points of a presentation; they can refer the audience to points which are difficult to communicate verbally, for example data or technical considerations; and they can be used as promotional tools for your organisation.

The design of the handout is crucial:

* Whenever possible the handout should be typed and professionally printed - spirit duplication (e.g. bandas) tends to produce low quality reproductions.

* Only the key points should be communicated on the handout - there's no need to write a long essay, the reader will ignore it.

* Attention should be paid to the handout's layout to ensure that it is well-spaced, and visually pleasing, not distracting.

* Poorly produced handouts should never be used.

In addition to thinking about their design, you should also consider when to use them:

* Handouts distributed before the presentation act as a guide for the audience, structuring the flow of topics. A problem might be, though, that the listener reads the handout and then ignores the presentation.

* Handouts distributed after the presentation might not be read at all as the listener feels he knows all that he wishes to know about the topic that has been covered.

A compromise position is to distribute the handout during the presentation. To prevent this acting as a distraction for the audience, you should:

* Forewarn the audience that they will receive a handout of the key points being discussed.

* Reiterate the key points on the handout before distributing it.

* Once the handout has been distributed say nothing for 2 or 3 minutes, to enable the audience to read it. When they have read it ask if there are any questions about its content.

* Then instruct the audience to put the handout away before continuing with the presentation.

If these points are followed then you should be able to maintain the attention of all the members of the audience.

MEMOS

A 'Memo', or memorandum, is a common means of communicating within an organisation. You can use a memo in four ways.

(i) to provide instructions to others.

(ii) to record a series of events of which the reader should be aware.

(iii) to make suggestions to others

(vi) for expressing opinions or points of view.

No matter what purpose the memo has you should normally only use it to convey a brief message, which is set out in a standardised layout. Each organisation, though, will tailor the layout to suit their own in-house style and design.

However, no matter the style and design, the memo should indicate the sender, to whom it is being sent, the subject being discussed, the date of writing, and the reference notation being used, as in the example below:

MEMORANDUM

From:	Peter Blake, Sales Manager
To:	The Sales Team
Subject:	Transferable Personal Skills Training
Date:	1 April
Reference:	PB/DH

I am pleased to inform you that the results of the above training have been conclusive. Since undergoing the programme, our sales have increased by 200%. Well done.

If you send copies of the memo to third parties for their information, indicate this by an additional heading - 'Copies To:' As the writer of the memo, you will keep a copy as should the receivers.

Memos are useful forms of internal communication as they can be used to record verbal discussions, not as minutes of a meeting but as a confirmation of something that has been agreed and as such they act as a formal means of verifying decisions. Also by circulating memos widely, perhaps in a 'Perusal File', all colleagues concerned will be aware of developments in other departments. Memos are also valuable as a means of keeping senior colleagues informed of new developments, allowing them to intervene if they are concerned about the way a matter is being handled.

Normally, you would not sign a memo, but if the memo is requesting authorisation of the payment of funds then the originator's signature should be provided to indicate that it is a bone-fide request.

In writing memos you should always bear in mind the need for brevity and clarity of expression, as senior members of staff receive many memos everyday and long ones will tend to be overlooked, or just quickly read through.

BUSINESS LETTERS

Most organisations must communicate with their customers and suppliers. While telephone conversations and face-to-face meetings play an important part in this communication process, the most common method of communicating in writing is by the business letter.

Business letters do not simply provide information they also play a much wider role in communicating with the external environment. Business letters help to create the corporate image of the organisation by the style of the letter-heading, its typeface, and by the way in which the letter is composed and typed. Business letters must be regarded as legal documents frequently committing the organisation to a specific course of action. They are also important conveyors of technical information which if incorrectly written could lead to serious consequences for the writer of the letter. You should pay careful attention, therefore, when writing business letters and you should follow a number of steps when composing them:

1. Determine the objective of the letter

2. Determine the layout of the letter

3. Follow the normal conventions for business letters

1. Determine the objective of the letter

The first step you must take in writing a letter is to determine what its purpose is. Four types of letter will be discussed here:

(i)   letters seeking or offering information
(ii) letters of complaint
(iii) letters of a standard nature
(iv) references and testimonials

(i) Letters seeking or offering information

You can gain or provide much information by letter. Problems will arise, though, if you do not have a clear idea of the information that is needed. The starting point for this type of letter is for you to note down in rough the specific information you require. When you have done this, you can draft a letter that explicitly includes the information that you request. If you include a broad request for information such as:

"Please inform me of the cost of a two week holiday to Europe" the person who receives the letter could waste a considerable amount of time contacting you to find out more specific information details.

When writing a letter requesting information you should ensure that the letter is written in an understandable way. Frequently, writers use words which are not considered jargon by themselves, but when read by other people cause a certain amount of confusion. A marketing student when undertaking a project might find that he has to write letters to obtain information from local companies. Some of the recipients of the letters might not be familiar with marketing terminology. Thus questions such as: 'Can you provide me with details of your marketing mix and above and below the line expenditures?' will be confusing to people who do not understand the meaning of the terms 'marketing mix' and 'above and below the line expenditures'. Instead the student should specifically state the information he requires: 'Can you provide me with details of:

       a) the products you sell
       b) the prices charged for the product
       c) how you distribute the products to customers
       d) how you promote the product i.e. advertisements, sales promotions, publicity and personal selling?'

You should present the information you require in a coherent form. Indeed, it may be wise to write a short covering letter which does not contain any requests for information, but explains why you are collecting it. The information required is then typed on separate sheets in the form of a questionnaire.

If your letter requesting information is broken down into a series of questions, then the person replying to the letter should be specific in the responses to each of the questions posed, in a complete and accurate form.

(ii) Letters of complaint

You should write letters of complaint in a similar way to letters seeking or offering information, that is they should be most specific in referring to the complaint, which you need to explicitly state. In addition, it is important that you are objective in your style of writing and the phraseology that you use, keeping clear of emotive language, simply relating the facts surrounding the grievance and what compensation is sought or further action is to be taken. Your style of writing should be non-threatening and should not contain any points that cannot be substantiated. You should always be polite and courteous, although it will be important not to be condescending.

If your complaint is justified then a letter of apology will have to be written. Such letters obviously need to offer an apology but in most cases a simple sentence will suffice followed by a brief explanation of why the problem arose and how it will be resolved:

"Dear Mr. Smith,

Thank you for your letter of 27 August informing me that the electric kettle you bought from us in July has ceased working. Please accept our sincere apologies for the inconvenience this will have caused. After contacting the manufacturers we are informed that there is a design fault with this type of kettle. If you would care to return the kettle to us,we will either refund its cost in full or provide you with an alternative model of similar value.

Yours sincerely"

If the complaint is unfounded then you will have to send a full explanation of why this is so to the complainant:

"Dear Mrs. White

Thank you for your letter of 30 May informing us that you are dissatisfied with the fuel economy of your new car and that you would like a free service to be carried out to rectify the problem.

After contacting the manufacturer I am informed that the fuel economy figures you quote are within the cars expected fuel economy range of 30 - 40 miles per gallon of petrol. Your engine, therefore, is performing satisfactorily and there is no need to service your car at this point in time.

Thank you for drawing our attention to this matter, if your fuel economy becomes much worse in the future then please contact us again and we will investigate the problem further.

Yours sincerely"

It may help if the letter is sent out from a senior member of staff to indicate to the customer that the company does take such complaints seriously.

If you cannot give an immediate response to the complainant then you should send a letter to this effect to them followed by regular up-dates informing them of the progress being made. It is important to try and maintain the complainant's goodwill if you hope to deal with them again in the future.

(iii) Standard letters

The term 'Standard letter' is used here to refer to any letter that is sent out to a large number of recipients. As such they fulfil a variety of purposes, for example inviting applicants to attend for interview, or inviting shareholders to a company meeting. The content of the standard letter will be the same, irrespective of to whom it is sent. You should, however, take care when writing such letters to personalise them and to maintain the quality of any reproductions that are used. Although the letter is standardised, you should personally address each letter to the recipient and the person who has written the letter and whose name appears on it should endeavour to sign each one personally.

Letters which are used for persuasive purposes, for example direct marketing letters need careful composition. They need to create an instant impact with the reader otherwise they will be immediately filed in the waste paper basket. To do this you need to use a bold headline or a dramatic opening sentence that gains the attention of the reader and encourages them to read further. You should use a varied typeface and short paragraphs that are not too taxing or threatening for the reader. The language that you use should be easily understood and you should include a clear 'selling' message that will motivate the reader to take action.

Often a good idea after you have signed the letter is to include a 'P.S' which should be hand written, followed by a 'P.P.S.' as it is felt that these are frequently the main parts of the letter that are remembered.

Two examples of direct marketing letters are given below.

Fast-Fit Motor Dealers Ltd.
67-74 Dene Street
Northtown
NO5 3PT

Telephone 019 66349

Our ref: 00222
Your ref:

25 June 19**

Mr D Gordon
54 Queens Avenue
Northtown NO6 JTT

Dear Mr. Gordon,

This is a different kind of letter.

This half is ours .

This half is yours

Your car has not been serviced
by us recently.

Obviously there will be a
reason for this - that is your
side of the story. The side we
would like to know.

Perhaps it is because you have
sold the car, or moved to
another address. Maybe you
were dissatisfied with the
service you received from us
last time.

Whatever the reason, please
let us know so that we can
either amend our records, or
improve the quality of our
service.

Please use the other half of
this letter to tell us why you
have not had your car serviced
by us recently.

Thank you

Yours sincerely,

John Williams

John Williams
Service Manager

EASTERN SUN TRAVEL AGENTS

19 The Mall
Northtown
NO4 6PD

25 January 19**

Your ref:
Our ref:

Miss S White
120 Western Avenue
Northtown
NO9 4PJ

Dear Miss White

A SPECIAL OFFER FOR LOCAL CUSTOMERS

After one of the wettest and coldest British winters in recent years
the demand for holidays abroad has never been stronger. Holidays for
this summer are fast running out.

As you have not yet booked a summer holiday for this year I thought
you ought to be aware of some of the special offers that we are
currently providing for our local customers:

10% per person off the Summer Sun short haul programme.
20% per person off our Summer Sun long haul programme
30% per person off selected cruises.

These discounts are EXCLUSIVE to past customers, but will only apply
to holidays booked before 25 February. If you book your Summer holiday
now you need only pay a 5% deposit, with the balance due 7 days before
your departure.

Over 100,000 holidaymakers will book their summer holidays with
Eastern Sun Travel this year - make sure you are one of these lucky
customers. Come along and see us now to book your holiday in the
sun.

Bring this letter with you to receive your special loyalty discount.

Yours sincerely

Kate Wynne

Kate Wynne
Manager

P.S   You will also receive free travel insurance
if you book before 25th February

P.P.S This will save you at least an EXTRA £25
off the cost of your summer holiday in the sun.

(iv) References and testimonials

A reference is a statement either produced as a letter or written on a special form which provides an account of an applicant's character, ability, qualities and interests with respect to a given vacancy. An example of a reference form is given below:

REFERENCE

NAME: Laura Jones

POSITION APPLIED FOR: Graduate Trainee - Controller

Could you please complete the following reference form by circling the response that is most relevant for the above applicant:

TEAMWORKING

| Always seeks to involve others | Works well as a team member | Makes good effort | Dislikes team working | A loner |

QUALITY OF WORK

| Consistently high quality | Good in most aspects | Of varying quality | Not acceptable |

FLEXIBILITY

| Rigid and inflexible | Not very flexible | Acceptable flexibility | Welcomes new methods |

ABILITY TO WORK UNDER PRESSURE

| Thrives on pressure | Works well under pressure | Accepts pressure | Positively dislikes pressure |

PROBLEM SOLVING

| Outstanding | Generally good | Acceptable | Usually unable to solve problems |

QUALITY OF DECISIONS

| Makes frequent errors | Mostly correct | Clear and always correct | Avoids making decisions |

PERFORMANCE AGAINST OBJECTIVES

| Does not meet any objectives | Does not achieve most objectives | Achieves most objectives | Achieves all objectives |

CREATIVITY/INITIATIVE

| Dislikes change | Does not initiate | Welcomes new initiatives | Regularly seeks change |

LEADERSHIP

| An outstanding leader | Leads well on most occasions | Does lead occasionally | Not at all a leader |

PERSUASIVENESS

Rarely able to convince others	Mostly able to convince others	Always able to convince others

PERSISTENCE

Positively persists	Fully determined	Can be dissuaded	Rarely persists

PLANNING OF WORK

Superbly organised	Generally well organised	Inadequate planning

COMMUNICATIONS - VERBAL

An outstanding communicator	Communicates proficiently	Needs to improve	Does not communicate well

How would you rate the applicant's overall suitability for the post?

Tick the appropriate response:

1 **OUTSTANDING:** leaves little room for improvement, consistently exceeds objectives

2 **HIGHLY COMMENDABLE:** regularly, but not always, exceeds objectives. Displays some outstanding characteristics, but not always.

3 **FULLY PROFICIENT:** fully acceptable performance. Normal objectives met and assignments properly handled.

4 **MARGINAL:** performance does not fully meet requirements of position. Some objectives met, but not consistently.

5 **UNSATISFACTORY:** below minimum requirements. Objectives rarely met. Needs constant supervision.

SIGNED.................   POSITION.........................
DATE........

Source: Adapted from a reference form used by Nissan (UK) Ltd.

Reference forms have the advantage that the same information is obtained about each applicant, whereas with a letter of reference the writer dictates its content.

A testimonial is a letter of commendation in support of the applicant. The distinction between a reference and a testimonial is that the reference is requested by the interviewer and is sent direct from the referee to the interviewer, whereas the applicant keeps the testimonial until such time as it may be requested by an interviewer.

References are more highly rated by interviewers than testimonials, especially if they are written in an objective way and draw the attention of the interviewer to the applicant's weaknesses as well as strengths. References must be based on fact and should never be defamatory, otherwise legal action could be brought against you especially if malice is intended. Reference letters usually include the following:

* An indication of how long the referee has known the applicant and in what capacity.

* The current duties and responsibilities of the applicant.

* The applicant's skills, qualities, aptitudes, capabilities and personal characteristics .

* Major achievements of the applicants.

* Major weaknesses of the applicant .

* A statement evaluating the applicant's suitability for the vacant post.

2. The letter's layout

Once you have established the objective of the letter you can then consider its layout. The layout of the letter should be pleasing to the eye and should create a favourable impression with the reader of you and your organisation. Letters in which incorrect spacing is used and the text is bunched in the top half of the page, or in which the paragraphs are too large,for example, will signify to the reader that you and (or) your typist is unaware of presentation conventions. If you ignore presentation conventions you will lose credibility and not appear professional. We shall next give some guidelines for the layout of business letters.

The letter should clearly state:

* Who the sender is .

* When the letter was sent .

* What the letter is concerned with.

* What action should be taken as a result of receiving the letter .

The three ingredients of a businesslike letter are: accuracy, brevity and clarity. In addition to these there are other important considerations:

* The image created by the printed letter head and company or institution logo.

* The quality of the paper.

* The quality of the typeface that is used (some dot matrix printer typefaces are inappropriate for business letters).

* The visual design of the letter and its spacing on the page.

* The provision of ample margins.

All of the above considerations need to be reviewed regularly to ensure that the most professional image possible is being created by all letters that are sent from the organisation. Sometimes the only contact customers have with an organisation is the letters they receive. If the letters are poorly written, incorrectly laid out, and do not use appropriate letter-heads or logos, then the recipient will not form a very favourable image of the organisation. You should make every effort,therefore,to ensure that all letters that are sent out by you will enhance the organisation's image in the eyes of the recipient.

3. Letter writing conventions

Certain letter writing conventions should be followed.

A number of guidelines exist for the writing of business letters:

* The sender's name and address should be written in the top right hand corner of the letter, unless a pre-printed letter head is provided. The sender's name should appear at the end of the letter.

* The addressee's name and address should appear in the top left hand corner of the first page.

* The date appears after the sender's address on the right hand side of the page. The date should be written in full, and abbreviations should not be used.

* In greeting the reader, the recipient's name should be used whenever possible e.g. Dear Mr. Blake. When this greeting is used the letter should end Yours sincerely. If the greeting Dear Sir/Madam is used the letter should end Yours faithfully. If the letter is more personal i.e.. Dear Georgina, then a more personal ending may be used - Best wishes.

* A title or subject line should be used after the greeting to inform the reader of the content/purpose of the letter. This line should be underlined.

* All letters should be closed with the writer's personal signature followed by your title and position. If the writer is not available to sign the letter before it is posted it may be signed in his or her absence, and the letters p.p. (per pro) used to denote that the person signing the letter is empowered to do so.

* Reference numbers should be used in a series of letters to link the correspondence together, and to ensure that replies are directed to the appropriate department or individual. Usually two references are provided: 'Your Ref:' and 'Our Ref:'.

* When enclosures are included with a letter it is important to indicate them by typing 'Encl' or 'Enc' at the end of the letter, on the left hand side of the page, after the signature.

As we mentioned previously, business letters are ambassadors for the sending organisation. Customers, and other recipients, base their impression of an organisation on its letters as much as anything. The letter reveals much about what the organisation is really like, as distinct from the image created by its advertising or other promotional campaigns. Every letter sent out, therefore, either further endorses or reduces the standing and prestige of the organisation in the eyes of the receiver. The standard of business letters must be maintained at all times.

MALAYSIAN ENCOUNTER TOURS LTD.

Kampong Taynton View
Jalan Bee Cheras
34090 Kuala Lumpur
Malaysia
Tel: 887794/98
Telex: MA 56489

Mr. Roland Wyatt
The Operations Manager   1 June 19..
Eastern Tours Ltd.
Northsea
NE42 6QB
ENGLAND

Our Ref: f/0303/88
Your ref: w/1001/88

Dear Mr. Wyatt

Educational Field Visit to S.E. Asia

Thank you for your letter dated 22 May.

We are pleased to confirm your reservation of 1 unit 40-seater coach
and English-speaking guide as follows:

22 October

9.00am - Report to South East Asia Hotel, 190 Waterloo Street,
Singapore and transfer group to Kuantan with sightseeing enroute.

24 October

9.00am - Report to Merlin Beach Resort Hotel in Kuantan and drive to
          Cherating, Dungun and arrive at Rantau Abang

25 October

9.00am - Report to Rantau Abang and drive to Kuala Trengganu with
          swimming and sunbathing enroute.

The invoice for M$4000 in respect of the above will be sent to you 10
weeks before your departure to Malaysia. We wish your party a
pleasant visit to S.E.Asia.

Yours sincerely

Ho Clement

Ho Clement
Tour Co-ordinator

Reports

A written report is a document that provides an account of something, of work carried out, or of an investigation together with conclusions arrived at as a result of the investigation. Reports, therefore, convey information, research findings, and put forward ideas and suggestions. Reports can be classified in a number of different ways.

A **formal** report is detailed, is well-structured and is sub-divided. An **informal** report is usually shorter, less structured and more generally used.

Routine reports are frequently used in business as a matter of internal procedure for the information processing system of the organisation. For example, monthly sales reports need to be produced detailing the sales of the products in comparison to the previous month.

Special reports are produced on an ad hoc basis . They are often 'one-offs' dealing with a non-routine matter, such as the development of a new product, or the success of a new training programme.

However, irrespective of the nature of the report, you can adopt a common style to writing reports.

THE FORMAT OF A REPORT

Reports are structured documents which contain discrete sections and sub-headings within each section. The structure will be based on the following format:

* A title page showing the title of the report, your name as the author, your host organisation, and date of publication .

* A contents page detailing all the sections of the report and their sub-sections, with page numbers.

* A summary of the main points raised in the report and the findings under the section heading 'Executive Summary'

* An introduction containing:

    terms of reference - for whom the report has been written, and the purpose of the report
    procedures adopted - how the information presented in the report has been obtained
    topics covered - a broad indication of the report's content.

* The content of the report broken down into discrete sections and subsections. Each section and subsection should have a title/heading, and be numbered. At some stage you may have to evaluate some aspect of the

report's findings. This is the most intellectually challenging part of the report and needs to be conducted in an objective manner, for example analysing the strengths and weaknesses of the situation before arriving at a judgement.

* Conclusions indicating what the report has found, and which make reference to the report's objective(s).

* Recommendations for future action to be taken.

* Appendices detailing information that is relevant but which would detract from the coherence of the text, or is too lengthy or detailed to include in the body of the report. Each appendix should be numbered and referred to in the text of the report. The source of all data included in the report should be written after the data: the originator/writer, date of publication, title of publication and page numbers.

* Bibliography - references to information sources used e.g. articles, books etc. with details of the writer, date of publication, title of publication, publisher and page numbers.

You should adopt a similar format with all reports, even informal ones, although some variation will occur depending upon the nature of the report and its purpose. However, like letters, reports need careful preparation as they can enhance your prestige if they are well researched, written and presented.

You should keep headings as simple and brief as possible. Sub-sections within each section should be numbered or lettered, and you should consider numbering each paragraph. By numbering the report in this way any paragraph can be located quickly:

    1.   MAIN SECTION HEADING
    1.1   Section sub-heading.
    1.1.1 Sub-ordinate point.

We shall now given an example of a report.

**THE HADRIAN LODGE HOTEL
MARKETING FEASIBILITY STUDY**

THIS REPORT HAS BEEN RESEARCHED AND WRITTEN BY:

**JANICE CLARK BA(Hons), MBA, M Inst M
MARKETING CONSULTANT**

Hotel Consultancy Services
Ltd.
Broadstreet House
Northbay
NO76 6TY

Tel: 0567 45637

May 19..

CONTENTS

1: EXECUTIVE SUMMARY

Detailed below are the main points covered in this report:

1.1 After a slow start to the decade, the hotel industry is now more buoyant in terms of revenue generated and profits earned. Indeed, investment in new hotels is a national trend that is mirrored locally.

1.2 As the hotel industry becomes more competitive, hotels have to be targeted at clearly defined market segments, offering them clear selling points. According to Mintel Market Research the prime consumer of hotel accommodation is the business person. New hotels, therefore, need to be located on sites proximate to such demand.

1.3 There is a well developed supply of hotel accommodation in the proposal's catchment area. However, these hotels are primarily suitable for the tourist market, as opposed to the business market.

1.4 The proposed development will be able to offer a number of unique selling points to the business person: large bedrooms; business services; meeting rooms; secure car park; and leisure facilities. No other local hotel is able to offer these facilities.

1.5 A number of factors will positively influence the demand for the new hotel: the local economy is now more stable; new companies are being attracted to the previously declining industrial sites; a new shopping centre is being built close by; a trunk road will be opened adjacent to the site later this year, enabling passing trade to be attracted.

1.6 The negative influences to the demand revolve around 2 other new hotels to be developed locally next year.

1.7 It is concluded that the strengths of the proposal outweigh the weaknesses, and that the new proposed hotel appears to be viable from a marketing perspective.

2: INTRODUCTION

2.1. Terms of Reference

2.1.1 According to instructions given by the Directors of Bay Islands Ltd. a marketing feasibility study has been conducted to investigate the viability of a new hotel to be developed at Eastsea, the Hadrian Lodge Hotel.

2.1.2 The sponsors propose to develop a 120 bedroom hotel on a 10 acre site adjacent to the A1(T). Included in the development will be restaurant facilities, a leisure complex, and a function room suitable for small conferences or private functions.

2.1.3 This report has been researched and written by Hotel Consultancy Services Ltd.

2.2 Procedures

2.2.1 Research for this report was conducted in two ways:

2.2.1.1 Reference was made to published data from reputable and reliable sources in order to provide background data on national, regional, and local trends in the hotel industry. A list of references is given in the Bibliography.

2.2.1.2 Personal interviews were held with representatives from the public and private sector who have an interest in the local hotel industry. A list of the people interviewed is given in Appendix 1.

2.3 Topics Covered

2.3.1 This report analyses the product, market, factors likely to influence demand, before evaluating the proposal and reaching a conclusion. No reference is made to financial aspects.

PREPARING THE REPORT

Preparing a report is a skilful process involving a number of TPS, such as research skills, intellectual skills, (analysis, synthesis, and evaluation skills), and writing skills.

Your starting point is to determine the report's objective for this will dictate to a great extent how you should research, write and present the report. Once you have clearly identified the information needs you can set about collating the information. When you have fully researched the topic under investigation and you have collated the information you can then apply your intellectual skills to argue your case and to arrive at your conclusions and recommendations. Just as with other forms of written communication, the report should be clearly written and presented, concise and relevant to the report's objective.

CONSTRUCTING THE REPORT

You construct the report once you have collected and analysed the data. Layout is of great importance in formal reports, especially as they contain a considerable body of detailed material which needs to be carefully structured in a coherent, logical and non-repetitive manner. The structure of your report should follow the format outlined above so that it is readable and flows easily. You should use straightforward language and take care with grammar and sentence construction. Just because you are writing a report it does not mean that you should use a note-style of writing.

The report should be written in the third person singular. You should avoid personal terms such as 'I' or 'We', the word 'It' should be used instead:

"I decided to interview the Tourism Planning Officer....."
should read

"It was decided to interview the Tourism Planning Officer...."

You should not use emotive language, and avoid using vacuous terms - terms which lack a precise meaning such as 'good', 'excellent' and 'most'. Indeed, at all times you should be striving for precision in your writing and remembering that the report needs to be concise and to the point, for example use 'Now' instead of phrases like 'At the time of writing'. 'Sales peaked in August' should be used instead of 'The highest level of sales in the year were recorded at the height of the summer season in the month of August'.

Thus, your aim when writing a report contrasts with the aim of a fiction writer. The latter can use all forms of creative writing style in order to amuse and entertain the reader. Suspense can been maintained until the final word of the novel. In contrast, when writing a report you should bring the conclusions and main findings to the front of the report so that the reader can decide as soon as possible how much, or little, he needs to read to find out what he requires.

The emphasis in report writing is on facts, and interpretation of the facts in a logical, intellectual way rather than an emotional manner. You should write reports objectively to allow the reader to gain an unbiased view of the topic under consideration. Always remember that reports are for the benefit of those who read them, rather than the person who writes them.

Recording Meetings

Another important aspect of written communications is the recording of meetings. In such circumstances it is important to minute accurately what has been said. In this section we will consider how you should record motions and minutes at meetings. To begin this section on meetings however, we will give an example of a notice of a meeting and an agenda.

Notice

The purpose of the 'Notice' is to invite all interested parties to attend the meeting. Thus it should contain the date, time, and place of the meeting, as well as its purpose, and should be circulated well in advance.

Agenda

The Agenda contains all those items (topics) to be discussed at the meeting, and should also be circulated in advance.

In writing an agenda you should ensure that the items listed do inform the people attending the meeting of the exact topic to be discussed. To indicate the importance of different items on the agenda you could place timings against each one to show how long will be spent discussing it. This will also assist with the time-management of the meeting, helping to ensure that sufficient time is allocated to each item.

NOTICE OF THE MEETING

Notice is hereby given that the Eighth Annual General Meeting of Eastern Tours Ltd. is to be held on Monday 15 June at 2.30 pm in the Assembly Rooms, Northsea to consider the Director's Report and Statement of Accounts for the year ending 30 April. The dividend will be declared, directors appointed, auditors appointed, and any other business considered. All shareholders are invited to attend, those unable to do so may appoint a proxy to vote on their behalf.

Date: 15 May
By order of: The Company Secretary, Eastern Tours Ltd.

AGENDA OF THE MEETING

1 Introduction by the Chairman

2 Reading of the Minutes of the previous Annual General Meeting and their agreement

3 Matters arising from the Minutes

4 The Directors' Report read by the Managing Director

5 The Statement of Accounts read by the Finance Director

6 Declaration of the dividend by the Chairman

7 Appointment of Directors

8 Appointment of Auditors

9 Motion number 1

10 Any other business

11 Closure of the meeting by the Chairman

MOTIONS

When a formal meeting is held no subject or topic should be placed on the agenda, and hence debated, unless it has been proposed as a motion. When proposing a motion, the proposer must have it seconded, that is another person must state that he wishes it to be included on the agenda and debated.

Motions should be written, signed by the proposer and seconder, and submitted prior to the meeting. However, at less formal meetings it may be possible for motions to be proposed orally, at the time of their discussion. All motions, though, should start with the word 'That':

'That an increase in wages of 10% be offered to the work force.'

The wording used should be clear, to the point, and unambiguous. If any person disagrees with the motion or its wording, he should re-draft the motion and get it seconded, and submit the amendment prior to the meeting taking place. Any amendments have to be voted upon before the original motion is discussed. If the amendment is successful then it is discussed, if not, then the original motion is debated. When a motion has been accepted, it becomes a 'resolution'.

MINUTES

Minutes are made of the discussion and debates that take place at meetings. They primarily record the decisions that were reached. When the minutes have been signed by the chairperson, they become legally binding, cannot be altered, and may be submitted before a court of law as evidence.

If you are required to write minutes then you should include the following:

* The date and place of the meeting.

* The names of those present, and the apologies received from those unable to attend.

* The items of business that were transacted, with the decisions reached. The minutes should follow the order of the agenda.

Care should be taken by the secretary to the meeting to ensure that:

* The minutes are accurate.

* The wording used is clear and unambiguous .

* The minutes are concise, to the point, and are self-explanatory.

* That all phrases are written in the past tense.

* That numbers are given to each item discussed, or sub-headings are used.

When minuting the decisions of motions, the minutes should commence:

'It was resolved that......'

You should include the names of proposers and seconders in the minutes, as well as the main arguments that support a particular motion. If a vote is taken, you should include a summary of the voting for future reference.

The minutes of the meeting should be circulated to all those attending it, and the absentees, as soon after as possible. This will allow them to establish whether the minutes taken were in fact a true record of the discussions, debates, and decisions reached. The minutes that are kept outline the history of the decisions that have been taken and help to inform new delegates to the meeting of what has occurred previously.

Our purpose in this chapter has been to discuss how you can communicate most effectively using written material. In earlier chapters we have investigated the use of other non-verbal communication techniques as well as aspects of verbal communication. It is important, however, to recognise that each of these areas of TPS are not discrete elements that are used separately when communicating with others. Frequently you will need to use both verbal and non-verbal communication skills in the same situation. In the next chapter we shall consider another aspect of communication, namely that of communicating numerically.

Chapter Six

DATA HANDLING AND PRESENTATION SKILLS

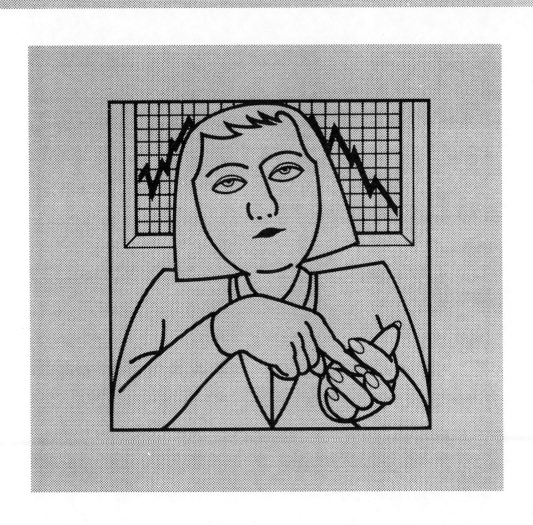

Chapter Six

DATA HANDLING AND PRESENTATION SKILLS

In this chapter we shall examine the skills of data handling and presentation. The chapter is divided into four parts:

(i) Basic arithmetic operations using such methods as ratios, percentages and indexes.

(ii) The presentation of numerical data using tables.

(iii) The presentation of data using graphs, charts and pie charts.

(iv) Statistical analysis of data.

It is important that you use numerical data skilfully. You will face many situations which require you to interpret data and communicate your conclusions to other people, for example, presenting a club or society's annual accounts to its members, or showing trends in the sales of a product to management. The skill of communicating data, therefore, is a TPS that you will need to master.

In this chapter we assume that you are competent at basic arithmetic - the addition, subtraction, multiplication and division of whole numbers, fractions and decimals. If you are weak in this area it is essential that you seek to improve your arithmetic by asking for remedial help from your tutors or by studying a basic school arithmetic book.

BASIC ARITHMETIC OPERATIONS

In this section we shall investigate three common methods of expressing data.

(i) Ratios.
(ii) Percentages.
(iii) Index numbers.

(i) RATIOS

A ratio is a method of showing the relative size of one item in comparison with another. Ratios are frequently used to compare relative sizes, quantities, costs, or sales. Thus, a ratio shows the number of times that one quantity is contained in another quantity of the same kind.

To work out a ratio, the quantities to be expressed need to be converted into the same units of measure. For example, to determine the ratio of 30 days to one year, we need to express the period of one year in days (365 days). Normally, the ratio is then divided by the highest common factor. The ratio is therefore:

$$\frac{30 \text{ days}}{365 \text{ days}} = \frac{6}{73}$$

This is written as 6:73, which means the ratio of 30 days to one year is as 6 is to 73. (Note the colon and that a ratio is a number without units such as days, pence or grammes).

Another example would require you to express £0.75p as a ratio of £2.50. Once again you must find a common unit of measure and so £2.50 is expressed in pence:

$$\frac{75}{250} = \frac{3}{10}$$

The ratio in this case is 3:10.

Ratios can be used for more than two quantities, for example when making a cake. The recipe might be 6 grammes of raisins, to 7 grammes of sugar, to 9 grammes of chocolate etc. The recipe works for any amount provided the ingredients are combined in the same proportions. Data expressed in this way can be used for working out simple calculations. For example, assume that a cash bonus is to be paid to 4 workers in the ratio of 9:11:13:15. If the total bonus is £480, work out how much each worker will receive:

First add the proportions together $(9 + 11 + 13 + 15 = 48)$ to give the total number of parts to the bonus. Then divide £480 by this number

$$\frac{£480}{48} = £10$$

Each part, therefore, is worth £10. Notice that this number is expressed in pounds. The cash bonus that each worker receives is calculated by multiplying his proportion by £10:

1st worker	9 x £10 =	£90
2nd worker	11 x £10 =	£110
3rd worker	13 x £10 =	£130
4th worker	15 x £10 =	£150
		£480

(ii) PERCENTAGES

Percentages are also ratios, and describe the rate of an item per hundred. If 15% of sales of the product come from the south of the country this means that for every 100 sales that are made in the country, 15 of them will be recorded in the south.

Expressing data as percentages gives a quick picture of the situation being described and is a common way of communicating data. Calculating percentages is straightforward. The first step is to express the data as a fraction. This shows it as a proportion of the total. The number to be expressed as a percentage is always divided by the base figure. Next this fraction is scaled up or down in order to express the fraction as a number divided by 100.

Using another sales example, assume that a total of 1000 units of the product are sold in the country, and that 250 of these sales were made in the west. The fraction used to work out the percentage is:

$$\frac{250}{1000} \quad \text{which is then expressed as} \quad \frac{25}{100}$$

The final stage is to convert this fraction into a percentage, by multiplying it by 100%

$$\frac{25}{100} \times 100\% = 25\%$$

Further examples are given below.

Example 1

Find 10% of £350

$$10\% = \frac{10}{100}$$

Therefore, 10% of £350 is

$$\frac{10}{100} \times £350 = £35$$

Example 2

Express 20 days as a percentage of one year

$$\frac{20}{365} = \frac{5.48}{100}$$

$$\frac{5.48}{100} \times 100\% = 5.48\%$$

This could be more simply written:

$$\frac{20}{365} \times 100\% = 5.48\%$$

(iii) INDEX NUMBERS

Using an index number is another way you can describe data, and is especially useful in showing trends. The purpose of index numbers is to show trends in a way that is easy to comprehend. This is done by comparing a set of figures with a base figure. First the base index is decided. This is commonly 100, but might be 1, 10, or 100. The base value (e.g. production output in year 1) is assigned the base index (e.g. 100). To calculate subsequent indices, each data value (e.g. production output in years 2, 3, 4) is divided by the base data value and then multiplied by the base index. If you are making a comparison of how production output has varied over time, then you could use index numbers to show the relative rises and falls in annual production. An illustration is given below:

The annual production output of a factory was recorded:

YEAR	PRODUCTION OUTPUT (TONS) (data values)
1	12000
2	14000
3	17000
4	18500

Year 1 is taken as being the base year against which all index numbers are compared. The index number is calculated in a similar way to percentages:

The year 1 index is 100 (the base).

The year 2 index is 14000 (the new production figure) divided by 12000 (the base year production figure) multiplied by 100.

$$\frac{14000}{12000} \times 100 = 117$$

The year 3 index is 17000 (the new production figure) divided by 12000 multiplied by 100.

$$\frac{17000}{12000} \times 100 = 133$$

The year 4 index is 18500 (the new production figure) divided by 12000 multiplied by 100.

$$\frac{18500}{12000} \times 100 = 158$$

Having taken 100 as the base index, it is easy to see that from year 1 to year 2 production output increased by 17%, from year 1 to year 3 by 33%, and from year 1 to year 4 by 58%. You can then draw interpretations from these index numbers, for example what accounted for such consistent growth.

There are many different types of indices, for example price indices and value indices. More sophisticated methods of calculating indices include such techniques as 'weighted indices' and 'several-item indices'. Such techniques are beyond the scope of this book and you should refer to a statistics textbook for a more detailed explanation of them.

THE USE OF TABLES

A useful way of presenting data is in the form of a table. Tables present numerical data visually. A good table shows data in a manner which highlights relationships between sets of data. At its simplest, a set of data gives values of a variable independent of any other factor. An example would be a table which shows the results of a machine which weighs all bags of flour after they have been filled to ensure that they equal or exceed the advertised weight; another would be a table to show the results of measuring the speed of cars on a motorway. Either of these examples could be presented as follows:

Weight of flour in each bag (kg)	Speed of each car on motorway (mph)
1.00	40
1.02	60
1.05	75
1.07	55
0.98	49
1.01	90
etc.	etc.

A more sophisticated version involves distinguishing classes of data items. For example, the machine weighing bags of flour might be able to distinguish between wholemeal flour, white flour and self-raising flour; a distinction between different lanes on the motorway could be made.

Weight of flour in each bag (kg)			Speed of each car on motorway (mph)		
Wholemeal	White	Self Raising	Lane 1	Lane 2	Lane 3
1.02	1.00	0.98	40	60	75
1.05	1.01	0.97	49	55	90
1.02	1.02	1.00	47	62	80
1.03	1.00	0.99	42	73	70
etc.	etc.	etc.	etc.	etc.	etc.

Notice that each bag of flour has a weight, and each car a speed. The weight of flour in a bag can vary. The speed of a car on the motorway can vary. Weight and speed in these examples are termed 'variables'.

Consider a burning candle , the candle gets progressively shorter. You might have recorded the following data observing a candle.

Time of observation (hrs: mins)	Length of candle (cm)
15.30	10.00
15.35	8.00
15.40	6.00
15.45	4.00
15.50	2.00
15.55	0.00

Most data collection and presentation concerns change of one variable in relation to change of another variable. Much data concerns change over a period of time. Most observations are recorded at intervals over a given period of time. In the example above the length of the candle was measured every five minutes. Examining the table it can be seen that as time progresses, the candle gets shorter. The length of the candle is dependent on the time. In this example, time is called the 'independent variable' and length of the candle the 'dependent variable'.

A more sophisticated version of the table might give not only the time of the observation, but also the time from the first observation:

Time of observation (hrs: mins)	Time from the first observation (mins)	Length of candle (cm)
15.30	00	10.00
15.35	05	8.00
15.40	10	6.00
15.45	15	4.00
15.50	20	2.00
15.55	25	0.00

Processing the data in this way helps to show more clearly what relationship exists between data items. Time remains the independent variable, but now we can consider 'elapsed time', rather than 'clock time'.

Note that by using time as a variable, we could choose to take observations when we wished - we are no longer dependent on a bag of flour falling onto the weighing machine, or a car coming along the motorway. Time is a continuous quantity, as is the length of the candle, as the following table shows:

Time of observation (hrs:mins)	Elapsed time (mins)	% Elapsed time (%)	Length of Candle (cm)	% of total candle (%)
15.30	00	00	10.00	100
15.35	05	20	8.00	80
15.40	10	40	6.00	60
15.50	20	80	2.00	20
15.52	22	87	1.20	12
15.54	24	96	0.40	4
15.54.5	24.5	98	0.20	2
15.55	25	100	0.00	0

Note that, within reason, a table can include any number of columns, although there is little point in including an extra column of figures unless it helps the reader's understanding of the table.

Here are some guidelines to consider when producing material in such a way:

* Consider the purpose of presenting the data as a table - there may be better ways of presenting it.

* Include only those figures which address the purpose of the table (some tables are huge and contain columns which could be irrelevant to the immediate purpose .

* Do not include superfluous data which does not add to the reader's understanding.

* Provide a table number and title for each table. If abbreviations are used when labelling, provide a key.

* Allow sufficient space when designing the table for all figures to be clearly written.

* At the end of the table indicate where the data, or the table itself, have been obtained.

THE GRAPHICAL PRESENTATION OF DATA

Graphs, bar charts, and histograms bring to life data from tables and allow for comparisons to be made relatively quickly. When using these visual methods for presenting data a disadvantage is that some of the detail and perhaps a degree of accuracy will be lost.

Data can be presented visually in many situations, for example showing trends in costs of production or trends in market share. Your aim is to present such data clearly so that the reader can quickly identify the patterns that exist and then draw inferences or conclusions. Sometimes it is important to present the data in such a way that any inconsistencies or unusual features stand out, or alternatives to show the relationship between various sets of data. To achieve this you can use a number of different graphical presentation styles:

(i) Graphs.
(ii) Bar charts.
(iii) Histograms.
(iv) Trend Graphs.
(v) Pie Charts.

Before addressing each of the above in turn, it is important that you recognise several distinctions between sets of data. In isolation, it might seem unimportant to distinguish between 'continuous' data and 'discrete' quantities. However, it is this distinction that helps you to determine what style of graphical representation to use. A continuous quantity is that which can (theoretically) be measured to any chosen degree of precision. Examples of continuous quantities are mass (kg), length (m), time (s) and rate of change (e.g. m/s, m/s^2). Notice that each example has a unit of measure (kilogrammes, metres, seconds, etc). Continuous quantities can be expressed in integers (2kg, 4m, 101s), fractions (21/72 inches), decimal fractions (27.36m) and negative numbers (-2.6 m/s). Discrete quantities, by contrast, can be expressed only as integers: 3 biros, 72 eggs, 14 sheep. In trying to determine whether something is a continuous or a discrete quantity, decide whether (in context) it is like a stream of water (continuous) or like people (discrete).

Only if both aspects of a data set are continuous quantities should you plot a graph (see below). For example, plotting the speed of a sports car as it accelerates away; plotting market share through a year. Money might appear problematic because the way in which you should treat it depends on the use you intend to make of it. Petty cash expenditure per day is straight forward because days are discrete. Therefore, technically, a graph would be inappropriate. By way of contrast, a factory always has a capital value, which may vary through time, and may conceivably be measured in fractions of a penny.

If a set of data should not be presented in the form of a graph, then alternatives include a bar chart and a histogram. These are also more appropriate ways of presenting discrete quantities because they permit the grouping of data. A simple example might be the number of eggs laid each day by a flock of hens. A more complex example might be the number of students in a class earning part-time wages, grouped in bands e.g. £0.00 - £9.99; £10.00 - £19.99/week, etc.) Bar charts and histograms allow such data to be presented accurately and usefully.

This shows us the second distinction to be made. The speed of a sports car through time can be plotted on a graph. If there are two sports cars, then two separate lines (curves) could be plotted on the same graph. If there are 1000 sports cars, then not only would it be impractical to plot 1000 separate lines (curves) on the same graph, but also our reson for testing 1000 sports cars is likely to be different from our reason for testing just one or two. For example, we may wish to find out how many can accelerate from 0-60 mph in under six seconds. The emphasis has shifted from rate of change (graph) to how many cars are in each category (bar chart or histogram).

(i) GRAPHS

Graphs enable you to present numerical data in a way that clearly shows the trends occurring within a given set of data. The normal way of drawing a graph is to use two axes - two straight lines drawn at right angles. One of the lines is drawn vertically, and is known as the vertical axis, or y axis, while the other is drawn horizontally and is called the horizontal or x axis. These two axes cross at the origin. The data to be presented on the graph will normally depict two sets of data, for example set A showing the months of the year and set B showing the sales of a product.

Pairs of data can be formed, for example for every A data value there will be a B value (the A data are called x-values and the B data y-values):

Months of the Year (The A data)	Sales of the product (The B data)
Month:	
1	70 units
2	70 units
3	65 units
4	50 units
5	40 units
6	41 units
7	33 units
8	20 units
9	53 units
10	60 units
11	64 units
12	69 units

The ordered pairs (an x-value with its corresponding y-value) are called 'co-ordinates'. These co-ordinates can be plotted on a graph. Plotting a co-ordinate on a graph requires two pieces of information - the value of x (the horizontal value), and the value of y (the vertical value). The x-value is always written first. A cross is then placed on the graph paper where '1' on the x axis meets '70' on the y axis. To do this accurately, you should use squared graph paper. An x-value is plotted with reference to the horizontal axis, and its corresponding y-value with reference to the vertical axis. This shows that every x-value relates to, and depends on its corresponding y-value.

Graphs drawn like this help the analysis of data. For example, if you simply look at the above table it might not give a very clear picture of the sale trends of the product. When such data are plotted on a graph, however, and a line is drawn to connect the co-ordinates, you get a visual picture. It is immediately apparent that sales of the product peaked during months 1-3 and 11-12. During other months sales fell with a low period during months 7 and 8.

When drawing graphs, you have to work out scales for the axes. The scale is how the axes are divided up to show the units that are being represented. Each axis should be divided up into equal sections, as on a ruler. The size of each section should be such that all the data values to be represented can be included on the axis. In the table above the x-axis should have twelve equal divisions, for each month of the year. The y-axis could commence at 0 units sold and then divided into equal sections, each representing 10 units of the product, you may have a maximum unit 80, making 8 divisions in all.

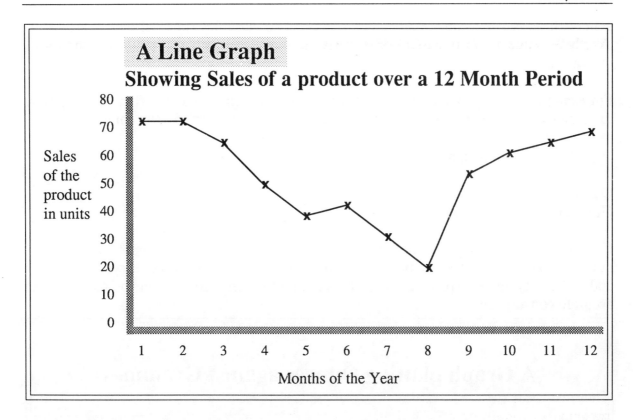

A Line Graph

Showing Sales of a product over a 12 Month Period

Sales of the product in units *(y-axis)*

Months of the Year *(x-axis)*

Note that the scale used for the y-axis does not have to be the same as that used for the x-axis. You should use scales so that the graph fits the area of paper you wish to cover. The axes are normally drawn with '0' as the origin. Sometimes, though, this might result in the coordinates all being plotted in one confined area of the graph. In such circumstances it is more appropriate to draw the axes starting at a higher value. When the axes start at values other than '0', they are referred to as false axes.

The choice of scales can greatly affect the visual impression that is given. By compressing the scale of the independent variable trends in the data can be made to look quite dramatic, whereas expanding the scale of the independent variable can reduce the visual impact of trends in the data. You should aim to keep such distortions to a minimum as the purpose of communicating graphically is to present the data in a clearer form than could otherwise be achieved. You should continually ask yourself whether your presentation of the data gives an accurate impression.

If you have to plot negative x co-ordinates on the graph (such as -4 or -6) you should plot these to the left of the vertical axis, whereas all positive x co-ordinates (4, 6) are plotted to the right. In a similar way, negative y co-ordinates are plotted below the x-axis.

INTERPOLATION AND EXTRAPOLATION

Graphs are useful for plotting one variable (or value) against another variable to show trends that might be occurring. There is, however, additional information, that can be gained from graphs.

Where there is a constant relationship between two variables (one variable increases at exactly the same proportion to the other variable) then it is possible to use the graph to work out values.

For example, if the weight of a product is expressed in ounces and a particular weight has to be converted into grammes then you could use a graph to perform the conversion:

Weights

Ounces	1	8	16
Grammes	25	200	400

If the table given here is the only data that you have available and you are to convert 13 ounces into grammes, then the best you might say is that 13 ounces lies somewhere between 200 and 400 grammes. However, if the data are plotted on a graph then you can make an accurate conversion.

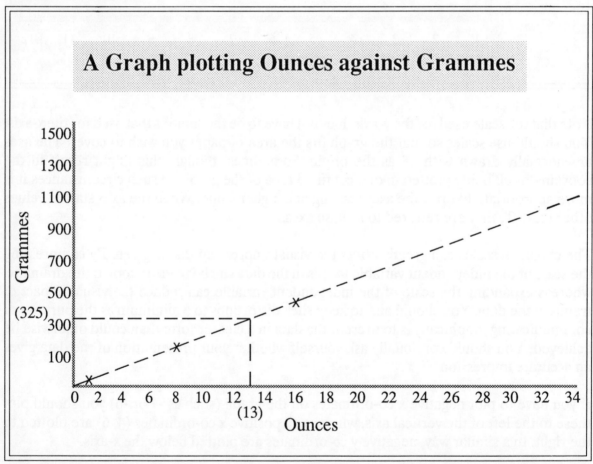

A Graph plotting Ounces against Grammes

The data will produce a straight line when you join the co-ordinates together on the graph. To convert 13 ounces into grammes, draw a vertical line up from the '13 ounces' point on the x-axis until it cuts the diagonal line. Then draw a horizontal line from this point to the y-axis. The point (325) at which the y-axis was cut indicates the number of grammes that are equivalent to 13 ounces. The process can be reversed to convert grammes into ounces. The process of finding equivalent values from a straight line graph is known as interpolation.

Extrapolation is used when the ounces or grammes to be converted lie outside the data presented in the table, for example converting 18 ounces into grammes. The constant relationship between the variables means that the straight line can be extended, at both ends, (see the dotted lines drawn on the graph) so that you can make further readings from the graph. The process of finding equivalent values that are beyond a given set of data is known as extrapolation.

Your interpolation and extrapolation will be accurate only if there is a constant relationship, at all values, between the variables. Should the co-ordinates not produce a straight line, when plotted and joined together, but a curve, you will be unable to obtain equivalent values. Curves will still be of benefit, though, in that they show trends that are occurring with the data.

(ii) BAR CHARTS

Bar charts use elongated oblongs, or bars, to show quantities of a given product or item, over time. On the x-axis will be plotted the days, months or years, and on the y axis the quantities of the product or item being considered. Bar charts provide a quick, clear presentation of data. In producing them it is important to ensure that the oblongs have a uniform width, and if a number of different products or items are being represented on the same bar chart that you use colours or shading patterns to distinguish between the different products or items.

Bar charts can be drawn either horizontally or vertically. The elongated bars may be either touching or separated from one another, depending upon the amount of data to be plotted. In constructing them, you must always consider their clarity and ease of comprehension for the reader.

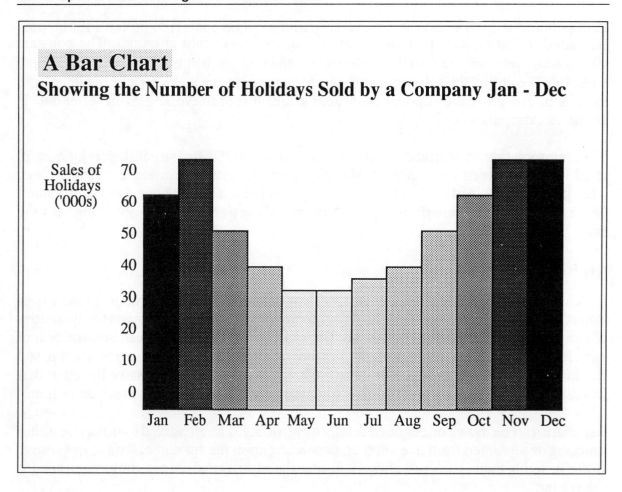

A Bar Chart
Showing the Number of Holidays Sold by a Company Jan - Dec

Sales of Holidays ('000s)

Sometimes, it may be appropriate to use a single percentage bar chart, for example when showing how a company's sales turnover is derived. The total length of this bar represents 100% and divisions are made to signify the percentage contributions of different products. For example the first quarter of the bar is shaded in one colour to signify that 25% of the sales turnover comes from lawn mowers; the next division is three-quarters along the bar to show that 50% of sales comes from garden tools - shaded differently - and the final quarter, 25%, shows that these sales come from garden accessory equipment.

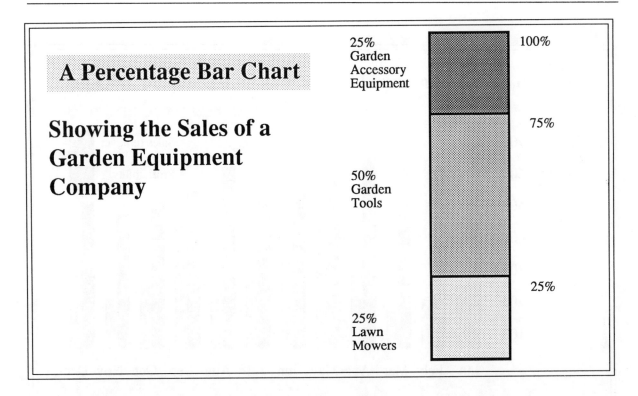

A series of percentage bar charts can be plotted against each other to show the trends that are occurring in sales over time, giving the reader a clear picture as to whether the sales of lawn mowers as a proportion of total sales are increasing faster than sales of garden tools. Where this type of presentation is used, normally all the bar charts will be of the same length.

In other circumstances it may be appropriate to use dual, or treble, bar charts. With these, for each time period being considered, two or three sets of data are presented. For example, the data might be company sales turnover and profitability. Here, both bar charts stand side by side for the time period in question.

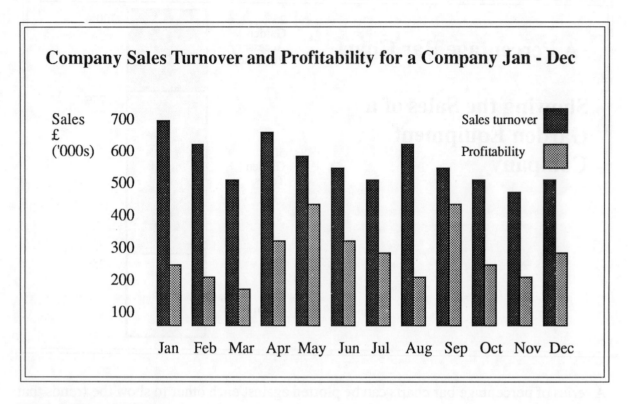

(iii) HISTOGRAMS

Histograms are widely used for illustrating grouped data. Grouped data are data that have been put into classes or bands in order to make the information easier to handle. Typically, a population is banded into age groups. The histogram then shows, for example, the average weekly income for each band, or average life expectancy, etc.

A histogram differs from a bar chart (which it resembles) in that frequency is represented not by length but by area. This might seem to be a technical point. In purely practical terms it means that a histogram is best drawn onto squared paper, and that the height of a rectangle must be calculated. Each square represent one (or a given number of) unit(s) in a population. For example, surveys often ask the age of the respondent. These ages are then banded in a manner appropriate to the needs of the survey. The following example illustrates this.

A survey of 1000 rail travellers was conducted in order to consider the proportion of passengers eligible for a concessionary fare. A question in the survey asked respondents to identify to which age group they belonged:

	(years)	(years)	No of Respondents
Child	5-15	11	132
Young Person	16-24	9	333
Middle Age (a)	25-44	20	200
Middle Age (b)	45-59	15	195
Pensioner	60-80	20	140
			1000

A histogram is drawn onto squared paper, with age along the x-axis. For each class, a rectangle is drawn. The width of the first rectangle is the class interval for children: 11 years. The height of the rectangle is calculated by dividing the number of respondents in that class (132) by the class interval (11 years). This gives a rectangle representing 132 children aged between 5 and 15 years. The other rectangles are drawn in a similar fashion.

The purpose of doing this would be to show rail use by age for any given age. Rather than using the precise age of each respondent (there might just happen to have been no-one aged 47 years interviewed in the survey, and therefore that age would have no bar on a bar chart), useful bands of ages are considered. Using the notion of area rather than height representing respondents means that the class interval can be variable.

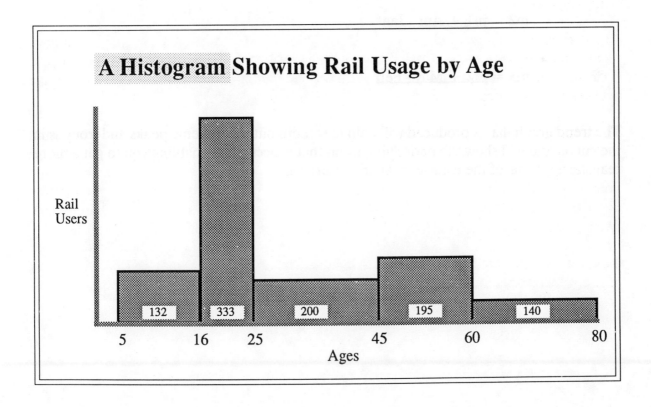

(iv) TREND GRAPHS

Straight line graphs and bar charts might not clearly show what is the underlying trend or pattern of data. To show a trend you could use a 'moving average' graph.

Moving average graphs, as their name suggests, plot the average figure for the time period under consideration. Thus, if the graph is showing monthly fluctuations in the data, where great peaks and troughs are being recorded, it might be more meaningful if you were seeking to identify an underlying trend in the data to look at the average quarterly value rather than the monthly sales value.

Using this approach, the monthly values are added up for the quarter and then divided by three to arrive at the average. This figure is then plotted on the graph at the mid-point for the quarter in question. Once the first average figure has been calculated, the second is worked out as below:

For a quarterly moving average, where Jan, Feb, Mar, Apr, May, Jun represent months of the year, and m1, m2, m3 represent the quarterly moving averages:

$$m1 = \frac{Jan + Feb + Mar}{3}$$

$$m2 = \frac{m1 + Apr - Jan}{3}$$

$$m3 = \frac{m2 + May - Feb}{3}$$

The trend graph that is produced will help to smooth out the extreme peaks and troughs in the curve, and will show the underlying trend that is occurring, enabling you to get a more realistic appraisal of the changes that are occurring.

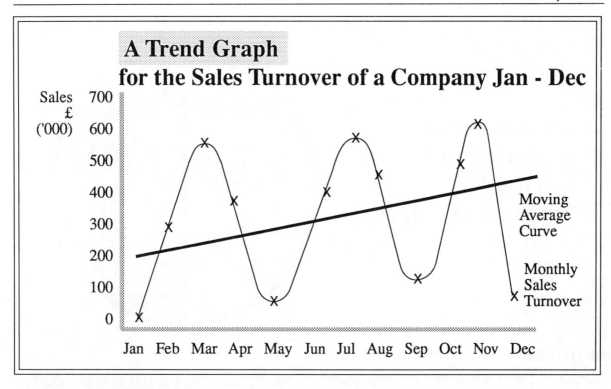

(v) PIE CHARTS

Pie charts are circles that are divided into proportionate segments that show how a 'complete whole' is to be divided up. From a pie chart you can very quickly establish the relative importance of the different segments. The pie chart is drawn by calculating the proportionate importance of each of the segments (for example 25% of the sales in our earlier example come from lawnmowers) and then by multiplying this figure by 3.6 (360 degrees divided by 100):

> Lawnmower sales contribute 25% of total sales, therefore on the pie chart this segment will account for:
> 25 x 3.6 = 90 degrees.

> Garden tools account for 50% of total sales which is
> 50 x 3.6 = 180 degrees.

> Garden accessories account for 25% of total sales, which is
> 25 x 3.6 = 90 degrees.

Once you have calculated the size of each segment in degrees you can draw the circle. Then using a protractor divide it into the appropriate segments. Give the pie chart a title and clearly label each segment. Include the percentages for each of the segments on the pie chart to give an accurate picture of the importance of each segment. You should draw the pie chart so that the size of each segment follows in a sequential pattern - the largest segment first, followed by the second largest and so on. If there are a number of segments to the pie chart it will probably be best to use colour or shading to denote each one, with a key indicating what each segment represents, otherwise too much text would be included.

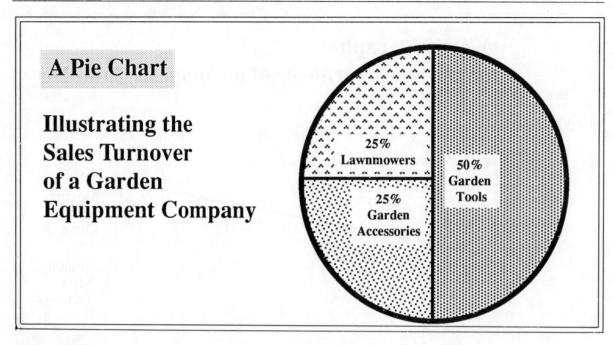

A Pie Chart

Illustrating the Sales Turnover of a Garden Equipment Company

25%
Lawnmowers

25%
Garden
Accessories

50%
Garden
Tools

SUMMARY

You should bear in mind a number of guidelines when presenting visual data to prevent any ambiguity in its interpretation:

* Think clearly about what you are trying to say when using a visual presentation.

* Give all visual presentations a title. The title should indicate what is being represented and leave no doubt in the reader's mind as to the nature of the data. The axes should be labelled, and clear indication given as to the scales being used, and the numerical quantities being referred to.

* All dates and time periods should be explicitly stated in the title, and on the appropriate axis.

* The source of the data should be indicated, especially when drawn from published material.

* Correctly drawn and presented visual material can provide a quick impression of patterns that exist in a set of data, patterns that might not be so readily apparent from tabulated figures. You must take care as a reader of such material not to be misled by techniques that might exaggerate or distort such patterns.

* Look out for axes not numbered from zero. The effect of this can be to make relatively small variations in the data seem more amplified. This technique as mentioned previously is known as the 'false zero'.

STATISTICAL ANALYSIS OF DATA

FREQUENCY DISTRIBUTIONS

The table below shows the mileages recorded by a fleet of vehicles in 1 week:

Mileages Recorded by Vehicles

482	502	466	408	486	440	470	447	413	451	410	430
469	438	452	459	455	473	423	436	412	403	493	436
471	498	450	421	482	440	442	474	407	448	444	485
505	515	500	462	460	476	472	454	451	438	457	446
453	453	508	475	418	465	450	447	477	436	464	453
415	511	430	457	490	447	433	416	419	460	428	434
420	443	456	432	425	497	459	449	439	509	483	502
424	421	413	441	458	438	444	445	435	468	430	442
455	452	479	481	468	435	462	478	463	498	494	489
495	407	462	432	424	451	426	433	474	431	471	488

A casual examination of this set of figures is unlikely to reveal anything other than the fact that most of the figures are in the 400s with an occasional one in the 500s. From a table in this form it would be very difficult to determine any patterns present in the data. For instance, are the numbers evenly distributed, or is there a certain small range which holds most of the numbers?

The statistical techniques discussed here will allow raw data such as that presented above to be summarised and presented in a form which facilitates identification of trends and allows the significance of the figures to be grasped. It should be noted, however, that as the crude data are converted into more convenient forms of representation, the fine details within the data are progressively lost.

UNGROUPED FREQUENCY DISTRIBUTIONS

A first step in the analysis of the data in the table could be to sort the figures into ascending order of magnitude and at the same time to note the number of times any figures are repeated. The next table has been produced in this manner and is termed an 'Ungrouped Frequency Distribution'. The table consists of a list of every unique mileage with its frequency of occurrence, that is, the number of times it occurred in the original table.

Ungrouped Frequency Distribution

Mileage	freq	Mileage	freq	Mileage	freq	Mileage	freq
403	1	434	1	456	1	479	1
407	2	435	2	457	2	481	1
408	1	436	3	458	1	482	2
410	1	438	3	459	2	483	1
412	1	439	1	460	2	485	1
413	2	440	2	462	3	486	1
415	1	441	1	463	1	488	1
416	1	442	2	464	1	489	1
418	1	443	1	465	1	490	1
419	1	444	2	466	1	493	1
420	1	445	1	468	2	494	1
421	2	446	1	469	1	495	1
423	1	447	3	470	1	497	1
424	2	448	1	471	2	498	2
425	1	449	1	472	1	500	1
426	1	450	2	473	1	502	2
428	1	451	3	474	2	505	1
430	3	452	2	475	1	508	1
431	1	453	3	476	1	509	1
432	2	454	1	477	1	511	1
433	2	455	2	478	1	515	1

Notice that the sum of the frequencies is equal to the number of items in the original table, that is, 120.

GROUPED FREQUENCY DISTRIBUTION

Though the data have now been organised, there are still too many numbers for the mind to be able to grasp the information hidden within them. Therefore the next step is to simplify the presentation of the data further. At this stage in the production of a grouped frequency distribution, the crude data are replaced by a set of groups which split the mileages into a number of small ranges called 'classes'. The following table is an example of a grouped frequency distribution based on the ungrouped frequency distribution shown in the ungrouped frequency distribution table.

Grouped Frequency Distribution

Mileages	Frequency
400 to under 420	12
420 to under 440	27
440 to under 460	34
460 to under 480	24
480 to under 500	15
500 to under 520	8
TOTAL	120

The overall range of mileages, 403 to 515, has been split into 6 classes each covering an equal sub-range of the total range of values. Notice that the class limits, that is the boundary values of the classes, do not overlap, nor are there any gaps between them; these are important characteristics of grouped frequency distributions.

The effect of grouping data in this way is to allow patterns to be detected more easily. For instance, it is now clear that most of the figures cluster in and around the '440 to under 460' class. The cost of being able to extract this piece of information is the loss of the exact details of the raw data; a grouped frequency distribution summarises the crude data. Thus any further information deduced or calculated from this grouped frequency distribution can only be approximate.

CHOICE OF CLASSES

The construction of a grouped frequency distribution will always involve making decisions regarding the number and size of classes to be used. Though these choices will depend on individual circumstances to a large extent, the following guidelines should be noted:

* Class intervals should be equal where possible.

* Restrict the number of classes to between 6 and 20; too many or too few classes will obscure information.

* Classes should be chosen so that occurrences within the intervals are mainly grouped about the mid-point of the classes in order that calculations based on the distribution can be made as accurately as possible. Examination of the ungrouped frequency distribution should highlight any tendencies of figures to cluster at regular intervals over the range of values considered.

* Class intervals of 5,10, or multiples of 10 are easier to work with than intervals of 7 or 11 (manually, that is; it is not a problem when using a computer).

CUMULATIVE FREQUENCY DISTRIBUTION

The next table contains an additional 2 columns to the data in the previous table. The entries in the column labelled 'Cumulative Frequency' have been calculated by keeping a running total of the frequencies given in the adjacent column. As expected, the final entry shows that the sum of all the frequencies is 120. The final column shows the same accumulated figures as percentages of the total number of figures.

'Less Than' Cumulative Frequency Distribution

Mileages	Frequency	Cumulative Frequency	Cumulative Percentage %
400 to under 420	12	12	10.0
420 to under 440	27	39	32.5
440 to under 460	34	73	60.8
460 to under 480	24	97	80.8
480 to under 500	15	112	93.3
500 to under 520	8	120	100.0
TOTAL	120		

This new table allows further observations to be made regarding the data being examined. For example, the table now shows that 80.8% of the vehicles travelled less than 480 miles, and that 6.7% (100-93.3) of the vehicles travelled more than 500 miles; 20% (80.8-60.8) of the vehicles travelled between 440 and 480 miles.

Because the figures have been accumulated from the lowest class to the highest, this table is called a 'less than' cumulative frequency distribution. The next table shows a 'more than' cumulative frequency distribution in which the frequencies have been accumulated in reverse order:

'More Than' Cumulative Frequency Distribution

Mileages	Frequency	Cumulative Frequency	Cumulative Percentage %
400 to under 420	12	120	100.0
420 to under 440	27	108	90.0
440 to under 460	34	81	67.5
460 to under 480	24	47	39.2
480 to under 500	15	23	19.2
500 to under 520	8	8	6.7
TOTAL	120		

Hence, the table shows directly that 90% of the vehicles travelled more than 420 miles and 6.7% travelled more than 500 miles. Simple calculations also allow 'less than' figures to be derived, just as 'more than' figures can be calculated from the 'less than' cumulative frequency distribution.

The data in a grouped frequency distribution can be represented diagrammatically using a histogram. Alternatively a graph could be drawn to represent the cumulative frequency distribution - this is known as an 'ogive':

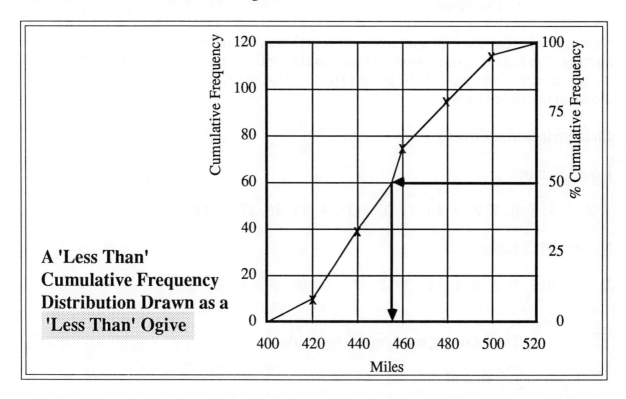

A 'Less Than' Cumulative Frequency Distribution Drawn as a 'Less Than' Ogive

Ogives start at zero on the vertical scale and end at the outside class limit of the last class on the horizontal axis. The vertical axis on the right of the diagram gives the cumulative frequency as a percentage, so that either scale may be used.

An ogive curve provides a useful and efficient method of determining 'percentiles'. Percentiles are points in the distribution below which a given percentage of the total lies. A percentile divides a set of observations into 2 groups. For example, using a 'less than' ogive, 25% of the mileages, in the example above, are below the 25th percentile (that is below 434 miles approximately), and 75% are above the 25th percentile. Certain percentiles are known as 'quartiles':

> the 25th percentile is the first quartile
> the 50th percentile is the second quartile (also known as the median)
> the 75th percentile is the third quartile.

Percentiles are a very useful way of expressing such statistics as

> "5% of the population of the U.K. own half of the individual wealth ."

MEASURES OF LOCATION

Measures of location or measures of central value are ways of expressing averages. The most common types of averages are:

* The Arithmetic Mean (or just 'the mean').
* The Median.
* The Mode.

Each one of these measures attempts to represent a collection of figures with a single number. The following discussion summarises the methods by which each is calculated and its significance. Reference will be made to the data in the ungrouped frequency distribution shown in the table below:

Children in Saville Street

House Number

1 2 3 4 5 6 7 8 9 10 11 12 13 14 15 16 17 18 19

Number of Children

1 0 6 0 3 0 1 0 1 1 5 2 2 2 0 3 4 2 0

The following notation will be used:

$\sum$ = sum of

$\bar{x}$ = mean value

x_i = single value

n = number of values

f = frequency.

MEAN

Calculation of the mean:

a) Ungrouped data:

      i) add together all the values
      ii) divide by the number of values.

The mathematical notation for the calculation is:

$$\bar{x} = \frac{\sum x_i}{n} \quad i = 1, \ldots, n$$

Using the values in the above table this gives:

$$\bar{x} = \frac{33}{19} = 1.74 \text{ approx}$$

b) Grouped frequency distribution:

    i)   identify classes and respective mid-point values
    ii) multiply each class mid-point by the frequency
    iii) add these values together
    iv) divide this sum by the sum of the frequencies.

The mathematical notation for the calculation is:

$$\bar{x} = \frac{\sum(f \times \text{Class mid-point})}{\sum f}$$

Using the values in the Grouped Frequency Distribution this gives:

$$\bar{x} = \frac{12 \times 410 + 27 \times 430 + 34 \times 450 + 24 \times 470 + 15 \times 490 + 8 \times 510}{120}$$

$$\bar{x} = 454.5$$

The arithmetic mean indicates what value each item would have if the total of all values were shared out equally. The mean is the most suitable measure to discover the result that would follow on from an equal distribution of something (consumption of beer per head, for instance).

MEDIAN

Calculation of the median:

a) Ungrouped data:

    i) arrange the data into ascending order of magnitude
    ii) locate the middle term in the series - this is the median. If there are an even number of numbers and there is no middle term then the nearest to the mid-point on either side will do.

Were you to arrange the data in ascending order of numbers of children, you would see that the median term in the Saville Street example is the 10th one and the value of the median is therefore, 1. In the mileages example, the middle term is the 60th and the median value is 452 miles.

b) Grouped frequency distribution:

      i) produce the equivalent ogive
      ii) read off the value of the 2nd quartile - this gives the median value.

The median is merely the value of the middle term when the data are arranged into ascending order of magnitude. Consequently there will be as many terms above it as below it.

MODE

The mode is usually derived from an ungrouped frequency distribution by determining the value which occurs most frequently. In Saville Street, the value occurring most frequently is 0 children. In the table showing the ungrouped frequency distribution there are several modes: each mileage which occurs three times is a mode of the distribution of mileages.

As the mode is the value that occurs most frequently, it represents the typical item. It is this form of average that is implied by such expressions as 'the average person' or 'the average holiday'.

DISPERSION

Quoting an average value, such as the mean, is an attempt to describe a distribution figure by a single representative number. Such averages, however, suffer from the disadvantage that they give no indication of the spread, or dispersion of the figures represented. For example, the following two sets of numbers have identical means but the range of values is much greater in the first case than the second:

      10 20 30 mean value = 20
      18 20 22 mean value = 20

The next figure further illustrates how two distributions with the same mean value can have different distributions:

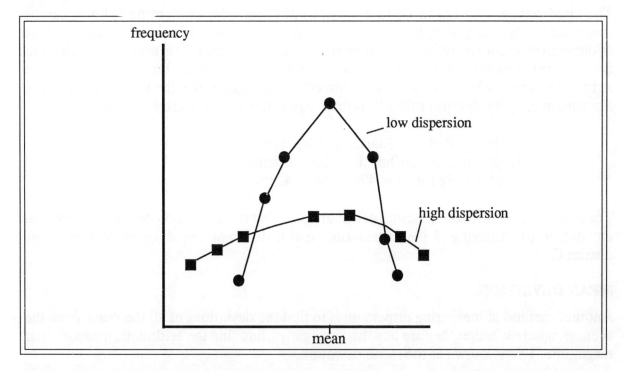

It is desirable to be able to describe the dispersion of data in a distribution with just a single figure. Four such measures will be described. They are the range; the interquartile range; the mean deviation; and the standard deviation.

RANGE

The range is merely the difference between the highest and lowest values:

Range = highest value - lowest value

The range of the distribution of mileages given in the ungrouped frequency distribution table is given by:

Range = 515 - 403 = 112 miles.

Unfortunately the range, like the mean is influenced by extreme values. If the majority of the figures in the distribution cluster around a certain value, but there are a small number having extreme values, then the range does not provide an accurate measure of the dispersion of the majority of the distribution. For example if in the ungrouped frequency distribution table one of the mileages had been 112 miles, then the range would be:

Range = 515 -112 = 403 miles

more than three times the previous figure, even though only one figure has changed.

INTERQUARTILE RANGE

The disadvantage with the range as a measure of dispersion, as identified above, can be overcome to some degree by ignoring the extreme high and low values so that the measure of dispersion is representative of the majority of the distribution. One method of doing this is to use the values at the lower limit of the 3rd quartile and the upper limit of the 1st quartile as the values from which the range is calculated. These figures give the interquartile range. For example, with reference to the 'less than' ogive, these figures are as follows:

Lower limit of 3rd Quartile (75th percentile) = 476
Upper limit of 1st Quartile (25th percentile) = 434
Interquartile range = 476 - 434 = 42 miles.

The main problem with this measure of dispersion is that it still is unable to take into account any degree of clustering in the distribution, and it does not use all of the values in the distribution.

MEAN DEVIATION

Another method of measuring dispersion is to find the deviations of all the items from the average, ignore whether they are positive or negative, and find the arithmetic mean of their magnitude. This is known as the mean deviation.

As an example, suppose it is necessary to find the mean deviation of the following set of numbers:

27 33 36 37 39 39 40 44 50 55

i) Sum of numbers = 400

Mean value = $\dfrac{400}{10}$ = 40

ii) Deviation from mean:

-13 -7 -4 -3 -1 -1 0 4 10 15

iii) Sum of deviations (ignoring sign) = 58

iv) Mean deviation = $\dfrac{58}{10}$ = 5.8

The mean deviation of the numbers is 5.8

STANDARD DEVIATION

The Greek letter σ is universally adopted to represent standard deviation. The formula for standard deviation is as follows:

$$\text{Standard deviation } (\sigma) = \sqrt{\frac{\sum(x-\bar{x})^2}{n}}$$

or where the figures come from an ungrouped frequency distribution:

$$\sigma = \sqrt{\frac{\sum f(x-\bar{x})^2}{\sum f}}$$

Setting out the calculation in the form of a table, and using the figures above for the mean deviation calculation, the calculation may be performed as follows:

x	$(x-\bar{x})$	$(x-\bar{x})^2$
27	-13	169
33	-7	49
36	-4	16
37	-3	9
39	-1	1
39	-1	1
40	0	0
44	4	16
50	10	100
55	15	225

$$\sum x_i = 400 \quad \sum(x-\bar{x})^2 = 586$$

$$\text{Standard deviation } \sigma = \sqrt{\frac{\sum(x-\bar{x})^2}{n}} = \sqrt{\frac{586}{10}} = 7.655$$

Note that by squaring the difference between the mean and a value, the minus signs disappear.

To summarise, the steps involved in calculating the standard deviation of a distribution are as follows:

> i) Calculate the arithmetic mean.
> ii) Subtract the mean from each value.
> iii) Square each value in (ii).
> iv) Sum the values in (iii).
> v) Divide by the number of numbers.
> vi) Take the square root of the result of (v).

Where the standard deviation is to be calculated from an ungrouped frequency distribution, in step (ii) the result would be multiplied by the frequency of the value, and in step (v) the sum of the frequencies would be used as the divisor.

Reference is frequently made to the variance of a distribution. This is the square of the standard deviation. In the example immediately above, the variance of the distribution is given by:

$$\text{Variance} = (\text{standard deviation})^2 = 58.6$$

and conversely, the standard deviation is the square root of the variance.

A COMPARISON OF MEASURES OF DISPERSION

Of the measures of dispersion in this section, the standard deviation is the most important, but also the most difficult to comprehend. Basically, the standard deviation provides a measure of the likelihood of any random value from the distribution being close to the arithmetic mean of the distribution. The greater the measure of deviation, the less likely it is that any value chosen at random will be close to the mean value.

Its importance lies chiefly in the considerable use made of it in analytical statistics, and a familiarity with it is crucial to making progress in more advanced statistical techniques.

The range is easy to calculate but is sensitive to untypical values. The range takes into account only two figures, those at either extreme, and gives no indication of the clustering of data. It is neither a reliable nor an accurate measure of dispersion.

The mean deviation has the advantage of using all of the figures in the distribution and is a measure of how far, on average, the values in the distribution are dispersed from the mean value. Its chief disadvantage is that it is not particularly well suited to algebraic treatment.

If the distribution of values is fairly symmetrical about the mean, bell-shaped, and the number of items is large, that is, it is more or less what is known as 'normal distribution' as shown in the next figure, then the following relations are approximately true:

Quartile deviation $= \dfrac{2}{3}$ of the standard deviation, and

Mean deviation $= \dfrac{4}{5}$ of the standard deviation

Thus in approximately normal distributions (which are of great importance in analytical statistics), the quartile and mean deviations may be used to approximate the standard deviation.

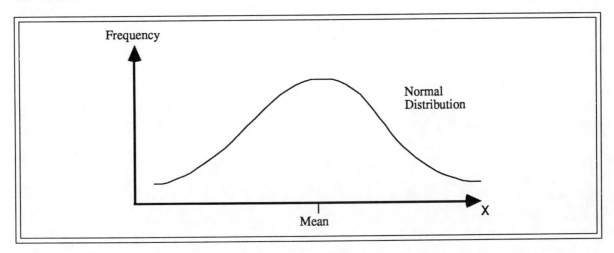

After having read this chapter it is hoped that you are now more aware of the value of communicating numerically. Communicating quantitative data is a TPS that is important in business and commerce where it is necessary to be able use statistics and to understand the implications of statistical analysis.

One rule deviation = ±(?) has under 1 deviation, etc.

Mean ± 6s includes = ±(?) The standard deviation μ

This is appropriate because normal distributions contain data of great importance in analytical chemistry). The quartiles and median deviations may be used to approximate the standard deviation.

After having read this chapter it is hoped that you are now more aware of the value of being able to summarise data using descriptive summarising data in a TPS, that is, on a scale measured sort. Furthermore it is necessary to be able to use statistics and to understand the implications of statistical analyses.

Chapter Seven

INTERVIEW SKILLS

Chapter Seven

INTERVIEW SKILLS

In the previous chapters we have looked at a range of verbal and non-verbal communication skills which you should develop. One of the purposes of doing this is so that you become aware of the various elements of these TPS and can apply them in a number of different situations. One situation that requires highly developed TPS is an interview. In this chapter we shall concentrate on the job interview: how you can improve the likelihood of being called for interview by writing an effective application form or curriculum vitae, and how to handle the interview. We shall also provide you with the guidelines to interview someone else. Whilst the chapter concentrates on job interviews, many of the personal skills discussed here are transferable to other types of interview.

MAKING AN APPLICATION

We all, from time to time have to make some form of application, whether it be for a new post, a training course, to join a club or society, or to enter college. Making an application requires careful thought because a second chance is unlikely if the application does not result in your being invited for interview. Applications are made in one of two ways: using a standard application form, or by sending a curriculum vitae.

APPLICATION FORMS

Your task in completing an application form is to convince the recruiter that you are the ideal candidate for the vacancy. This is an important point. Once you have recognised this, you will ensure that the application form is completed to the highest possible standard, and to the best of your ability.

Recruiters receive many applications for every post and are constantly looking for reasons (valid or otherwise) to reject applications, especially in the initial screening process, known as the pre-selection. Your first objective, therefore, is to overcome this hurdle in order to be called for interview. Half-hearted applications are generally easy to detect and weed out. As a rule, therefore, only those applications into which you are prepared to invest time and commitment are worth pursuing. There is usually only one opportunity to apply for a particular job. A successful applicant will have assessed the main requirements of the post and tailored the application to reflect these requirements.

WHAT THE RECRUITER IS LOOKING FOR

Most recruiters draw up a list of criteria that they use for evaluating each application. A frequently used approach is to develop a profile of the likely, successful candidate, based around seven broad criteria.

Profiling the Candidates

      1 Physical appearance, personality, and character.

      2 Successes to-date e.g. exams, work experiences etc.

      3 Intellectual ability.

      4 Skills and competencies - including TPS.

      5 Hobbies and leisure time pursuits.

      6 Personal qualities - i.e. assertiveness, self-confidence etc.

      7 Personal situation - mobility, family ties etc.

This profile has three purposes:

    a) To draw a picture of what the recruiting organisation sees as a successful applicant so that appropriate advertisements can be placed requesting applications from individuals matching the profile.

    b) To be used at the pre-selection stage to screen the applications.

    c) To be used in the interview to determine whether or not the applicants match the desired profile.

Thus, before completing the application form you must 'read between the lines' of the advertised vacancy and draw a profile of the applicant that you think the recruiter is looking for. The next step is to determine whether you match the recruiter's desired profile. If you think that your profile does match that which the recruiter is looking for, then complete the application form. Should you meet most, but not all of the recruiter's criteria, however, then you should still apply as it is very unlikely that the 'ideal' candidate will exist.

COMPLETING THE APPLICATION FORM

Once you have established that your profile is suitable for the vacancy then you must set about completing the application form. In completing this task you should follow certain guidelines:

* Do not write answers on the actual application form until you have answered all questions in rough. You should give a great deal of thought to answering each question.

* Check the rough copy for grammar and spelling errors.

* Always use black ink for writing - application forms are photo-copied and black ink will print out best.

* When completing the application form write legibly and take care not to make any mistakes as untidy applications are likely to be rejected.

You should pay great care and attention to completing the application form - not only how it is completed, but how the questions are answered. Application forms tend to be broken down into various sections reflecting the stages of the seven profile criteria discussed above. Each section of the application form will provide the recruiter with further insights into the applicant's profile. A number of sections are common to most application forms:

Personal details: name, address, vacancy applied for, qualifications etc.

This section might appear relatively straightforward to complete, but you must pay attention to ensure that you answer it completely and legibly. This will be the first part of the form that the recruiter reads so it will be vital to make a favourable first impression.

When detailing your qualifications bear in mind the nature of the vacancy. Can you use any projects that you have completed or options that you have studied at college to illustrate a special skill or competence that you have upon which the recruiter might look favourably?

Skills questions: can you speak languages, use a computer, drive etc.?

Skills are important to recruiters and you need to emphasise your competence in them. You need to take care though, to indicate that the skills that you possess will help you to do the job better, rather than be seen to be applying for the post because you want to use your skills.

Achievements: successes, accomplishments, assignments completed etc.

The majority of people have achieved something in their lives and it is important to show this on the application form. To complete this section you need to list all the achievements that you consider to have been important to your own personal development in your business, college, or social life.

You could mention a great variety of achievements: work experiences, examination successes, leading groups in leisure time, being a member of a successful activity, overseas travel, or sporting achievements. In mentioning your achievements, however, you should add a brief note showing what you have gained from them and any new skills you have developed as a result. The space on the application form will dictate how many achievements you can mention and the detail that you can provide for the recruiter.

Proof questions: asking for evidence about work experience, training

There will be questions on the application form asking for details of previous work experience, training and education - 'proof questions' - requesting evidence that shows you have the experience and qualifications for the vacancy.

Your answers to these questions should be factual, giving dates, the name of the organisation where the experience was gained, and the position held, with stress being placed on the successes you achieved.

Part-time jobs can impress the recruiter, especially when the special responsibilities of the job are highlighted, or the skills that you developed are mentioned.

If you have had a certain job or activity which was very interesting or especially relevant to the application, then you should elaborate further to explain its relevance. An example is given below:

> EASTERN TOURS LTD., NORTHSEA, 1987 to date
>
> **Tour operator's overseas manager in Bangkok, Thailand**
>
> This post has been of great benefit as it involves working in a foreign country ensuring that the tour clients gain satisfaction from their holiday. All client and company difficulties that are encountered have to be overcome, often involving great use of tact, initiative and interpersonal skills.

The Crucial question

There often tends to be an open-ended question(s) on application forms to which much importance is attached by the recruiter. Answers to these questions are frequently decisive:

> 'Why have you applied for this post?'
>
> 'Why do you think you will succeed if you are appointed?'
>
> 'Explain how your background will assist you if you are offered a post with this organisation?'
>
> 'Successful managers are able leaders, effective problem solvers and competent decision takers. Can you provide any evidence that shows you possess these qualities?'

To answer these questions competently you will have to have a clear understanding of:

> a) what the post applied for entails
>
> b) the skills and competencies you can offer that match the recruiter's requirements

c) why you wish to be successful in obtaining the post.

Before answering this type of question, it is important to know as much as possible about all these three areas. You should also ask yourself why this question is being asked, what is its purpose, and what will it tell the recruiter about me.

When answering such a question, you need to show how your qualities and experience fit the needs of the organisation. If you concentrate on **your** needs and wants and what **you** expect from the position, then your application will probably be unsuccessful. You should whet the recruiter's appetite when reading the response to this question, and include points that you can elaborate on in the interview.

Needless to say, you should give much thought, attention and creativity to answering these 'crucial' questions, the answers to which often hold the key that will open the door to the interview.

Referees

You need to select your referees with care. They should be people who know you well and hold respected positions in the community. You have to obtain their consent before they are mentioned as referees. It will be useful if the referee knows why you are seeking the position and what qualities and strengths you have that make you a suitable candidate.

Concluding Comments

Before you finally commit the rough draft to the application form you should ask yourself a few final questions:

* Have you answered all the questions on the application form?

* Have you left any time periods in your career unexplained?

* Do the answers you give address the questions asked?

* Has your tone in answering the questions been positive?

* Is the style of your presentation appropriate?

* Will the recruiter gain a favourable impression of you as a result of reading the application form?

And before you post the form to the recruiter:

* Are any additional items to be included with the application form e.g. examination certificates, photograph etc.?

If you bear in mind all of the above points then your chance of being invited for interview will be much improved. Some organisations, though, will not ask you for an application form, but will wish to see your curriculum vitae (C.V.).

THE CURRICULUM VITAE

Your C.V. is another means of communicating with the recruiter, and as with application forms you need to give attention to its design and submission. Normally you should not use a C.V. where the recruiter issues an application form. Use a C.V. when, for example, the advertised vacancy says:

> 'send full details to...'

or simply asks for a C.V. If you are making a speculative application, a C.V. with a covering letter is essential.

THE PURPOSE OF THE C.V.

The purpose of your C.V. is to summarise your personal details and experience. Whereas application forms are structured with questions and spaces for replies, you can design your C.V. as you think fit. Your C.V should include information relevant to the recruiter. Thus, each C.V. that you produce has to be tailored for the specific requirements of each position for which you are applying. A standard, 'mass-produced' C.V. is not the most effective means of presenting yourself for a specific job.

THE STYLE OF YOUR C.V.

An important point about the style of your C.V. is that it should be easy to read and concise, using brief, clear statements. Your C.V. will have a stronger impact if actual facts or figures are included, such as grades achieved in examinations, and successes that you have enjoyed at work, for example increasing sales turnover by 100% in 12 months! There is normally no need, however, for sentences to be used as a note-format will suffice.

You should use certain key verbs, such as:

accomplished	contributed	produced	developed
established	implemented	initiated	mediated
motivated	negotiated	arranged	convinced
devised	sustained	tested	wrote

When applying for posts which demand creativity, you should use a creative approach in designing the C.V., for example writing it as if it were a press release that gives your details. Alternatively, you could provide an additional 'fact file' that includes further details and examples of your creative work. You will need to give this approach careful consideration and pay attention to detail. If you are sending a fact file it must encourage the selector to read it rather than discard it in the waste paper bin.

THE CONTENT OF THE C.V.

As we have indicated above, the content of your C.V. will depend upon the position you are applying for. A C.V. to impress an advertising agency will be of a different style and content to that intended to impress an accountant.

Your C.V. has to provide the recruiter with a picture of your accomplishments and experiences, as well as your potential capabilities. When you write your C.V., however, while you must use facts, adopt a style that allows the recruiter to make favourable assumptions about you.

Once you have decided on the style and content of your C.V. you need to follow a number of guidelines.

You should produce an initial first draft and check the following points:

* The length of your C.V. should not normally be more than two A4 sides - the C.V. is a summary, not a report. The recruiter will receive many C.V.s and needs to be able to read through them quickly, gaining an initial first impression of your suitability.

* The various sections of the C.V. should be well spaced with ample margins. A tightly packed C.V. will be difficult to read and digest.

* The style of writing should be 'snappy' using verbs that suggest dynamism. Sentences, if used should be short and to the point. Just include facts.

* The tone of the C.V. should be positive and optimistic creating a strong and favourable image.

You should then get another person to read through your C.V. to confirm its appropriateness, and to make sure it creates the intended impact. The next stage is to:

* Have the C.V. professionally typed on high quality paper.

* Post the C.V. with a covering letter.

* Keep a copy of the C.V. and read it before the interview.

As with application forms, the immediate objective of using a C.V. is to obtain an interview. The golden rule for achieving this is to relate your skills and accomplishments to the recruiter's needs. To support the C.V. and to motivate the recruiter to read it you will also have to write a covering letter. On the next two pages we show examples of a typical covering letter and a C.V.

Flat G
College Halls of Residence
Wall Street
Southwall
SO6 5RF

30 November 19..

Ms W J Wilkes
Personnel Director
Gamble UK LTD.
33 Western Road
Westcliffe
WE24 9UH

Dear Ms Wilkes

<u>Marketing Assistant, Post MA24</u>

I read with interest the above career vacancy that was advertised in 'Marketing', 29 November, and would like to be considered for the post. Please find enclosed my Curriculum Vitae.

As you will see from my CV, I am in my final year at polytechnic reading for a Business Studies degree, specialising in the Marketing Option. The work placements that are integral parts of the degree have enabled me to gain valuable experience of two important activities of the Marketing Department - advertising and selling. The successes I achieved on placement, plus my studies at polytechnic, have given me a clear understanding of Marketing and its relevance to business. These experiences have also shown me the importance of marketing people developing effective transferable personal skills.

The positions of responsibility I have had at school and polytechnic have further developed these skills. I work well with others, am capable of leading others and taking decisions. Being treasurer of the Nomadic Society has shown me the importance of administrative skills and communication skills.

Your company appeals to me because it is involved with marketing fast-moving-consumer-goods. The work experiences I have already enjoyed have been in this sector, and will enable me to make an effective and rapid contribution as a Marketing Assistant to the Detergent's Product Manager, using my planning and analytical skills.

I am free to travel to Westcliffe for interview at any time during December or January. I look forward to hearing from you in the near future.

Yours sincerely

Anne Williams (Miss)

CURRICULUM VITAE

PERSONAL DETAILS

Name: WILLIAMS, Anne, Alison

Date of Birth: 23rd January 1967

Nationality: British

Marital Status: Single

Home Address: 14 Woolcot Terrace, Northsea, NE45 9TH
Tel: 0909 76783

Term Address: Flat G, College Halls of Residence, Wall Street, Southwall, SO6 5RF
(5 October-13 December).

EDUCATION and QUALIFICATIONS

1978-1985   Trinity School, Northsea.

1983   'O' Levels: English Literature (A), History (A), Mathematics (A), English Language (B), History (B), Geography (C),French (C), Physics (C), Chemistry (C).

1985   BTEC National Business and Finance: 3 Distinctions, 5 Merits.

1985-date   Southwall Polytechnic.
BA (Hons) Business Studies Sandwich degree. Option subjects: Marketing Management, Market Research, Quantitative Methods, Buyer Behaviour, Marketing Communications.
Final year project: "The Effectiveness of Advertising Expenditure for Tour Operators".

POSITIONS OF RESPONSIBILITY

School: Head of House - organising the prefects and motivating the children.
Hockey Captain - arranging fixtures, planning a tour, liaising with teachers.

Polytechnic: Treasurer of the Nomadics Walking Society - collecting expedition funds, maintaining accounts, presenting the accounts to the AGM.

WORK EXPERIENCE

Summer 1986   NBC Advertising Agency, London - work responsibility for 5 accounts, liaising with the client and buying media space.

Summer 1987   Procterlever Household Division - work placement, sales rep, servicing existing accounts and prospecting for new ones. Increased sales in the territory by 30% in 3 months.

OTHER SKILLS/HOBBIES

Full driving licence, overseas expeditions, jazz music, Shakespeare.

COVERING LETTERS

A covering letter must always accompany a C.V. Sometimes it is also wise to include one when sending an application form, especially when you have had limited previous correspondence with the organisation to which you are applying.

The purpose of the covering letter is to introduce you to the recruiter and to encourage the recruiter to read your attached C.V. or application form. You must give thought and attention to writing the covering letter. It is a vital component of the selection process.

Writing a covering letter

Covering letters should be brief, not exceeding one A4 side of high quality paper. If your handwriting is neat then it is good to write the covering letter by hand, supported by a typed C.V. If your handwriting is poor then you should have the covering letter typed.

You should always follow standard letter writing conventions as we discussed in Chapter Five. However, you need to bear a number of additional guidelines in mind:

* Always write a rough draft first.

* State explicitly the post for which you are applying and any reference numbers quoted in the advertisement.

* Indicate where you saw the vacancy advertised, or how you heard the details about it, or why you are making a speculative application.

* Stress the factors relevant to the application such as your previous work experience, skills, knowledge, interests, aptitudes etc.

* Include relevant information not given in your C.V., such as your motivation for applying.

* Inform the recruiter of convenient interview dates and any dates when you will be unavailable for interview.

As we discussed at the beginning of this chapter, making applications is important. Normally, you will have only one opportunity to be called for interview. If your application form is poorly completed, if your C.V. is ill-conceived and your covering letter unstimulating, then it is unlikely that you will be called for interview. If you pay careful attention to succeeding at the pre-selection stage, however, you could well be rewarded by being offered an interview.

SUCCEEDING AT THE INTERVIEW

You will need to master interview skills because interviews are the most common means of selecting employees. The personal skills you develop here will also have relevance in different types of interview situation such as appraisal interviews, market research survey interviewing, and indeed even for being interviewed for a radio or television programme. In the section that follows, however, we continue the theme of applying for a career vacancy and consider a number of steps that have to be followed for the interview to be successful.

Preparing for the interview

To walk ill-prepared into an interview is foolish. You have to carry out research beforehand into a number of areas:

* The recruiter's business - what is the nature of the organisation, its markets and products, who are the consumers and competitors, what position does the recruiting organisation hold in the market place? This information can be found from company reports, press articles, and informal discussions with other employees of the firm.

* The responsibilities involved in the job, what will be expected of you, where will you fit into the organisation? It is very helpful to have had a discussion with the person for whom you will directly be working prior to the interview. By contacting this person before the interview you will be showing that you are keen to be selected for the vacancy.

You need to collect as much background material as possible. You will also have to review:

* Why you have applied for the post, your motivations and ambitions, where the post fits into the logic of your career development.

* Why you will find the job interesting.

* The skills you will be able to offer the employer.

* Your relevant previous achievements.

The clothes that you are to wear for the interview will require preparation - do they need dry cleaning, should you wear a new pair of shoes, what about your hairstyle, what will be appropriate for the interview, do you have to conform to certain standards of appearance and dress or would a more individualistic style be appropriate? Appearance and grooming are important because they help to create that vital first impression that the interviewer will gain of you.

Whenever possible, visit in advance the place where the interview will be held. This will give you an idea of how long it will take you to travel there on the day of the interview. Allow sufficient time for the journey so that unforeseen problems and delays (e.g. rush-hour traffic) do not make you late for the interview.

It is helpful to know what kind of questions are likely to be asked in the interview. Not only will this help you to prepare, it will also boost your confidence because you are unlikely to be taken by surprise. A list of typical and general questions is given below. Questions specific to the vacancy can be worked out by considering what questions you would ask each candidate were you the interviewer. For each question, work out your best answer using the guidelines below. Rehearse the interview the evening before, a friend acting as interviewer asking the questions. You should also prepare several questions to ask at the interview.

ON ARRIVAL

You should plan to arrive before the interview is scheduled to start. This will allow you time to gather your thoughts and calm your nerves. Be polite and courteous to everyone you meet - they may be future colleagues.

THE INTERVIEW

When you are invited into the interview room you should enter with a purposeful and confident walk, erect posture, and with a smile. You should greet the interviewer, or the chairperson if it is a panel interview, with :

> "Good morning/afternoon Mr./Mrs./Miss...pleased to meet you. My name is..."

accompanied by a firm handshake, pleasant facial expression, and strong eye contact. When you are asked to sit down, adopt an erect posture, with your hands folded in your lap, making sure that you maintain eye contact with the interviewer.

The interviewer will then take control, probably by outlining how the interview is to be organised. Then the questioning will commence. If your research and preparation have been thorough then a number of the questions will come as no surprise, questions like:

> "Why are you applying to this organisation?"

> "Why did you choose that particular course to study at college?"

> "What other organisations have you applied to?"

> "Where do you see yourself in five years time?"

> "What do you know about....(a technical point)....?"

> "How would you define......(a technical term).....?"

> "What skills or qualities do you possess that make you a suitable candidate?"

"What do you know about our business?"

"Who do you see as our main competitors?"

"What would you say are the main difficulties facing us?"

"What has been your greatest achievement?"

"What are your weaknesses?"

"How do your friends perceive you?"

When answering questions you need to remember a number of points:

* Always look at the interviewer and other members of the panel.

* Use effective verbal and non-verbal communication skills - don't fidget, avoid distracting mannerisms, control facial expressions, use appropriate gestures, try to hide your nervousness by controlling your voice and speaking with varied tones and pitch, and different speeds of speech. Use pauses in speech to stress important points.

* Always be positive and optimistic when you are replying to questions, look for opportunities to highlight your achievements, turn unsuccessful elements in your career to-date into successes.

* Never be derogatory, cynical, facetious, or sarcastic. Rather, use humour to show the warmth of your character and personality.

* Be honest, don't invent answers. If you cannot answer a question say so - this will earn more respect from the interviewer than a garbled invention.

* Answer the question that is posed, not the one that you wish had been asked. Recognise those questions requiring brief answers and those intended to produce a more in-depth response. Don't use one-word answers, always elaborate.

* If you do not understand a question, ask for it to be repeated.

One purpose of the interview is to allow you to communicate with the interviewer using your well-developed verbal and non-verbal communication skills. In addition, the interviewer will be seeking to establish your intellectual skills and so a problem may be set, or specific situations put before you to solve:

"Sales of our product have been declining, what would you do?"

"How would you motivate other people who are working with you?"

"The quality of the products produced fluctuates greatly, how can this be overcome?"

These problems are not posed to test your in-depth knowledge of the given situation, but to establish whether you can think logically and solve problems in a structured way.

When the interviewer's questioning has finished you will be given the opportunity to ask questions. Valid questions which you could ask are those relating to:

* The job, the organisation, its employees, products and processes.

* Future career prospects.

* Additional staff development and training which you might receive.

You should ask only three or four questions at most, after which the interviewer will conclude the session by thanking you for attending and informing you of the next stage in the selection process. You should always use a concluding handshake to end the interview on a positive note, accompanied by pleasing facial expressions - remember to smile even if you think the interview has not gone terribly well.

You should thank the interviewer for giving you the opportunity to discuss your application in more detail, and should then walk out of the room in a confident and purposeful manner.

Your hard work does not end here as there are follow-up procedures to complete.

AFTER THE INTERVIEW

You should regard each interview as a valuable learning opportunity. To learn from each one and to develop your repertoire of TPS you need to analyse each interview carefully.

Make notes as soon after the interview as possible on the questions that were asked and the responses that you gave. This will be useful to you if you are offered a second interview, and will help you to think of more effective ways of answering such questions. Following this you should critically evaluate the TPS that you used, writing down your perceived strengths and weaknesses. Spend time on analysing where your weaknesses were shown and think about how you might improve them.

The first interview will probably be used by the recruiter as a means of drawing up a short list of candidates for the second (final) interview - your last hurdle before they offer you the job.

THE SECOND INTERVIEW

The first interview will have been a screening process, rejecting applicants thought to be incompatible with the organisation's needs. The second interview will establish from the short list of applicants which one has the skills, qualities, experience and potential to succeed in the vacant post.

In preparing for the second interview you should follow similar steps as you did for the first. The main difference between the two interviews will be the way they are organised. Second interviews are frequently spread over a two day period and include a variety of activities.

The Night Before

Second interviews for more senior posts frequently start the night before when the candidates are invited to dine with senior managers from the recruiting organisation. Recently recruited employees may also be present. It will probably be stated that the evening session is to be informal, but the senior managers and other employees will be observing your social behaviour which may be fed back to the interviewers (if they are not present). Thus, you will need to display TPS of a high standard to ensure that another favourable first impression is created:

* You will have to display the appropriate etiquette as the hosts will be observing how you cope with such situations, and evaluating the image you will portray when you work for the organisation.

* You should be careful about your verbal and non-verbal behaviour so that the observers develop a favourable impression.

* You should prepare intelligent work-related questions and topics for conversation beforehand as this will show an interest in the organisation and its work.

* Alcohol should be consumed only in moderation.

During the evening it may be possible to steer the conversation around to the proceedings of the next day. You should do this sensitively in order to find out a bit more about how the day will be organised and the skills and competencies that the interviewers will be looking for. Typically, though, the recruiters will be keen to see the full range of TPS as discussed in this book being displayed by the successful candidate(s).

The Next Day

The format of the interview day will vary according to the interviewing practice of the recruiting organisation, and as we have already stated you should, if possible, try and find the likely format beforehand.

The organisation could provide a variety of activities for the candidates:

* Interviews by different people, with different numbers of people on each panel, each with a different objective.

* Written and scientific tests, such as psychometric tests, to determine the mental agility of the candidates, their aptitudes, and suitability for the work in question.

* 'In-tray' exercises, a type of situational analysis, where certain tasks or problems relevant to the vacancy have to be completed in a certain period of time.

* Group exercises where a problem has to be solved by the candidates working as a team. This identifies those with leadership skills, those who can work effectively with others as well as each individual's intellectual skills.

* Case studies which are completed individually, to establish the knowledge and understanding of the candidates, and their ability to analyse, synthesise, and evaluate a problem, before taking a decision.

* Formal presentations which may be spontaneous, for example having to speak for three minutes on a particular unknown topic or on a topic chosen by you. These entail using a broad range of TPS.

* Group discussions to determine the ability of the candidates to develop persuasive arguments and to defend their views when questioned by others.

The TPS we have discussed previously, and those which we will discuss in the remainder of this book, will be of use to you in second interviews where a variety of activities are performed by the candidates. Clearly, you must obtain as much information beforehand about the type of tests you are likely to encounter and you should endeavour to practise the skills involved.

Prepare thoroughly before the second interview. You should plan a short presentation on a topic of your choice. Try, however, to choose an interesting or slightly different topic that highlights a pertinent element of your character, your leadership skills for example. Plan such a presentation so that it appears well-structured and organised - the interviewers will be looking for this, see Chapter Eight.

If you are involved in group discussions ensure that you make a contribution, rather than sitting back and saying nothing. The interviewers will be looking for your ability to relate to others. Take care, though, to ensure that you do not dominate the discussion to the extent that you appear to be insensitive to the views of others. You should accept and acknowledge the views of others, and wherever possible develop them even further. If you can give an indication of your leadership potential then all well and good. This might involve the summarising of the arguments that have been made, and inviting comments from quieter candidates.

If role-playing exercises are used you should firmly slip into the role to be adopted, but be careful not to over-exaggerate your behaviour. If the role-playing involves performing a situational task, such as completing work in the 'in-tray' then you need to prioritise the work in the 'in-tray' so that you complete the more pressing tasks first. Should you be asked to solve problems, then you need to identify the underlying causes of the problem before you take action to overcome them. Be ready to justify the decisions that you reach.

Situational tasks are favoured by some interviewers because they enable a number of traits and skills to be identified, such as the candidates' abilities to solve problems and take decisions, as well as their ability to maintain relationships with others, or to show sensitivity to the feelings of others. When attending a second interview, you should try to anticipate a number of different situations that might be put before you, and think about possible ways of handling these situations.

You may need to consider some additional points:

* A second interview will be more related to the work involved with the post than was the first interview. Therefore you might need to do some further research.

* Interviewers for a technical post will be more interested in technical knowledge and competence than was the case with the first interview - you must emphasise such competencies if you have them.

* You need to keep a positive frame of mind at all times. You should try to project the appropriate image that the recruiter is looking for.

* The person for whom you will be working will probably be a major influence on the decision made at the second interview.

* Recruiters will be looking for evidence that you will be committed to the employing organisation and will be able to follow a structured career path.

If you remember all of these points, as well as the previous ones made in this chapter, then you will be well placed to succeed at the second interview.

INTERVIEWER SKILLS

Hopefully the person who is interviewing you has well developed TPS which will make you feel at ease and allow you to communicate to the best of your ability.

You may, at some later time, be called upon to carry out interviews as an interviewer. In this section we will examine some of the skills you will need to have if you are to conduct a successful interview.

Many interviewers are not formally trained in effective interviewing, but are expected to have developed such skills as part of their career progression. The importance of the interviewer managing the interview efficiently cannot be overstated as the face-to-face interview is still the most commonly used method of selecting new recruits. If you adopt an inappropriate style as an interviewer then it could result in your organisation employing a candidate who is not the best suited for the post in question.

Candidates attending for interview will naturally be nervous and anxious, some will be highly stressed. As the interview is to some extent a 'false' situation, in that all the participants will be playing specific roles which may not be a true reflection of their typical behaviour, it will be important for you as the interviewer to organise the interview process carefully so that an accurate assessment can be made of each candidate.

A number of potential problems might arise if you are inexperienced as an interviewer:

* You may not have established a clear profile of the likely candidate prior to the interviews, making it difficult to assess the suitability of each candidate.

* You might dominate the interview to the extent that the candidate has hardly any opportunity to speak.

* You might assess only the candidates' interpersonal skills, or you might be distracted by the physical appearance of the candidates, ignoring their other qualities.

* Although you might have produced a list of questions to ask, you might not have evaluated what an appropriate response is, reducing the value of such questions.

If you avoid these pitfalls an interview can be an effective way of collecting information about each candidate, enabling you to make a suitable choice. However, a key factor will be whether or not you understand the data you need to collect from each candidate.

One way of deciding the type of information to collect is to identify the skills, competencies, and characteristics of those employees currently undertaking roles similar to that for which the applicants have applied. By studying people who are already successful at carrying out the work you can draw up a profile of the likely candidate. Once you have done this you can devise questions that you can ask all candidates. Their answers should show whether or not they are suitable for the post. For this to work, though, you must ask each question in the same way to all candidates, and you must listen to each response to see which candidate appears to be the most suitable.

Interviews are primarily used for obtaining information. If you wish to gain insight into how well the candidate is likely to perform in the post, then situational analysis should be used. This should give a systematic assessment of a candidate's suitability to undertake certain job responsibilities, rather than you having to rely on assumptions based on the candidate's previous employment experience.

In a situation interview you present the candidates with either real or hypothetical problems that they might encounter were they to be appointed. The candidate's task is to decide how to respond to each problem. This method of interviewing is useful if the candidate has no previous experience of the type of work involved with the vacancy. You can then probe the candidates on their responses, to provide further insight as to their suitability.

It is important that you listen carefully to a candidate's responses. Make notes or record the interview. You will have to develop the skill of probing the candidates through the subtle use of open-ended questions beginning with 'What..?, How..?, Which..? and When?' Posing questions in this way invites candidates to talk about an issue, enabling them to reply at an intellectual level. This will indicate to you the candidates' knowledge and understanding of the issue. If you probe further you can discover the candidates' ability to develop logical arguments or uncover their motivations, perceptions, beliefs and attitudes.

Use 'Why ...?' questions in moderation only as these can feel quite threatening to candidates, requiring them to justify what they believe about a particular issue.

Situational interviewing helps to reduce the subjectivity that often creeps into the interview process and allows you to adopt a more objective stance from which you can evaluate each candidate against work related criteria.

Irrespective of the type of interview that you use to select the successful candidate, however, you should follow certain guidelines to help candidates relax and contribute to the best of their ability:

* You should select carefully the physical environment where the interview takes place to ensure that:

  - the temperature is not too hot or cold
  - there will be no distractions such as telephones ringing, or third parties entering the room
  - the layout of the chairs will allow the candidate to communicate freely
  - there are no physical barriers that might impede the interview such as tables or equipment.

* You should be well-briefed on the candidates and have studied their application forms or C.V.'s in detail.

The interview needs to be planned and structured. There should be an introduction, the questioning period (for both the interviewer and interviewee), and a conclusion. In the introduction you should explain to the candidate how the interview is to be conducted, you should introduce the members of the panel, and help to relax the candidate. The questioning period should include a variety of different types of question, most of which will have been pre-planned and designed to elicit information that will show whether the candidate matches the desired profile. You should then allow time for the candidates to ask questions before concluding the interview by informing them of the next stage in the process.

* The questions you ask should be clearly phrased so that they are unambiguous and easily understood, and designed to draw out the qualities of the candidate. If a candidate struggles to answer a question, allow time for thought before probing more deeply.

* Ask questions in a warm, friendly tone of voice. If the answer that is given is incorrect do not admonish the candidate. Acknowledge correct answers by nodding your head, smiling, and giving positive verbal support.

* At no time during the interview should you be patronising or condescending.

* You can apply pressure to the candidate by carefully listening to the answers that are given, and asking for clarification of points that were not clearly explained. If you adopt an assertive, rather than an aggressive manner this will this will show how the candidate responds to such pressure.

* Do not dominate the interview. The candidate should be given the opportunity of speaking for at least 60% of the time. If a panel interview is to be held, the same rule applies. A chairperson should manage the interview inviting colleagues to ask questions. Ideally, one person's sole role should be to observe the proceedings paying particular attention to the candidate's non-verbal behaviour noting whether it supports or contradicts what he is saying.

* When the interview has concluded you need to complete an assessment form to indicate how well the candidate performed against the criteria which you had established as being important.

If you follow the above procedures you will adopt a professional approach for the interview which should allow you to identify the most suitable candidate for the vacancy. Interviewers who have had no previous experience need to be informed of the skills required. Indeed, before being faced with a real interview, you should use role-playing situations to practise and to receive feedback on the TPS being employed by both the interviewer and the interviewee.

In this chapter we have considered interview skills, and highlighted ways in which you can improve the success of the selection process either as an interviewee or interviewer. Another skill area that draws upon a broad range of TPS is that of making a formal presentation. We shall discuss this topic in Chapter Eight.

Chapter Eight

PRESENTATION SKILLS

Chapter Eight

PRESENTATION SKILLS

At some stage in your career it is more than likely that you will have to make an oral presentation. It may be a highly formal event, perhaps speaking at a conference, but most commonly it will be of a less formal kind, for instance informing colleagues of new working practices, trying to convince a customer that the new product on offer is what she is looking for, or explaining to new employees how your organisation operates. Some people, such as teachers and lecturers, spend much of their time presenting information to others and enjoy doing it. Other people, though, do it infrequently and find it a nerve wracking experience.

No matter in what situation you have to make a presentation, or the frequency with which you do it, or the size of the audience you face, you can apply similar principles to make your presentation more effective. In this chapter we will examine some of the principles which can improve your presentation technique.

PREPARING THE PRESENTATION

You must prepare all presentations. Very few speakers can make a successful presentation without preparation. Your starting point is to establish why you are making the presentation, and then to set yourself clear objectives that you must achieve in delivering it.

SETTING OBJECTIVES

You should begin by considering the needs of the audience - what will the audience be expecting to hear and what do they wish to gain from hearing the presentation. These are the objectives of your audience, to whom we shall return shortly.

Your objectives are equally important. You might want the audience to accept and agree with your views or to change their behaviour in some way as a result of hearing you speak. You may simply want to give information in an instructional or explanatory way. The objective of an instructional presentation might be to increase the knowledge of your audience, which you can subsequently test by asking questions, or by requiring the audience to perform what they have learnt. If you are giving an explanatory presentation you may be trying to improve the understanding of your audience.

Once you have clearly established the purpose of the presentation and set your objectives, the next stage in the preparation process is to consider the nature of the audience.

THE NATURE OF THE AUDIENCE

We have already identified that it is important to consider the audience during the preparation stage. The skills you will use when making a presentation to an audience of one will be virtually identical to those you will require when making a presentation to an audience of one hundred. With a smaller audience, however, there is more scope for including the listener(s) directly in the presentation and it requires a different presentation style.

Similarly, when you know all the members of the audience personally you can adopt a more informal style. In contrast, if the members of your audience are drawn from quite varied backgrounds with different expectations of the presentation, you will have to try and meet as many of their differing needs as possible.

It is vital, therefore, to know who the audience is, what their role is, and what they are expecting to learn. Linked to this is the need to be aware of what the audience already knows about the topic under consideration. Are they experts or novices? This will clearly determine how you pitch the content of the presentation.

CONTENT PREPARATION

Next you must pay careful attention to preparing the content of the presentation.

DECIDING ON THE TOPIC

Decide on the specific topic to be covered in the presentation taking into account the objectives of the presentation, the previous knowledge of the audience, and what it is they are to learn.

DETERMINE THE CONTENT OF YOUR PRESENTATION

Pay careful attention to the content of the presentation. Try and make sure that what you say :

* Is interesting.
* To the point.
* Can be clearly understood.
* Is appropriate for the nature of your audience.
* Can be feasibly presented in the time you have available.
* Will achieve what you set out to achieve.

You should not overload the audience with information, as you can make only a certain number of points in the time available. If the presentation is very short, not lasting more than a few minutes, then make only one or two points. If your presentation is longer then obviously you have more scope to expand on what you have to say. Be careful with presentations which are too long, however, as the audience is likely to lose concentration and remember little of what is said.

If you are trying to make a number of points you must follow a logical sequence, so that each point builds upon the previous one. The presentation needs to be broken down into manageable stages and you must give it a structure.

THE STRUCTURE OF THE PRESENTATION

Your presentation should be divided into three distinct stages each of which needs to be allocated a specific time. The stages are:

1. The Introduction.
2. Developing your argument.
3. The Conclusion of your presentation.

1. THE INTRODUCTION

In the introduction you should:

* Welcome your audience.

* Identify yourself and the topic on which you will speak.

* Explain the purpose of the presentation (its objectives).

* If the presentation is one of a series, then re-cap on the previous ones.

* Outline what you are going to say and how you will say it.

* Explain what will be expected of the audience in terms of their participation.

* Tell the audience whether they should ask questions during, or after, the presentation.

In preparing the introduction you should aim to whet the appetite of the audience and to stimulate their interest. To do this successfully requires a little imagination. Many presentations begin with the speaker saying:

'Good morning, the purpose of my talk today is to ......'

While this is business-like, direct, honest, and down-to-earth, a more interesting introduction might be one which tempts the audience:

'In the next ten minutes I am going to tell you how the profitability of your company can be increased by 50%.'

Or a startling statement such as:

> 'If you do not adopt the proposals I am about to make, you may well find that our competitors will outstrip us in the next five years!'

Another means of introducing the presentation might be by way of quoting statistics, or research findings:

> 'Did you know that only 30% of British companies are geared towards marketing their products successfully? In the next 30 minutes I am going to show you how your company can adopt a more positive approach to marketing and improve its efficiency and profitability.'

You could begin your presentation with a straight quotation :

> 'I wish to introduce my talk by referring you to a quotation from Peter Drucker, one of America's leading business academics and business consultants:
>
> "The further away your job is from manual work, the larger the organisation of which you are an employee, the more important it will be that you know how to convey your thoughts in writing and speaking."
>
> Ladies and gentlemen, the purpose of my presentation is to help you improve your communication skills.'

You may use a rhetorical question to gain the audience's interest and attention:

> 'Are you dissatisfied with your communication skills? Do you find the audience falls asleep when you talk? Do you want to be more persuasive? If your answer to each of these questions has been 'yes' then listen closely for the next 45 minutes........'

Finally, involving the audience in some way during the introduction might help to gain their attention, either by asking a general question, or one specific to an individual. Alternatively, you could use a handout with a series of questions which the audience must complete. You can then use their answers to focus attention in a specific direction. In using this approach you must take care not to embarrass any member of the audience or to create an air of tension that might deter audience participation.

Clearly, you need an imaginative and creative introduction to gain the attention of the audience and stimulate their interest. Try to avoid apologetic introductions:

> 'I will only take 15 minutes of your time.....'

or ones using cliches:

> 'Unaccustomed as I am to public speaking......'

If you are going to speak to the same audience on a number of occasions then try to vary the style of introduction on each occasion.

Avoid gimmicky introductions, and ones which are blatantly patronising or condescending. Never speak down to your audience.

2. DEVELOPING YOUR ARGUMENT

During this part of the presentation you should specifically state your key ideas in a logical sequence. To convince the audience that your ideas are valid, however, requires you to do more than simply state them. You must support what you say. This is achieved in a number of ways. These are:

(i)   Establishing your credibility with your audience.
(ii) Providing supporting rationale.
(iii) The pattern of the presentation.
(iv) Answering questions.

(i) ESTABLISHING YOUR CREDIBILITY WITH YOUR AUDIENCE

The audience must trust you if they are to accept what you are saying. You establish this credibility in a combination of ways:

* Demonstrating that you have knowledge and understanding of the topic.

* Referring to learned sources of relevant information.

* Showing sincerity and integrity, and recognising the views of others.

* Appearing to look composed and confident during the presentation.

* Using your verbal and non-verbal communication skills effectively.

You will enhance your credibility by being thoroughly prepared and by delivering what you are saying with enthusiasm, belief, and commitment. Indeed, these qualities are contagious and if you show that you are enthusiastic the audience will be more likely to share this enthusiasm.

(ii) PROVIDING SUPPORTING RATIONALE

To convince the audience that your views are correct you should provide supporting rationale in a number of ways:

* Make reference to similar situations - analogies. This helps the audience to understand the point that is being made as they can relate the new knowledge to a familiar, similar situation.

* Draw examples from personal experiences. By including a personal story or two you not only demonstrate the truth and relevance of your major

point, but you also add interest to the presentation, which might help your audience to remember what you have been saying.

* Refer to research findings and empirical data. Material produced by other people can substantiate what you are saying and help to make your views more credible.

* Include interesting quotations from a respected authority.

* Ask the audience to support what you are saying. If members of the audience can support what is being said from their own experiences then this will add credibility to the points you are making.

In addition to the above points, pay attention to the structure of your presentation.

(iii) THE PATTERN OF THE PRESENTATION

You can use various patterns for presenting your message:

a) The Main Idea First

Using this method you propose your main recommendation first and then provide supporting rationale. If your time is restricted then this is a feasible approach. It is business-like and logical.

This pattern will be unsuccessful, however, if your audience does not know the details surrounding the issue under consideration or if you do not expect them to agree immediately with the recommendation that you are proposing.

b) The Build-up Pattern

In this style of presentation you set the scene surrounding the issue, giving background information and details before arriving at a proposal. You would then introduce supporting rationale.

This is a feasible approach to adopt to persuade an audience which knows little about the topic under consideration, or which might be sceptical towards your proposals. You will need more time for this approach, however, and you will need to think how the various arguments can best be developed.

c) The Choice Pattern

A variation of the build-up pattern that is useful if you are making a presentation on a problem-solving issue, is to detail the criteria which identify the most appropriate outcome, before proposing alternative solutions and evaluating them against the criteria. In this way you inform the audience of the alternative solutions that you have considered and they will understand why you have rejected them.

This approach is fine if you have time available to develop all the arguments. Part of its success, however, will depend upon the audience agreeing with your evaluation of the alternatives.

d) The Informative Pattern

The patterns we have discussed above are useful if you are trying to persuade the audience of something. Other considerations are necessary if your presentation aims to provide information for the audience.

When you present information it is important to structure your delivery so that the audience is able to assimilate it. You can adopt various approaches to achieve this. Firstly, you can deliver the information in chronological order. This is appropriate if the presentation is an updating session informing the audience of developments since the last session.

You could use a variation of such an approach if you are informing the audience of how to perform a certain task. In this case you can break down the task into steps and discuss each step separately until you have built up the overall picture. Use this approach when it is important for the audience to understand the development of a concept.

Another useful pattern is the cause-effect approach. With this pattern of delivery you discuss the cause of something before analysing its effects.

A final pattern can be employed when a complex topic is being discussed. To reach the complex issue it is best if you start the content of the presentation at a relatively easy level before building up to the more difficult issues. It will be important to make sure, however, that the audience grasps each point before moving onto the next level of complexity.

With any of the patterns of presentation we have discussed you must carefully organise the key ideas in your presentation. Draw up a flow chart which lists the topics to be covered in order of precedence. Question the logic of the order to confirm that the audience will be able to follow the development of your argument.

Pay particular attention to the way you develop the argument, and to the links within the presentation which add to its flow and assist your audience in remembering what has been said.

e) Linking Techniques

Linking techniques are a valuable device as they add further structure to the presentation, and allow the audience to see how the argument has developed so far, and where it is heading.

Before making a new point , preview it. Stress the topic headings you are using and repeat them to act as 'sub-headings'. Summarise important points to ensure the audience have grasped the message. For example:

> 'So, to summarise this point it can be seen that....... The next stage in the argument is to consider the effect of transferable personal skills training on the motivation of the sales force. The area that I will now draw your attention to is the role of transferable personal skills training. The role of transferable personal skills training is multi-dimensional......'

You can reinforce these markers in the presentation with handouts, direct aids, or projected aids. The purpose of using them is to make the structure of the presentation explicit. Think also about how you use your voice. Slow and speed up the pace of your delivery, stressing certain words, repeating key phrases.

The success of your presentation, therefore, will in part be dependent on the content, and whether or not you present and substantiate the key ideas clearly and with due conviction and the use that you make of linking techniques to guide the listener through the presentation. You might provide an outline of the topics to be discussed in the presentation for the audience, either on a handout, by a direct aid, or a projected aid.

(iv) ANSWERING QUESTIONS

While you must give thought and attention to the introduction and development of your arguments, you must also consider how to answer questions.

At some stage during the presentation you may be asked questions by the audience. The questions might require you to clarify a point, or they might be extending the content of your presentation into a different area. No matter what the questions are, however, they should be treated in a similar way:

* You should welcome questions from the audience: not only do they show that the audience is interested and listening to what you are saying, but questions give you an opportunity to engage with what is of direct concern to the audience.

* Repeat the question, or rephrase it, so that all members of the audience can hear it. You will frequently find that those who ask questions speak in soft tones of voice.

* Try to answer each question that is posed directly. Do not ignore the question and answer some other that you would have preferred. This will substantially reduce your credibility with the audience.

* Give short answers if possible so that you can answer more than just one or two in the time available.

* If you cannot answer the question, say so directly. Your audience will soon realise if you are giving a less than truthful answer. You could try to elicit the correct answer from other members of the audience, who might have the necessary experience or information.

* If you cannot answer a question or get other members of the audience to answer it, tell the person asking the question that you will find out the answer after the presentation and will provide it at the next session or forward it. Always obtain the information and make sure that the person who asked the question receives it, or recommend a particular source of information from which the answer might be obtained.

* Never ridicule a member of the audience for asking a question. Welcome audience participation as it adds further interest and stimulation to your presentation. If you make the audience feel foolish because of the nature of the questions they ask, then they will stop participating.

* If you get one questioner who is particularly persistent to the extent that she is dominating the questioning session, assert yourself and politely refuse to answer any more of this individual's questions, by offering to answer further of her questions after the presentation.

* As the questioning period is coming to an end, indicate this to the audience by saying something like "I'm sorry but there is only time for 3 more questions."

3. THE CONCLUSION OF YOUR PRESENTATION

The final part of your presentation is the conclusion. This will have a number of purposes:

* To answer any final questions that the audience might have.

* To summarise the main points discussed.

* To emphasise the key arguments.

* To commit the audience to a change in behaviour or a programme of action that they can follow.

* To introduce the next step/course of action/presentation.

Do not introduce new material in the conclusion, but reiterate the key points of your presentation. Draw the audience's attention to the objectives that you initially set and try to measure whether they have been met. To do this, put questions to the audience:

'Now that you have heard my presentation, what does transferable personal skills training mean to you? How will it help you in your future careers?'

If you have prepared and delivered the presentation well such a conclusion should bring it to a successful close. All that remains to be done is to thank the audience for their attendance, attention, interest and participation.

BRINGING THE PRESENTATION TO LIFE

In addition to preparing the structure of your presentation you should also pay attention to bringing it to life, personalising it, and making it enjoyable to listen to. This will help to maintain the attention and interest of the audience.

Particularly where the presentation is formal it will be important to consider ways of livening it up, making the content interesting to listen to, and preventing boredom setting in with the audience. You can use a number of techniques for this purpose.

The first point to remember is that the audience is made up of individuals. Therefore, you should seek to acknowledge their existence. If you know their names, then use them during the presentation. Make eye contact with all members of the audience, not just to select individuals. Show that the message directly applies to the audience, rather than speaking in abstract terms. Think about using the techniques we discussed in Chapter Three under the heading of figurative language. Use metaphors, hyperbole and similes to add a touch of humour to the presentation, but be careful not to overwork them. When using humour, your role is not to be a stand-up comedian, but a witty speaker. Do not offend the audience and do not let the humour detract from the objectives of the presentation.

VISUAL AIDS

To add a further dimension to your presentation you could incorporate carefully designed visual aids. Visual aids offer you a number of benefits:

* They add structure the presentation.

* They act as an aide-memoir/notes for you during the presentation.

* They act as 'memory joggers' for the audience, helping them to remember what you have said.

* They can help to clarify difficult concepts.

* They are a good way to communicate data/statistics/technical details.

* They stimulate the interest of the audience and help to hold their attention, especially if they are creative e.g. cartoons.

By being skilful in their design, creative in their production and implementing them as integral parts of the presentation further interest can be created for the audience, helping to bring the presentation to life.

(i) DIRECT AIDS

Direct aids can be directly written on, such as chalk-boards, dry-boards, and flip-charts. These can be used for a variety of purposes:

* Displaying data in tabular form/graphs/pie charts so they can be more easily understood.

* Displaying key words or phrases that help to structure the presentation.

* Summarising points.

* Illustrating how calculations are carried out.

* Displaying pre-printed posters/leaflets/cartoons/photographs.

* Noting down points raised by the audience, or building up a concept step by step, thus helping the audience to follow the development of the argument or presentation.

If possible prepare most of the visual aids in advance of the presentation and build them into the presentation plan. In using direct aids refer to the following checklist:

* Keep the visual simple: use only key words.

* Use co-ordinated colours to add to its appeal.

* Only use visuals that are neatly produced and are legibly written.

* Do not overload the visual with too much information, write only a few lines on each flip-chart.

* Write in large letters so that all the members of the audience will be able to read the message.

* Always direct the audiences' attention to the visual when referring to it - use a pointer.

* Make sure the visual aid can be seen by everyone, do not stand in front of it, but beside it.

* Only display the visual aid when referring to it.

* Speak to the audience, not to the visual aid - it is only an aid.

In addition to written visuals aids, you can use models, prototypes or the actual physical item itself.

(ii) PROJECTED AIDS

As technology advances, improvements are made in the means of projecting messages onto a screen, or screens. The two most commonly used methods of visual projection are overhead projectors (OHPs) and slide projectors. The advantages of using these are that the visual might be more visible than direct aids in larger rooms, as they enable your written words to be magnified and projected onto a screen. In addition, they are sometimes easier to use and to refer to. Indeed, careful slide design can add a strong visual impact to your presentation.

USING AN OVERHEAD PROJECTOR

You use an OHP by writing onto an acetate slide which is then projected onto the screen. These transparencies can be hand drawn or a printed or typed message can be copied onto the slide by some photo-copiers.

When using the OHP bear in mind the following points:

* Always face the audience, do not speak to the screen, or look at the projector.

* Stand or sit to one side of the projector, never behind it.

* Switch off the OHP between each transparency, otherwise the light and noise from it will distract the audience.

* When drawing the audience's attention to a particular aspect of the OHP slide, point to the transparency, never to the screen.

* Make sure the projection plate of the OHP is clean.

* Carry a spare bulb in case the one in the projector blows.

Overhead projectors can be used for projecting a variety of different material in addition to the single transparency:

* Overlays. Here, a series of slides are hinged onto a single mount which are laid on top of each other. At appropriate stages in the presentation new slides are overlaid in order to build up a point, concept or scenario as the presentation progresses. This is an effective way of developing a complex picture or argument in discrete stages, helping the audience to understand the message as it evolves.

* Revelation Technique. Using this, certain parts of the transparency are hidden behind masking paper. When it is appropriate to refer to a particular point it is revealed from under the masking paper.

* Movements. These can be illustrated on the OHP, for example iron filings being attracted by a magnet.

If you are going to use any of the techniques mentioned above it is important that you practise them beforehand if you are to achieve the correct effect during the presentation.

USING SLIDE PROJECTORS

Using 35mm photographic slides in a presentation is another effective means of communication. Recent advances in computer graphics now permit, clear images to be produced of graphs, tables, pie charts, maps, as well as conventional images, direct onto 35mm slide film.

All the points raised above for using an OHP apply to the use of slide projectors. You need to pay additional attention, though, to the projector itself, for instance ensuring that it is correctly positioned and is not too noisy.

PREPARING PROJECTED AIDS

Just as direct aids have to be carefully prepared so to do projected aids. A number of guidelines for their preparation are given here:

* Keep the slides simple, write separate messages on separate slides. Write only 6-7 words per line, any more will be difficult to read. Allow only 10 lines, or fewer, on a single slide.

* Use co-ordinated colours.

* Write legibly, or better still use slides produced by a desk-top publishing word processing package. Use both upper and lower case letters. A minimum height of 6mm will be required for projection purposes.

* Use charts and graphs instead of tables.

Once you have produced a transparency it should be mounted on a cardboard frame. This will prevent the slide from curling up at the edges when it is being projected, and allows for easier handling and storage. Another benefit of the cardboard frame is that cue notes can be written on it that draw your attention to the key points you should be raising about the slide.

SKILLED USE OF PROJECTED AIDS

Remember, when using the projected aid to:

* Make sure the screen can be seen by everyone, and speak to the audience not to the screen.

* Use slides to support what you are saying; ensure the presentation does not simply become a commentary of the slides.

* Dim the room lights when showing the slides, but do not switch them off.

* Use efficient equipment, check that it is working before making the presentation. Make sure that the projector operates quietly and does not distract the listeners.

* Memorise the order of the slides so that every time they change you know the content of the next one, reducing your need to be continually looking at the screen.

* Do not use too many slides - their over use is monotonous.

As well as using direct and projected visual aids you could also consider using films or videos as another means of stimulating the audience's interest. Commercial organisations such as Video Arts for example, provide well-produced training videos that have clear objectives, are well-structured, expertly acted, and which can liven up a presentation. Videos and films though, should not simply be used to entertain the audience. Pose questions to the audience prior to watching the video, and return to these questions afterwards to draw out the salient points of its message.

QUESTIONING THE AUDIENCE

Questions have a role to play in most presentations as they are a form of direct audience participation. The questions you put to the audience should be open ones, and hence should commence with:

'What', 'Why', 'How' or 'Where?'

Your purpose in using questions should be to motivate the audience by challenging them, or intriguing them. After a period when you have been doing all the talking and the audience has simply been listening, use questions to get them thinking and to involve them more. Think about how you phrase questions:

* Use simple wording that can easily be understood.

* Make sure the questions are reasonable and are answerable.

Do not use trick questions or ones which will make members of the audience feel foolish.

WRITING THE PRESENTATION PLAN

When you have set your objectives for the presentation, and considered the characteristics of the audience, and when all the elements that constitute the content of the presentation have been carefully prepared, you are then in a position to write your presentation plan.

The plan is the king pin of the presentation, it acts as a game plan, ensuring that all the previous points discussed in this chapter will fall into place on the day of the presentation. Without an explicit and clear plan all the preparation that has been carried out will be futile. The plan ensures that the delivery of the prepared material takes place as intended in a logical and interesting format.

To produce a plan divide an A4 sheet of paper into four columns:

PRESENTATION PLAN

KEY	PRESENTER ACTIVITY	AUDIENCE ACTIVITY	RESOURCES
Introduction	Welcome the audience Outline the presentation		OHP
5 mins	Using a video Ask questions at end	Listen	
Development			
2 mins	Definition	Note taking	
2 mins	Amusing anecdote	Listen	Cartoon
5 mins	Background details	Note taking	
3 Mins	Introduce the video	Listen	
15 mins	Play video	Watch and take notes	Video
5 mins	Ask 3 Open Questions	Answer Questions	
Conclusion			
5 mins	Reiterate key points	Listen	OHP
	Cover arrangements for next week	Note taking	

THE KEY COLUMN

This column serves two purposes. Firstly, it is used to divide the presentation explicitly into the three distinct stages of introduction, development of the argument and conclusion, serving as 'tram-lines' to prevent you deviating from this structure.

Secondly, timings are placed in this column against distinct stages of the presentation to ensure that all the points that you need to make can be covered in the time available, and also to act as a guide for you when giving the talk. By checking the timings in this column against the lapsed time of the presentation you will know whether to speed up or slow down your delivery.

Allocating specific times to specific parts of the presentation is essential and cannot be overstressed, for otherwise you will not know whether time is available to make all your planned points. A presentation can be ruined by running out of time before it has run its carefully thought out course. Similarly, you will appear unprofessional if you finish an hour long presentation in 15 minutes.

Once you have prepared the content of the presentation and you have determined a structure, place timings against each section, and add them up to make sure that all the time you have available for the presentation is being used and the presentation will not overrun. The content of your presentation should be noted in the next column - 'presenter activity'.

THE PRESENTER ACTIVITY COLUMN

The purpose of this column is to provide the structure for your presentation. Note down each stage of the presentation and include certain key words as a memory jogger. Outline the content of your talk here not in sentence form but in the form of single words or phrases.

Do not use a pre-worded script during the presentation but develop the exact wording of your speech as the structure progresses, elaborating on the key words on the presentation plan. By so doing you will achieve a more natural delivery, which allows you to maintain stronger eye contact with the audience as you do not need to look down at a script. During the presentation place the plan on a lectern or table. Many speakers place a watch beside their notes. Otherwise ensure that a clock is within easy view. At intervals check that the timings are running to schedule and that you are delivering the content of the presentation according to the plan.

If you are familiar with the topic under discussion then a single sheet should be enough for most presentations lasting up to one hour. If the topic is unfamiliar or complex, however, then you might need additional sheets but these should be kept to an absolute minimum. The fewer sheets there are the less likely that you will lose your place.

By using a presentation plan you will not need to resort to cards with points written on them. The use of cards is frequently distracting and clearly indicates that as a presenter you are unsure of your material.

THE AUDIENCE ACTIVITY COLUMN

It is important to plan all the ways in which the audience will be involved in the presentation - hence the audience activity column. Specify when you expect the audience to listen, when they are to write notes, and when you will ask them questions. Think how you will ask the questions. Should they be directed to named individuals or delivered as open questions for anyone to answer? Anticipate the likely responses to make sure that you are asking the right questions.

If you are giving a longer presentation change the type of audience activity at least every 20 minutes. This means that you should not speak for more than 20 minutes at any one time.

To break up the presentation use a variety of activities:

* Ask questions.

* Form small groups and hold discussions.

* Circulate handouts and ask the audience to read them.

* Play videos, films, audio tapes or tape/slide sequences.

* Ask the audience to take notes.

* Give a demonstration.

THE RESOURCES COLUMN

Note all the additional material that is to be used during the presentation in the resources column. Use just one or two word descriptions in this column, for example, 'definitions handout', 'cartoon OHP', or 'video'. Before the presentation check to make sure that all the necessary resources are to hand, that they will function correctly, and that they are in the right order.

The presentation plan can be used in a diagnostic sense as it will show you whether you have devoted too much or too little time to a particular aspect of the content. The presentation plan forms the key to a successful presentation as it enables you to structure your talk in a logical way. Presenters who do not structure their talks will appear to be unprofessional and incompetent.

REHEARSING THE PRESENTATION

Once the presentation plan has been produced you might find it helpful to rehearse the talk in private before giving the actual presentation. Although this might feel a little strange at first, most public speakers do it, as it highlights areas which need strengthening, and through added familiarity with the material and the sound of your own voice, boosts confidence. Rehearsal will enable you to confirm all the timings and to make sure that the presentation does not overrun or finish to soon. It will also give you the opportunity to become familiar with the structure of the presentation as well as the aids you are going to use.

It is best to try and rehearse the presentation in the actual room to be used on the day. This allows you to become familiar with the surroundings and will highlight possible distractions that might arise during the presentation. Check all the equipment you are going to use to make sure that you know how to work it, and that it does work.

During your rehearsal, as well as concentrating on the content and structure detail of the presentation plan, you should also pay attention to the other aspects of your presentation style. These were discussed in detail in Chapters Three and Four and we shall re-emphasise some of the points below.

1. DELIVERY STYLE

Your physical presence gives a message to the audience even before your presentation starts. As you walk into the room or onto the stage, or as you are being introduced, the audience will form a first impression of you. Try not to look anxious. You will establish a more favourable first impression if you look confident. If you are familiar with the room within which your presentation is to take place this will help to reduce your nervousness.

The next stage in the rehearsal process is to work through the presentation plan and actually deliver the talk to the empty room. Pay attention to the following:

* The space between you and the audience - are you too far, creating a barrier to communication?

* The physical barriers of the room - should you stand in front of or behind the desk?

* Body language - are you using appropriate and complementary body language? Have you any distracting mannerisms? Do you move around too much ?

* Verbal communications - can people hear you clearly? Are you varying your tone of voice and are you using intonation, inflection and different speeds of speech? Is your grammar correct and have you checked your verbal mannerisms/distractions?

* Personal appearance and grooming - are you appropriately dressed?

* Are you using visual aids efficiently in the presentation?

If possible a friend should be invited to the rehearsal to provide additional feedback on points about which you might not have been aware, such as sniffs, coughs, shrugs, ear-scratching, 'er's and 'um's'. Otherwise you could record the rehearsal and play it back and analyse it. The purpose of the rehearsal, though, is not only to practise the style of presentation but also to practise your activities and those of the audience.

2. PRESENTER AND AUDIENCE PARTICIPATION

The rehearsal session should also allow you to become familiar with using your presentation plan. You should work through the activities outlined on the plan to confirm that they are feasible. Test the memory-jogging words and terms to make sure that they do direct you in the right direction. If you find that your notes are too brief, then add further comments to the plan.

Practise the questions that you are going to ask the audience and consider their likely responses. What will you do if one of your open questions is not answered? What will you do if you direct a question at a specific individual and that person is unable to answer? In these situations you need to adopt a sensitive approach to prevent the audience feeling embarrassed. Rephrase the question, or give clues to the correct answer.

At no time should you reject answers out of hand, for this will discourage further contributions from your audience. Acknowledge and reward even partly correct responses to encourage further audience participation.

Make contingency plans for signs that the audience might be losing interest. Such signs include the audience reducing their eye contact with you, a person talking to her neighbour, somebody writing when she is not supposed to, people looking out of the window or even falling asleep. If you see these signals then change the audience activity.

The second purpose of the rehearsal, therefore, is for you to consider and practise the presentation. Familiarise yourself further with all the equipment you are going to use. Write on the board. Find out where all the switches and heating controls are, and even where the nearest toilets are - a member of the audience might not have planned ahead!

Rehearsing thoroughly for the presentation, knowing all the material to be used, and critically evaluating all the skills to be employed, should reduce your nervousness and apprehension. All that remains to be done is to deliver the presentation.

DELIVERING THE PRESENTATION

This is the shortest section of this chapter for the key to a successful presentation is preparation, planning and rehearsal. If you have taken care to follow the guidelines we have already proposed then the presentation will be delivered extremely competently and professionally. There might be disturbances and distractions during the presentation, however, and you need to know how to deal with these.

DEALING WITH DISTURBANCES AND DISTRACTIONS

You might have to face disturbances and distractions during the presentation. Somebody might arrive late, or a member of the audience leave early. Noise could be a problem if you have aircraft passing overhead or a car alarm goes off. A member of the audience could faint. The power supply to the room might be cut off, or the bulb in the OHP cease to function. The list of possible distractions and disturbances is endless. The way to deal with each of these depends upon the circumstances. However, a number of generalisations can be made:

* Remember that you are in control of the audience and must take the lead. If you have to evacuate the room, it is your responsibility to manage this in a calm, orderly manner.

* If the distraction is only temporary, such as a member of the audience arriving or leaving, stop talking until the distraction has finished. Simply explain why you are pausing.

> * No matter what the distraction or disturbance is, remain calm and collected. If you become irritated you will not be able to think as clearly.

Once you have delivered the presentation, all that remains to do is evaluate it.

EVALUATING THE PRESENTATION

You improve your TPS every time you use them. This improvement will be greater if you evaluate the effectiveness of your skills and learn from the process. Following a presentation you can get feedback from a variety of sources:

> * You can get a formal evaluation of the presentation by asking the audience to complete a specially designed questionnaire, that focuses on the TPS you used. (Ask your tutor for a copy of such a questionnaire).

> * Complete a self-evaluation questionnaire yourself.

> * You may get informal feedback from comments made by members of the audience.

> * You could make a recording of the presentation and then analyse it.

By adopting a systematic approach to evaluating the presentation you should be able to identify your strengths as well as areas you could improve. In this way you should find that your presentation technique improves and you become more confident about making presentations.

SPECIAL TYPES OF PRESENTATION

In the previous sections we have covered points which have a wide applicability and you should bear them in mind when making a presentation of any kind. It is essential to plan, prepare and rehearse a presentation before delivering it. There are, though, a number of situations that require you to adopt a slightly different approach. We shall discuss two of these below.

MAKING A SHORT PRESENTATION

In certain circumstances the time you have available for the presentation might be limited. At meetings, if there are a number of points on the agenda, each speaker, or proposer, might be given only a few minutes to make a point by the chairperson. Management teams receiving presentations from consultants pitching for a particular contract might only allow the presenters 10 or 15 minutes to present their views. Applicants being interviewed for a career vacancy might be required to make a 10 minute presentation on a certain topic. In these situations you must adopt a special approach.

Obviously, time is of the essence and everything you say must count. You will not have time to deviate from the central theme of the presentation. If your presentation, for which time is short, is to be successful, bear the following points in mind:

* You must clearly understand the purpose of the presentation and set explicit objectives.

* Consider carefully the nature of the audience and what they will be expecting from the presentation.

* When competing against others then try to find out what approaches they will be adopting.

* Present the main idea first, and then justify it. Get to the heart of the issue as soon as possible. You will have little time for considering alternatives in great detail.

* Once you have made the recommendation, give the audience reasons for accepting it - therefore, stress its advantages and benefits. How will they gain? Will they enjoy improved profitability or reduced costs? To do this you must be clear about what will motivate the audience before making the presentation or by establishing this at its outset.

* You can produce a report providing greater detail that is given to the audience prior to the presentation, giving them further background information. You can then refer to data contained in the report during the presentation.

* Remember, time is short so the style of your presentation should be clear, to the point, but at the same time creative and imaginative, and based around a well structured format.

As your time available for the presentation is limited, it will be essential to ensure that the audience is not overloaded with information - you can make only two or three points effectively in a short period of time. If you are presenting data, then be creative rather than using a mundane tabular form. It will be crucial to rehearse the presentation to ensure that you can make all the points in the time available. Your delivery will need to be meticulously paced so that you do not overrun.

A further constraint you may find with a short presentation is that you might not be able to rehearse in the actual room which you will use. In these circumstances clarify beforehand what equipment will be available, how the furniture in the room will be laid out, and what the seating arrangements will be. Make sure that you have all the necessary back-up material of all visual aids to hand. For example, make photocopies of all the OHP slides which you want to show as a precaution in case the OHP is unavailable or not working on the day.

Making a presentation in an unfamiliar setting requires you to assess the situation as soon as you enter. Quickly appraise the physical surroundings. If there are problems with the room decide immediately how you can overcome these. Spend as little time as possible gathering your thoughts, or arranging the material you are going to use. You should have covered these details in your preparation process, thus allowing you to start the presentation as soon as possible. If you demonstrate an amateurish approach at the outset you will not create a favourable first impression, especially if the previous presentations have been highly professional.

In a short presentation you can realistically aim only for the creation of a professional and favourable image with the audience. You should show that you have grasped the nature of the situation under examination, and are able to make recommendations that are logical and feasible and of benefit to the audience. You should encourage the audience to solicit further information from you. Short presentations, therefore, require a slightly different approach to those where more time is available.

GROUP BRIEFINGS

Group briefings also require special consideration. They tend to be more informal than persuasive or informative presentations as you will frequently know the people present. Nevertheless, you still have to adopt a structured approach:

* Notify all parties to the briefing session in advance of its time and place, and that they will be expected to attend.

* Prepare the room in which the briefing will take place. Arrange the seats in a circle or horse-shoe, and try to prevent the briefing from being interrupted, for example transfer all incoming telephone calls elsewhere, put a 'Do Not Disturb' notice on the door.

* Set objectives for the session and prepare, plan and rehearse as you would for any presentation. You will find, however, that as you become more familiar with the processes involved the need for detailed rehearsal will be reduced.

* You will find that you have more frequent and spontaneous interactions with the audience. You will need to pay attention to possible questions that might arise, and give some thought to handling them. If a question is asked that you cannot answer, admit to this and arrange to find out the answer after the briefing session.

* Keep the briefing session brief! It is likely that the audience will have other things to do.

Briefing sessions are of value in a number of situations. It is important to keep the group informed of progress that is being made and helps to reduce the likelihood of rumours developing and spreading. The morale of the group will be improved if you give praise for work which is completed on time and to a high standard. If working relationships are changing then keep the group fully informed of new developments. You can use de-briefing sessions as follow-up exercises after an event to find out why an activity was successful or unsuccessful.

In this chapter we have discussed the TPS that you require when making a presentation. Presentation skills will not be mastered, however, purely by reading this chapter. It is only by practising that you will find where your strengths and weaknesses lie. Critically appraise your own performance in giving a presentation and ask others to evaluate your performance. It is only in this way that you will be able to improve your presentational skills.

The next chapter considers two more important TPS - selling and negotiating skills.

Chapter Nine

SELLING AND NEGOTIATING SKILLS

Chapter Nine

SELLING AND NEGOTIATING SKILLS

"The art of management lies in persuading other people to want to do whatever it is that one wishes them to do. An effective communicator is far more likely to succeed in this respect."

Peter Youdale, Chairman, Pirbic Group
Management Consultants.

Selling and negotiating skills are of value far beyond simply encouraging customers to buy your company's products. These personal skills are highly transferable. When being interviewed for a job, you have to 'sell' yourself to the recruiter. If you are a manager making a presentation to colleagues, you will frequently have to 'sell' your ideas before they are accepted. Negotiations take place in a wide variety of situations, from determining who will carry out certain tasks or negotiating new terms and conditions of employment.

In all situations where you have to display such skills, there are certain principles in common. The selling skills you would use when encouraging a customer to buy the product will be similar to those used when encouraging colleagues to accept a new idea. The purpose of this chapter is to make you aware of the constituent components of these selling and negotiating skills.

SELLING SKILLS

Everybody has sold something at some time in their lives, and everybody is involved in selling, whether they realise it or not. To be successful at selling you need skills beyond simple instinct (although this will, of course, help). At the heart of effective salesmanship lies the controlled use of TPS.

Successful selling requires you, as the salesperson, to be well-prepared. Few salespeople are able to sell their product (no matter what it is) unless they have given prior thought and consideration to the situation which faces the customer. We shall consider two different selling situations in this chapter:

> 1. A formal sales presentation - in which you make a presentation to a large group of buyers.

2. One-to-One selling - a more informal setting in which you are selling in to a single customer.

1. THE FORMAL SALES PRESENTATION

All of the skills covered in Chapter Eight apply to sales presentations. The purpose of this section is to elaborate the special considerations that you need make when giving such a presentation. In this section we shall look at the following points:

(i)   Setting objectives.
(ii) The nature of the audience.
(iii) Structuring the presentation.
(iv) Delivering the presentation.
(v)   The venue.

(i) Setting objectives

In Chapter Eight we stated that all presentations must have an objective, a purpose. Sales presentations are no different. The purpose of a sales presentation, however, is to influence the audience in some way, and so you need to adopt a slightly different approach. Your audience will have a reason for listening. As it is a formal sales presentation, they know that you are trying to sell something. Thus, the starting point for your presentation will be to establish its purpose both from your point of view and from the audience's. Before the presentation pose yourself some of the following questions:

'What is the purpose of the presentation from the audience's point of view?'

'What do the audience expect from the presentation?'

'What are the audience's objectives in attending?'

'What is your purpose in making the presentation?'

'What are your expectations from the presentation?'

'What are your objectives?'

In answering such questions it is likely that you will come up with answers that are similar to these:

to communicate ideas
to provide information
to persuade the audience to buy.

Only when you have established a clear understanding of your audience, especially their readiness to buy, can you set explicit objectives for the presentation. If the audience are unfamiliar with you and your product it is likely that your presentation will concentrate on building their awareness and communicating information to them. If the audience already know your product, however, then your purpose will be to persuade and to sell.

(ii) The nature of your audience

Once you have established the purpose of the sales presentation and you have set your objectives, you need to consider the nature of your audience:

- who will comprise the audience?
- who are the members of the audience who will make the decision to buy?
- what is the status and standing of the audience?
- what is the level of their technical ability and comprehension of jargon?
- what kind of presentation do they expect?

These factors will be crucial in helping you to structure the presentation and decide on its content. In particular, you need to identify the key decision makers in the audience so that you can observe their reactions closely during the presentation.

If you notice that these key decision makers are losing interest (which may be clearly indicated by their body language) then your presentation is proving ineffective, and you will have to introduce a different tactic. Prior to making the presentation, you will need to find out what will motivate the key decision makers to buy the product - are cost savings the deciding factor, or is it product quality? If the audience is made up of senior managers of the host organisation, who have little contact with the product being considered, how much will they know about its technical qualities, will they be lost if you give a detailed technical analysis?

You need, therefore, to undertake research into the nature of your audience before making a sales presentation. If you understand their motivations, needs, technical abilities, and status, designing your message and structuring the presentation will be straight forward.

(iii) Structuring the presentation

The structure of a sales presentation will be essentially the same as for the other types of presentation we discussed in Chapter Eight:

* Introduction:
    - to communicate your plan for the presentation
    - to establish a rapport with the audience.

* Development:
    - to convey the key message of the presentation
    - to develop the sales argument
    - to provide supporting evidence, facts, data.

* Conclusion:
    - to reiterate the main points raised
    - to emphasise the key selling points
    - to encourage the audience to respond positively to your message.

The main purpose of a sales presentation is to influence the audience favourably towards the product. Frequently you will want a definite decision from the audience, it will not be sufficient to provide them with information and conclude the presentation. When you require a decision, however, you must provide the audience with sufficient information to enable them to arrive at a decision.

To decide on the type of information to provide which will allow the audience to reach a decision you will need to be aware of their motives, in other words why they will be interested in buying the product. People buy products because of the benefits they gain from using them. A major element of your sales presentation, therefore, will be to emphasise the benefits the audience will enjoy from buying the product.

Untrained sales presenters often emphasise the product's features in the presentation, describing them in some detail. While such a description of the product has a role to play, the main part of your presentation should be devoted to showing how it will benefit the audience. You should show the features of the product to be benefits of the product. For example, consider the two following statements a salesperson could make during a presentation:

The Product Description:

'Our new carburettor is electronically controlled by micro-chip technology'

The Benefit Statement:

'which means that you will improve the fuel consumption of your vehicles by 15%, saving your company £20,000 per year'.

From the above you can see that two words link a descriptive phrase with a benefit statement:

'.....which means....'

The main thrust of your sales presentation should be on highlighting the benefits of the product. You could provide impartial evidence, for example, by referring the audience to articles published in the press, or to testimonials from satisfied customers. You can make comparisons with competing products to show the differences that exist and why your product is superior.

To assist you in developing your sales arguments you should draw up a product features-benefits table:

PRODUCT FEATURE	PRODUCT BENEFIT
A hatchback car with 5 doors.	Easy accessibility for the family.
A 1600cc engine.	Lively performance.
A 5 speed gear box.	Economical fuel consumption.
Steel braced radial tyres.	Harder wearing and better road holding.

Such an approach helps you to get a clear idea of the main selling points of your product and the benefits it offers. You should make a similar analysis of competing products so that you can identify their unique selling points and counter them in the presentation.

When you have presented the arguments for buying your product to the audience, offer them a set of options as to what they could do next. Would they like you to expand on any part of the presentation? Do they require further information? Would they like you to make another presentation at a later date? Would they like to buy the product on the spot? You need to obtain some form of commitment from them at the conclusion of the presentation rather than letting it end with matters undecided and 'up in the air'.

Thus, although the structure of your sales presentation is the same as that discussed in Chapter Eight, your content will be such that it should influence the audience to follow a particular course of action. Your delivery of the presentation will also require competent use of TPS.

(iv) Delivering the presentation

Establishing your credibility with the audience is crucial. Customers will not buy a product from someone they do not trust. Audiences will judge much of the value of your presentation from their perception of your status and character.

The rapport that you develop with the audience will be important in helping to establish your credibility. Rapport does not just occur, you will have to use a range of TPS to build up such a rapport:

* Use effective body language:
  - smile at the audience
  - maintain eye contact (shifty eyes suggest dishonesty)
  - control your gestures
  - maintain a composed posture
  - make sure your appearance and dress are appropriate.

* Vary the way you speak:
  - use strong intonation
  - allow pauses in the speech
  - emphasise certain words
  - always make sure that you are audible to everyone in the audience.

* Be interesting in the way you make your presentation:
  - be humorous
  - be clear in expression
  - avoid jargon
  - use simple concise language.

* Show enthusiasm:
  - look as though you believe in what you are saying
  - convince the audience that you believe it
  - put over the message energetically, not in a lack-lustre manner
  - do not look bored.

* Be relaxed and confident:
  - try not to be nervous
  - do not fidget
  - avoid being apologetic
  - exude confidence in what you are saying.

(v) The venue

In addition to considering special aspects of delivering the sales presentation you must also think about the venue to be used.

Sales presenters pay great attention to the venue used for their presentations. The accommodation should suit the type of audience and their expectations - their number and status. In some cases you might have to hire special function suites in hotels for the occasion and provide hospitality for the delegates. The seating arrangements should be such that you can interact comfortably with all members of the audience with no barriers to communication.

The venue you use can add further credibility and prestige to your presentation and can help to ensure that the audience is influenced to act in a certain way.

You need to consider all of the points we have discussed here as well as those considered in Chapter Eight when making a sales presentation. With a sales presentation, however, you must give more thought to the audience, the structure and content of your message and the physical environment in which you will make the presentation. If you pay attention to these then you will achieve a more successful outcome.

2. ONE-TO-ONE SELLING

You should take a different approach when selling to individuals to that discussed above. When selling to groups there will be less scope for audience participation. With one-to-one selling, however, if you are skilful you will involve the customer much more in what is happening. There are a number of steps you should take in this type of selling:

(i) Listening first.
(ii) Explaining the product benefits.

(iii) Handling objections.

(iv) Closing the sale.

(i) Listening first

Before you can start to sell a product you must first establish your customer's needs. How else will you be able to decide what is the most appropriate product to give your customer satisfaction?

To establish the customer's needs you must ask questions and listen to the answers given. You should develop a repertoire of questions designed to establish the true needs of customers. This will be the starting point for the sale - posing questions and listening to the answers. As the customer gives you answers you should probe further. Below we give an example of a typical introductory conversation between a salesperson and a customer.

"Good morning sir, how can I help you?"

"I want to buy a new lounge carpet."

"Before I show you the types of carpet we stock, may I ask you a few questions? Firstly, are you looking for a hard wearing carpet or one which is less durable?"

"I need to buy a hard wearing carpet as we have two young children who play in the lounge with their toys."

"I take it then that you will also be needing a stain-resistant carpet?"

"Yes, you know what small children are like spilling food and drink everywhere."

"And a carpet that is washable?"

"Exactly."

As the questioning continues the salesperson is able to build up a picture in his mind of the product that will most closely meet the consumer's needs. Once he has arrived at that point he can then confirm the conversation:

"Right, let us see where we are then. You are looking for a hard wearing carpet, that is stain-resistant, easily washable, that is not foam backed, that is patterned, comes with a guarantee, and is reasonably priced."

"Yes, that's exactly what I am looking for."

We sometimes call this the 'agreement staircase' as both salesperson and customer reach an agreement as to what the customer wants. Once the 'agreement staircase' has been climbed, the salesperson is then in the position of being able to select those products which meet the criteria identified by the customer. If the customer disagrees with any of the summarised points the salesperson should clarify them before proceeding to the next stage which is explaining the product benefits.

(ii) Explaining the product benefits

When you know the type of product the customer is wanting to buy you can decide which of the ones you stock will meet the needs of the customer. While demonstrating them and describing their features, you should be stressing the benefits the customer will derive from buying the product. We will continue the conversation about the carpet.

> "Let me show you this carpet here, Mr. Evans. It is stain-resistant to the extent that just a wipe over with a wet cloth will remove the stain. With other carpets you would have to use a carpet shampoo which is not only expensive, but leaves spot marks where it has been used."

A features - benefits table (as explained earlier in the chapter) would be useful at this point as it will give you a clear understanding of the unique selling points of the product and how it differs from the competitors.

After you explain each benefit you should seek the customer's acceptance of it. We go back to the carpet sale example:

> "You can see the value of this stain-resistant carpet can't you Mr. Evans?"

If the customer does not accept the benefit then you should find out why this is so, and try to overcome it. Indeed, you should try and show that you welcome any objections that are put forward by the customer.

(iii) Handling objections

It is natural that many customers will have objections to the products they are buying. Objections are positive signs that the customer is interested in buying the product, but requires further clarification on particular points before the purchase decision is made. Thus, you should welcome objections and handle them positively.

If the customer objections relate to some of the product features then you might find it possible to re-work the various features and benefits so that they do meet the customer's requirements. Returning to the carpet showroom:

> "It was really a larger patterned carpet that I was looking for."

> "Yes, I can see your point but a larger pattern would show stains and dirt more than this pattern. With growing children you will have a lot spilt on it in years to come. Indeed, these smaller patterned carpets are fully guaranteed against stains which you cannot get out."

You can handle objections which are based on a lack of knowledge by the customer by providing the necessary additional information.

If the customer's main objection is to the price you are asking, you might ask whether the concern is about the quality of the product or simply the price. Indeed responding to objections with questions is a very effective way of dealing with them. Let us see how the carpet salesperson is able to deal with such an objection:

"Unfortunately, the price of this carpet is more than I wanted to pay."

"Well, Mr. Evans, are you concerned more about price than quality?"

"No, I do want to buy a quality carpet."

"Well, it might seem more expensive now, but it will last while your children grow up."

By countering objections with a question, the answers you get may provide further insight into what the customer is thinking so allowing you to stress further benefits.

Some objections will be fundamental with the customer showing a clear disinterest in the product, and in such circumstances there is no point in trying to pursue the sale. If you have climbed the agreement staircase with the customer, however, and you handle the customer's objections ably and courteously, then the customer should be ready to buy your product. You can now close the sale.

(iv) Closing the sale

As a salesperson, the most important part of your role is closing the sale - it is what you are employed to do, selling the product to the customer. Identifying when the customer is ready to buy will involve you in listening to what the customer is saying and interpreting his non-verbal behaviour. Among the signals that a customer begins to give when buying a product to show that he is interested in making the purchase may be some of the following:

* The objections to the sale will cease.

* The customer will start to express strong interest in the product - 'Yes, I do like the colour', 'It will match the wallpaper', 'The guarantee will be most useful.'

* A customer may begin to give strong eye contact with complementary body movements - to nod his head, smile and adopt an open non-defensive posture. The customer might make positive actions such as keeping a firm hold on the product rather than putting it down.

You should respond to these buying signals and start to close the sale. Rather than simply asking if the customer wishes to buy the product, you could adopt one of two closing techniques. These are:

a) The Assumptive Close.
b) The Alternative Close.

a) The Assumptive Close

The assumptive close assumes that the customer is ready to buy the product, and so you, as the salesperson, need to make a statement which signifies that a sale has been made. Let us see how our carpet salesperson would do this:

> "Will it be O.K. if we come round and fit your new carpet next Thursday?"

The onus is now on the customer to indicate that he does not wish to buy the carpet - it is easier to say 'yes', than it is to say 'no'.

b) The Alternative Close

With this approach, you offer the customer some kind of choice. Our carpet salesperson might say:

> "Would you like to pay for the carpet with cash, by cheque, or on credit?"

The salesperson, acting on the assumption that the customer wishes to buy the product, offers a choice between alternatives. In making a choice, the customer signifies that the sale has been agreed.

When the sale has been closed the salesperson should ensure that appropriate after-sales-service is provided for the customer.

The example we have used above shows a number of skills involved in selling. At the beginning of this chapter we stated that selling skills are highly transferable. For instance if you were attending a selection interview you may try to translate your achievements into benefits that will appeal to the recruiter:

> "Last summer I gained my Duke of Edinburgh Gold Award. What this means is that I am now confident when leading others. I am happy tackling new tasks and using my initiative to overcome problems."

You should draw up your own features - benefits table.

Similarly, at a selection interview, if the interviewer were to raise objections to you, use sales techniques for handling them:

> "It appears from your C.V., Mr. Wilson, that you have little experience in selling."

> "That's true. What I have to offer is motivation and determination. Does your company recruit only people with a track record in sales?"

Here, the interviewee acknowledges what the interviewer has said, states his/her own 'product benefits', and asks the interviewer to evaluate the interviewee's strengths in relation to the vacancy.

Selling skills can be transferred, therefore, to a variety of different situations. In the next section we shall look at negotiating skills which are equally transferable to a number of different circumstances.

NEGOTIATING SKILLS

You will need to use negotiating skills when you have to resolve differences. Your aim in a negotiating session is to reach an agreement that serves the best interests of both parties and encourages the development of a long-term relationship based on trust and respect.

Disagreements can arise in many diverse situations, ranging from the negotiation of the terms to build a new power station in China to resolving a domestic conflict in the home between parents and children. Each negotiation situation requires the parties to it to use TPS and you will become a successful negotiator if you can master the necessary TPS.

To be a successful negotiator you need to:

> a) Plan meticulously.
> b) Be controlled in the use of your interpersonal skills.
> c) Understand fully the nature of the conflict.
> d) Design strategies to overcome the conflict.
> e) Recognise all the outside forces likely to affect the decision making of the other parties involved.
> f) Set yourself targets and objectives for a successful outcome.
> g) Have a series of alternative outcomes planned as 'next-best-solutions'.
> h) Apply pressure when necessary to the others involved in the negotiation.
> i) Recognise and build on your own strengths, both in terms of the strength of your argument and your own strength as a negotiator.

The skills demanded of a negotiator are the same as those used by a sales person making a presentation. As a negotiator, you must listen to what others are saying and interpret their body language. You must be able to communicate persuasively using both verbal and non-verbal means. You may work in a team of negotiators so your skills in working with, and leading, others will be important. In many negotiating situations you will face pressure and stress and your ability to cope with these may well prove crucial.

Negotiations involve a complex combination of TPS. The purpose of this section is to break the negotiating process down into its constituent parts so that we can examine each of these skills in more detail. We will consider three stages in this process:

> 1. Understanding the nature of the conflict.
> 2. Setting objectives and devising strategies.
> 3. Generating alternative solutions.

1. UNDERSTANDING THE NATURE OF THE CONFLICT

Disagreements arise when people are in conflict over a particular issue. To resolve a conflict requires the joint efforts of all those involved. Before negotiations can take place, however, all of the parties involved must understand fully the nature of the conflict. To gain a better understanding of this, you should analyse the conflict from the perspective of each of the parties involved.

For instance, let us take as an example a conflict that arises between a car-hire company negotiating to buy five hundred new cars from a motor manufacturer. The buyer, the car-hire company, will naturally seek the best possible package from the seller, the motor manufacturer. The car-hire company expects this because it is buying in bulk. The seller, on the other hand, will be interested in maintaining the profit margin on the sale of the cars. The starting place for understanding the true nature of the conflict is to analyse this situation from both the buyer's and the seller's perspectives. To do this you need to follow a systematic process.

i) Identify the issue under negotiation:
   - the purchase of the five hundred cars.

ii) List all those issues which are important from the buyer's perspective:
   - the discount expected on the normal price of each car
   - the time period over which the payments for the cars can be made e.g. four instalments
   - the warranty facilities offered by the manufacturer
   - discounts off further cars that the car-hire company might purchase in the future
   - the delivery dates for the five hundred cars.

Then look at the same topic from the seller's perspective:

iii) List all the issues important from the motor manufacturer's perspective:
   - the minimum discount on the price of each car to maintain acceptable profit margins
   - the need to ensure prompt payment of the full cost of supplying the cars
   - the standard warranty terms to be offered to the buyer
   - the need for an early decision to purchase so that the cars can be manufactured
   - an agreement from the buyer to purchase additional cars in the near future.

When you have completed both lists, analyse each of them to identify the most important considerations for each party. You should identify the outcomes desired by each party as clearly as possible. The next step is for you to consider each desired outcome and evaluate whether or not the other party to the negotiation would be willing to accept it. This will help you to gain a clear understanding of the perspective and stance of each side and allow you to identify issues that can be resolved at the outset so that some agreement is reached before the more contentious issues are tackled.

To negotiate on behalf of one party you would need to develop arguments which counter some of the likely claims and proposals of the other party. This demands a wide understanding of the conflict, which will probably require research into developments outside your own organisation. Were you negotiating on behalf of the car-hire company you would need to be aware of new car prices being charged by other motor manufacturers, as well as the terms, conditions and warranties on offer elsewhere.

Such preparation and planning is vital. When you have a clear understanding of the nature of the conflict, you can then set your objectives and devise appropriate strategies for attaining them.

2. SETTING OBJECTIVES AND DEVISING STRATEGIES

You need to set clear objectives before negotiation begins and these are frequently linked to the outcomes you wish to achieve. These objectives act as your bargaining framework around which your discussions will take place. They enable you to identify the important issues where you recognise little movement is possible on your part, as well as those areas where you feel concessions can be made. Objectives also clarify your expectations from the negotiations.

If you enter the negotiating session with high expectations you will achieve more than if you have less ambitious objectives. Those who expect a lot frequently gain more than those who do not. Thus, set your target levels high. Your targets, though, need to be flexible. The other party will be thinking in a similar way but with many objectives diametrically opposed to your own.

When your objectives have been set, you will need to devise strategies to achieve them. To be a successful negotiator you should always minimise your losses - seek to gain as much as possible from the session without making too many concessions. To achieve this anticipate the arguments that the opposition will be using during the negotiations and produce counter arguments in advance. In a similar way you need to devise arguments which support each of your claims and to prepare a number of alternative solutions.

3. GENERATING ALTERNATIVE SOLUTIONS

Negotiating requires you to use creative skills to look for alternatives acceptable to both you and the other party. Neither you nor the opposition will wish to lose face as a result of the agreed outcome. Before the negotiating begins, therefore, consider as many different solutions to the conflict as possible. Rank these in order of preference, with your preferred outcome ranked in first position. This should be the outcome that most closely meets the objectives you have set. Alternative outcomes that require you to make major concessions should be ranked at the bottom of the list.

By generating alternative solutions you will enter the negotiating sessions with a positive frame of mind which is open to creating the necessary movements and concessions required to reach an agreement. A skilled negotiator, though, will tend to concede on points that are less important than the other party believes them to be, and so the negotiation concludes with them accepting a next-best-solution.

SKILLS FOR NEGOTIATING

You will require a range of TPS for successful negotiating. As we have already mentioned you must plan and prepare. You must be as knowledgeable as possible about the issue under discussion. During the negotiation sessions you will make use of your communication skills. In this section we shall consider some of the more critical skills which you will have to develop. These are:

> (i) Your listening skills.
> (ii) Your use of body language.
> (iii) Your verbal communication skills.

(i) Listening skills

Your ability to listen and to understand what the other party is saying is crucial. The process of negotiation involves considerable personal interaction. A common dilemma is that while you are listening to the other party, you are also thinking about your response and counter-arguments. To some extent this distracts your listening.

One way of trying to ensure that you do not misinterpret what the other person is saying is to confirm at regular intervals what has been said in the form of a brief summary. You might phrase it something like this:

> "So what you are saying here is that you are willing to move on the price for the deal but you are not willing to budge on the delivery dates that you can give us."

This type of recap helps prevent misconceptions from arising on either side as to what has been said, and confirms that all parties have kept track of the way the negotiation is developing. It also helps to keep your concentration more finely tuned to what the other party is saying. To ensure that this process does not dominate the negotiating session, however, you will have to be a quick thinker in order to steer the discussion onto your own arguments after making the summary.

(ii) Body language

If you control the use of your body language during negotiation it will help you considerably. In Chapter Four we noted that a person's body language can show whether there is any discrepancy between the words spoken and his true feelings. For example, a negotiator may say that he is happy with the way the session is developing, yet has a worried look on his face. Similarly a negotiator may say that you can rely on his word, yet does not look you in the eye when saying it. Both are giving signs that what they are saying does not reflect their innermost feelings.

To be a skilful negotiator you must be a perceptive reader of body language and adept at using it to communicate to the other side. For example, consider the following actions:

* Forceful, downward hand moving gestures:
    - these should be used to emphasise important points, or to indicate that a strong stance is being adopted.

* Open postures, upward facing palms of the hands combined with strong eye contact:
    - these signify honesty.

* Nods of approval coupled with smiles :
    - indicate that agreement is being reached.

* Folded arms, crossed legs, closed postures:
    - indicate a defensive stance and signify that the person is putting up barriers to negotiation.

The body language that you use, therefore, must support and endorse what you are saying in the negotiation.

(iii) Verbal communication

The only way to negotiate is to talk to the other side. When you are doing this there are certain key rules you should remember:

* Speak clearly and forcefully. This allows the other side to understand what you are saying and will indicate your strength of feeling.

* Control your speed of speech. Increase the speed to make a point and then allow pauses to let the other side assimilate it. Long pauses in the negotiating process can put pressure on the other parties to break the silence and also the deadlock.

* Do not use emotive language. Your emotions will no doubt be aroused during negotiations, but it is crucial that you do not allow these to influence the proceedings. Make an effort, therefore, to remain calm during the negotiations.

* Stick to the important issues. At times the discussion might digress from the key issues involved. If this occurs steer the discussion back to the important issues. Digressions are distractions and waste time.

In addition to the TPS outlined above, you will also have to pay attention to your other personal skills. For instance, be assertive, think about how you should work with others and be critical in the way you think. These are all skills in their own right and we will discuss them in detail in subsequent chapters. You should be aware, though, that you will have to use them all if you wish to be successful in the negotiation.

THE NEGOTIATING PROCESS

Negotiations move through distinct stages. The stages are as follows:

> 1. The first stage of the process will involve listening to the arguments put forward by the other party, assessing their underlying logic, and formulating counter arguments.

> 2. The second stage identifies areas of agreement where movement is made towards finding a solution.

> 3. The final stage is when agreement is reached.

Progression through these stages is neither smooth nor easy. You will feel frustrated, you may become emotional and, at times, you may feel that you have reached deadlock. You will have to overcome all of these if you are to reach a successful conclusion to the negotiation. Indeed, it may be that the negotiation will move forward at quite a slow pace. We shall now examine each stage of the negotiation process that you are likely to encounter.

The early phase

The starting point in any negotiation is to find out what the other party expects to get out of it. What are they hoping to achieve and what are their desired outcomes? You should try to get them to 'lay their cards on the table' as soon as possible and clearly identify what they want as an outcome from the negotiation. This will allow you to see how close the anticipated desired outcomes that you arrived at in your planning stage are to the actual desired outcomes of the other party.

To do this ask open questions that start with:

> "How", "Why", "Where", "When", and "What"?

Put pressure on the other side by asking probing questions. But when you have to reply to one of their questions answer only the question asked. Take care not to digress from the question asked or to provide them with any further insights into what is your next-best-solution in case you have to make any compromises.

Once you have identified all the issues, if it is clear that the other side are unwilling to accept your position immediately, then you will have to think about using the strategies and counter arguments that you have already planned. Your arguments should aim to show that their desired outcomes are based on ill-founded logic. Using the example of the car-hire company negotiating for the purchase of the cars, take the part of the negotiator for the car manufacturer and assume that you are trying to counter the buyer's argument for a bigger discount:

> "You want a 30% discount on the purchase price. Come on, you have to recognise that this is completely unrealistic. You must know that in the motor

industry a car manufacturer's profit margin on this type of vehicle is only 20%. If we were to agree to a 30% discount, we would be making a loss on the deal."

If you are to succeed using this sort of tactic then all the arguments that you put forward need to be objective and based on fact, rather than on speculation.

As the negotiations progress you should try and settle all those issues that can quite easily be resolved in this early phase and carry forward the more contentious ones to the middle phase. Returning to our negotiation on the car purchase, the car manufacturer's negotiator might say:

"Before negotiating the price discount, let's first of all discuss the warranty facilities to be offered with the cars. I think that our initial talks indicated that we both have similar views on this, and hopefully we can reach an agreement on the warranty quite quickly."

The middle phase

The middle phase is where the hard bargaining takes place. The early phase is a testing period for both sides, and to some extent sets the terms of reference for what is to follow. Now your objective is to reach agreement on the issues where there is some diversity of opinion. The starting point is to select an issue and to identify the areas of agreement. The negotiator for the car manufacturer might say:

"Well, we have now agreed the warranty terms, let's return to the price discount. You've heard our view, we cannot offer you anywhere near a 30% price discount. At best we can manage a 9% discount. How do you feel about that?

You may well have to offer concessions at this point if agreement is to be reached. If you are a weak negotiator you might offer major concessions whereas if you were a more effective one you will have a number of minor concessions to use in this give-and-take period. Effective negotiators will also explain why a counter-proposal is unacceptable before putting forward their own. Again returning to the car sale:

"Unfortunately, a 9% discount is not acceptable given the size of our order. We would be looking for a discount of 12%, especially if we commit ourselves to buying more cars from you."

"12% discount on the first order is still rather high. However, we could agree to it if you sign a contract to purchase a further five hundred vehicles from us."

When putting forward arguments to counter a proposal it is important not to use them all in one go, but to ration them so that you can come up with further arguments if the other party has still not conceded.

This phase of the negotiating process is normally the most involved and fraught. The session might have to be halted so that both sides can appraise the progress that has been made or modify their strategy and stance in some way.

In many circumstances for the conflict to be resolved satisfactorily, it is likely that both you and the opposite side will have to make movements to reach agreement. If neither side is prepared to make any movement you will reach a deadlock. In these situations it will be important to ask questions to find out why the opposition is not prepared to move, and for you to establish the underlying cause of the deadlock. Until you both understand this, you will not be able to propose alternatives to progress the negotiations.

A useful strategy that you can use in deadlock situations is the 'conditional bargaining' approach:

> "If you accept this, then we will accept..."

Here your every concession has a condition attached to it. In this way you will put further pressure on the other side to move their position, showing that you are willing to make concessions.

Sometimes, though, the other party will seem resolute and unwilling to make any concessions to reach an agreement. In these situations, you will have to adopt a strategy to break the dead-lock. You may have to resort to more drastic measures such as:

* Seeking the services of an impartial mediation, conciliation or adjudicating body.

If this proves unsuccessful then you could try the following:

* Threaten to use the influence of the media to highlight the unreasonableness of the opposition.

* Try to bring pressure from third parties to encourage the opposition to break their dead-lock.

An agreement will be reached only if the interests of both parties are met. Both you and the opposing team of negotiators have to accept this and must work towards reaching such a position by making movements and concessions. Indeed, either you or the opposing side might help the other by identifying those forces that are hindering the agreement process, and by suggesting solutions.

Another approach you could try is to break down the issue which is causing the dead-lock into its constituent parts, to see whether you can agree upon the various components individually, before putting them back together again. This might help to move the negotiation process forward and can be seen as a positive move by both sides.

To add further pressure the other party may start to pose threats:

> "If you don't give us the deal we are looking for, we will simply take our business elsewhere."

The use of threats is a sign of weakness and desperation, and your response should be to acknowledge that it is a threat and ask that it is withdrawn. If the dead-lock persists then you could adopt the following procedures:

* Agree to disagree - do not waste any more time and effort. Often reaching this type of agreement will help to reduce some of the tension.

* Draft a statement that fully outlines the issue that cannot be resolved, indicating the crucial difference between both sides. Look for the solutions for overcoming these disagreements - e.g. set up a joint working party.

* Move the negotiations forward onto those points that can be agreed.

You will continue to be dead-locked in your negotiations if either side has no intention of reaching an agreement. If both sides are prepared to make concessions, however, and to accept their next-best-solution then you should be able to reach a mutually acceptable agreement.

A tactic which is sometimes used during negotiations is to apply pressure and create stress for the other side in the hope that this might force them to make concessions. You may find that the other side try to apply pressure on you in a number of ways. Examples of these would include:

* Emotional outbursts or personal insults - these might be used to try to get you to lose your temper and hence your controlled thought processes.

* Accusations of incompetence - this tactic might be used to upset you and undermine your confidence.

* Threats to walk out or to refer the negotiations to a higher authority might be bully tactics to encourage you to reach agreement.

* The hard and soft negotiator. The other party might assign distinct roles to members of the same team, one might be willing to offer concessions which will lull you into a false sense of security, while another might be the taker who spots your weaknesses and takes immediate advantage.

When faced with such pressure you should:

* Stay calm and show the irresponsibility of such tactics by indicating that they will have no effect.

* Appeal to the better nature of the opposition to act more rationally.

* Call a halt to the negotiations until such time as the opposition are prepared to retract what they have said and are willing to resume businesslike discussions.

Pressure and stress of one kind or another will be inevitable in a negotiation and can be quite unsettling if you are an inexperienced negotiator. Stress affects your emotions and thinking ability; as a negotiator, therefore, you need to practise facing up to and coping with such pressure.

From the above discussion it is clear that you will need to demonstrate a range of skills while negotiating if you are to reach a satisfactory agreement. When an agreement has been reached, you will then enter the final phase of the negotiating session.

The concluding phase

The agreements that you reach need to be ones that will be respected by all parties. To ensure that this will happen each finalised agreement needs to be repeated during the concluding phase and noted down in fine detail. If either party disagrees with what is being said or written down, then you need to clarify the position and make any necessary amendments. When both sides are satisfied with the agreements reached you should end the session, hopefully with you and the opposition parting on friendly terms.

The focus of this chapter has been to consider persuasive TPS. To be a successful persuader you will need to develop effective personal skills in addition to competent communication skills. Some further aspects of personal skills will be discussed in Chapter Ten.

Chapter Ten

PERSONAL SKILLS

Chapter Ten

PERSONAL SKILLS

In the previous chapter we investigated the persuasive skills required for effective selling and negotiating. Certain personal characteristics and skills contribute to a successful performance in these persuasive areas.

ASSERTIVE SKILLS

Assertiveness is the art of clear and direct communication. Being assertive enables you to:

* Express your personal feelings to others.

* Be direct and ask for what you want.

* Say 'No' clearly and firmly without causing offence when you do not want to follow a certain course of action.

* Take responsibility when necessary.

* Say what you mean clearly and confidently.

* Stand up for your rights.

Being able to express your feelings and to stand up for your rights are important skills in that they help you to establish relationships with other people.

Some people are naturally assertive and do not think twice about expressing their feelings or views. Others, however, tend to be non-assertive and more reticent, and find it difficult to say 'no', or refuse unreasonable requests. If you are a non-assertive individual you must realise that being assertive does not involve aggression, but simply firmness.

There are many situations when it is appropriate to be assertive, for example when making a request, refusing a request, coping with refusal or standing up for your rights. We shall now consider a number of such situations.

MAKING A REQUEST

Some people find it difficult to make a request of others, whether it be a formal request such as a demand for information, or an informal request such as asking a colleague to have lunch.

When you make a request of others it is important to be direct and positive and make sure that your message is as clear as possible. You can achieve this by maintaining strong eye contact with the other person, smiling, speaking in a pleasant tone of voice, and not being aggressive. If you are nervous about making the request, then it will help if you practise before actually asking the other person. This should improve your confidence, and will reduce the likelihood that you will 'dry-up' and be unable to make the request coherently and concisely.

One way of making the request is to turn it into a question:

> "Could you get me this report, please?"

This would mean that the other person would have to say 'no' if they wanted to refuse your request which is more difficult to do than to say 'yes'. If you ask the question in a polite and pleasant tone of voice, the other person will find it even more difficult to refuse your request. It is easier to refuse requests that are posed rudely, aggressively or impolitely.

REFUSING A REQUEST

Sometimes it is necessary to say 'no' to a request from someone else, but before doing so, decide whether or not the request is reasonable. If you think that the request is out of order and you cannot accept it, then adopt a firm polite manner. You could say something like this:

> "I'm sorry, but the report is in another section of the building and I can't get hold of it".

If the other person is persistent then you will have to justify your refusal:

> "The Managing Director has it at the moment and I can't get it until she has finished with it."

COPING WITH REFUSAL

When you make a request which is refused you need to make a swift recovery and hide your disappointment. You might make a face-saving statement such as:

> "Oh, well, not to worry, I'll read it when she's finished with it."

If the person who has refused your request is not in a position to do so, because, for example, they do not have the necessary authority, then adopt a firm approach and repeat the request, perhaps in a different form:

"Can you type this letter for me please? Its urgent!"

"I can't do it right away as I have other typing to do."

"I appreciate that, but the letter must be typed this morning."

"Well, come back at lunch time and it might have been typed."

"I'm afraid that's not good enough, I'll leave it with you and telephone at 11 o'clock to see whether its been done."

"Very well then, I will see what I can do."

"Thank you."

In such situations it is important not to take 'no' for the answer, but to show your determination and maintain the pressure on the other person until the request is accepted. It might be that you have to alter your tone of voice if the request is not accepted, but at no stage should you lose your temper, for this will probably increase the other person's determination not to give in.

STANDING UP FOR YOUR RIGHTS

People who are timid often find it difficult to say 'no' even to unreasonable requests from others. If you are asked to do something which is in breach of normal practice you must stand up for your rights to prevent yourself being put upon.

In this situation it is important to assess the circumstances quickly and to confront the other person immediately. Do not apologise but reply in a firm, polite and steady voice. For example, consider the following exchange:

"John, I've put you down for some overtime on Saturday. I want you to start at 9.00am."

"It's not my policy to work overtime. Why don't you ask someone else to work on Saturday."

If the other person still persists, then repeat the objection, but in a firmer manner:

"Be reasonable, John, everyone has to take their turn at working overtime."

"According to my contract of employment, working overtime is purely a voluntary matter. It is not something I want to do. You will have to find someone else."

SHOWING APPRECIATION

Just as it is important to be able to stand up for your rights so too is it important to be able to show your appreciation of others when the occasion calls for it. Paying compliments is one way of showing your appreciation. It helps to encourage loyalty from others. Showing appreciation of a job well done will develop the other person's self-confidence and help to develop personal relationships.

All too often managers fail to complement their staff for work that is well done. A few simple words of gratitude in such circumstances will encourage good work in the future. Individuals are motivated by knowing they have completed a task which is appreciated by their superiors. When people feel that the quality of their work is not appreciated, they are discouraged from maintaining standards. Tell other people that you appreciate what they have done as this will encourage them to act in a similar way in the future:

> "Thanks a lot. Typing that letter so quickly has really helped me."

MAKING APOLOGIES

Everybody makes mistakes and there will be times when you need to apologise. It ought to be possible to apologise without losing face. There is no need to be over-apologetic, just a simple:

> "I am sorry that this happened"

> or

> "I am sorry that you feel this way about it"

is usually sufficient. Indeed, if the other person is particularly irate then an apology, no matter how simple, may defuse the situation.

When you apologise, don't use an aggressive tone of voice as this might show that you are not sincere in your apology. Once the other person has accepted your apology it is important to take steps to remedy the situation and to try to ensure the same problem does not arise again.

MEETING PEOPLE FOR THE FIRST TIME

For some people, meeting others for the first time is a daunting prospect. Notice how some people blush, avoid eye contact, or stammer or mumble their words when they first meet you.

If you find it difficult to meet people for the first time then you might adopt a few simple pointers. The first step is to 'break the ice':

* Shake hands, smile and be friendly: "Hello, my name is ..., how do you do?" Try not to seem aggressive.

* Keep eye contact but do not stare as this may be interpreted as aggression.

* Look at the others when they are speaking as this shows you are interested in what is being said. Do not look out of the window or stare at the floor. Always show that you are trying to follow the conversation.

* Try to keep the conversation going in a friendly way. Follow the guidelines suggested in Chapter Three.

* Hide your nervousness as it can be distracting to the other person. Control your body language.

When your meeting with the other person is drawing to a close, finish the conversation on a positive note:

* Always part with a few friendly words such as "It has been nice meeting you", shake hands and end with a smile.

DEVELOPING FRIENDSHIPS

If you want to develop friendships with other people you must not be too self-centred. It is important to recognise when your friends are having problems and to offer help.

You might feel ill at ease about offering such help and it is important to recognise that some people are reluctant to accept help. For example when a friend suffers a bereavement it is all too easy to avoid her for a few days, and not say anything about her loss. Should a friend be made redundant, it is tempting to stop meeting her in the pub. If a friend is experiencing emotional problems, for instance as a result of the breakdown of a long-term relationship, she may be irritable, making her company difficult to enjoy. Although your friend might appear to be rejecting you, she does still need your support.

Good friends do not ignore each other in times of difficulty, they help each other. You need to be assertive, to engage in free and direct communication, but in a sensitive way that respects the feelings of the other person.

The first step in the process of supporting a friend is to identify that she is facing a difficulty. Some people do not like to talk about their problems and 'bottle them up'. Signs to look out for are:

* Changes in temperament. A humorous person may lose her sense of humour. A calm person may become angry. A quiet person may become even quieter. In fact whenever the person behaves differently to her normal behaviour this could be a sign that he is facing some difficulty.

* Change in habits. People facing problems often adopt different routines - a punctual person might forget meetings; a careful worker might become sloppy.

* Change in appearance and grooming. People facing difficulties often allow their appearance to become slovenly and unkempt.

The above characteristics are just some of the signals that will show that a friend is experiencing a difficulty. People respond to such pressure in their own way. Only by knowing someone well, and recognising when she changes mood or behaves in an abnormal way, will you recognise that she has a problem. You will easily recognise dramatic changes in behaviour. Sometimes, however, a difficulty builds up over time (for example a problem at work) and it is not always easy to recognise the symptoms.

When you establish that a friend has a difficulty, try to help in the following ways:

* Imagine how your friend is feeling. You will need to find out what lies at the root of the problem. It is likely that your friend is emotionally distressed and so you need to be sensitive in the questions you ask. Begin with questions such as: "What ...?", "How...?", "Who ...?", "Where ...?" Avoid questions beginning with "Why ...?" at first as these require your friend to give an explanation and initially this might cause further upset. It is best to try and establish the facts of the difficulty at first, rather than to try and justify it.

* Try not to express value judgements about what your friend says. Do not be overly critical about what she/has done, or is finding difficulty with. The last thing your friend wants is you to compound the difficulty by telling him off.

* Do not rush at this stage. If your friend starts to cry, then encourage it. It is a form of emotional release, helping to reduce pent-up tension.

* Avoid saying too much at this stage. Allow your friend plenty of time to gather her thoughts. Do not be tempted to speak during these silences. Let your friend lead the conversation.

When you have a clear idea of what the difficulty is, try to understand how your friend must be affected by it. Try to imagine how your friend is feeling - angry, sad, shocked, annoyed, frustrated, let-down, lonely, etc. Imagining how a friend is feeling and seeing the difficulty from her point of view is known as empathy.

The next step is to show sympathy. Sympathy means showing compassion, appreciating your friend's difficulty and offering words of comfort. It is important for your friend to realise that she does have emotional support and that she is not alone at this time of stress. You might offer support with phrases such as:

"Yes, I understand how you feel, you must be very angry/upset/frustrated..."

You can also show support through your non-verbal behaviour such as holding your friend's hand or giving her a hug.

Try not to dismiss the difficulty as unimportant even if you feel that the difficulty is only a minor problem. It is obviously distressing your friend. Phrases such as:

"Come on, pull yourself together, you ought to grow up."

are not going to reassure your friend.

Be as sympathetic as you can and perhaps follow these suggestions:

* Address the difficulty head-on, for example if your friend has suffered a bereavement, do not ignore the issue, say something like "I am so sorry that your mother has died. I know you will miss her. She was a lovely lady."

* Choose your words carefully so that you do not cause further stress, try not to 'put your foot in it.' For example if a friend has just been made redundant do not say: "You'll never find another job at your age." Instead be positive and say: "With your skills and experience it won't be long before you are back in work."

Talking about the difficulty and offering sympathy often helps to alleviate stress. When your friend is calmer try to provide additional support. It might be that simply staying with her is all that is required. Alternatively, you might have to do something else to help, such as informing other people of the difficulty - relatives in the case of bereavement, or the college or employer if your friend is unable to attend. Try and do this with the minimum of fuss. Your aim is to reduce any further potential sources of stress.

When helping a friend in this way it is important to decide whether additional, professional guidance is required, for example should the doctor be called, or a marriage guidance counsellor. Only when you fully understand the difficulty and appreciate how your friend feels can you make such a decision.

Everybody needs good friends. Good friends support each other at times of crisis and distress. Sometimes being a friend is not easy, it may involve you in much emotional upset. The TPS discussed here will be useful for coping with such stress.

BEING PERSISTENT

A number of situations discussed in this book require you to be persistent and to persevere against obstructions and difficulties.

When sales staff try to sell a product they have to be persistent, trying to overcome the customers' objections. If you are applying for a job you will probably find that you have to make a number of applications, and attend a number of interviews before being offered a post. When you gather information you may well be faced with difficulties. For example, the information that you require may not be readily available in a published form, which means that you have to instigate your own survey. Planning the survey, implementing it, and analysing the results will all require perseverance.

In all these examples you need to be assertive. If you are not assertive and persistent, then it is unlikely you will achieve what you set out to do. People who are not persistent often lack the will-power to overcome objections and difficulties that they encounter. To illustrate some of the TPS you could use in such circumstances we will consider one specific situation.

Let us examine a very common situation - 'seeing the right person'. You will face many situations that involve you in trying to find the right person in a certain situation. For example, salespeople who go out and visit business customers without appointments (known as cold-calling) frequently encounter the customer's secretary before meeting the customer. Often the salesperson requires considerable perseverance to persuade the secretary to let her see the customer. A customer (after buying a product) may discover it is faulty and wishes to complain to the manager of the shop where it was purchased. The shop assistant at the counter may refuse to get the manager and try to deal with the customer directly.

Be persistent in such situations. Decide what you want from the situation and make sure that you get it. The salesperson mentioned above will want to see the potential customer. The dissatisfied customer will want to see the manager of the shop. Nevertheless you might have to accept something which is next-best as the person you want to see might genuinely not be available. Therefore, you may have to accept an alternative, for example you could make a firm appointment to see the person or arrange to telephone at a specific time.

If you are going to get to the person you want to see you will have to be assertive. Be direct and to-the-point. Give clear reasons why you must speak personally with that specific person and why no one else will do.

Place yourself in the position of the salesperson trying to get an interview with a potential customer. Your conversation with the secretary may follow a pattern such as this:

> "Good morning, my name is Julie Grant from Prospect Manufacturing, could I please see Mrs Brown, your Buying Manager?"

> "Do you have an appointment?"

> "No, I don't. I want to speak to Mrs Brown about a new product our company has produced that is currently saving firms like yours £250,000 per year. I know that you buy a similar product from Stapleton Engineering, but our product is right up-to-date and much more economical."

> "That may be the case but Mrs Brown does not see salespeople without an appointment."

> "Yes, I appreciate that and apologise for calling without an appointment. I will only take a few minutes of Mrs Brown's time to introduce myself, and then I can make an appointment to see her for a longer time on my next visit."

> "Mrs Brown is too busy to see you now, even for a few minutes, you really should have made an appointment."

"Would it be possible for you to let Mrs Brown know that I am in reception, and wish to see her? She will probably have seen the advertisements for our product in the press and might be interested to learn how much she will save by using it."

"Very well, but I can't promise anything. Take a seat."

"Thank you."

In this conversation the salesperson is not prepared to accept 'no' as an answer. Every time the secretary says no she acknowledged it, and then continued to show how important it would be for the Buying Manager to see her, implying that if she did not the firm would lose money. Note that you should not give excuses for arriving without an appointment.

Throughout this type of encounter it is important to create a favourable first impression. If the secretary does not like you, for whatever reason, then it is unlikely that she will arrange a meeting with the Buying Manager. To help to create a favourable first impression, you need to speak pleasantly but firmly, not to lose your temper or become impolite. Maintain strong eye contact throughout the conversation and be friendly. Try not to appear nervous. It is important to attempt to interpret the secretary's body language. If it becomes obvious that the secretary will not budge and refuses to telephone the Buying Manager then if you continue to be persistent this will simply antagonise the secretary. In such a circumstance accept a next-best alternative, and ensure that you leave with a firm commitment either to speak to the Buying Manager in person or over the telephone.

Being persistent requires patience and tenacity. Like all the other TPS discussed in this book you will develop it over time. The example considered above is one approach that you can adopt to 'see the right person'. However, to support the TPS already discussed in this example, you will also have to be a positive thinker.

BEING POSITIVE

Being positive is really a frame of mind, an attitude, a way of thinking about situations. People who are positive thinkers always look on the 'bright-side'. No matter how difficult or disastrous a situation has been the positive thinker will try and identify something good that has arisen from such a situation. Positive thinking is to some extent the skill of receiving information, and identifying the good in it.

In contrast, negative thinkers always highlight the worst side of situations or events. These people tend to be critical, looking for faults, rather than good points.

To be positive involves being assertive not only with other people, but with yourself. Sometimes you will face difficult situations and it will be all to easy to complain about them. Complaining about situations in a negative way, simply to be critical without suggesting ways of overcoming the problem, is unhelpful - other people involved with the situation might also adopt a negative approach. In difficult circumstances both yourself and the others involved need to think positively and to look for good points.

When people think negatively a lot of time can be wasted moaning and feeling sorry for themselves. This just makes the matter worse. People who are negative in their approach to their jobs lose motivation towards their job. They lack enthusiasm and put the blame elsewhere, for instance on the organisation for which they work or the people they work with.

If you do face difficulties try to assess the situation and learn from it. Perhaps you could be more persistent, not accepting 'no' too soon. After any negative encounter carry out a self-evaluation process. Regard all experiences as part of a learning process. Indeed, it is from unsuccessful encounters that you learn most - a positive point in its own right.

To summarise - be positive. Adopt a frame of mind that always looks for successes rather than failures. Do not ignore difficulties but identify the cause of the problem and take steps to overcome it. Self criticism, while important, is on its own rather negative. Be constructive and try to improve what you do.

Being positive is a TPS you should adopt frequently. Everybody suffers from upsets and disappointments, no matter what they are doing. You will overcome difficulties more quickly if you think positively. There will be times during the TPS training programme when you will feel frustrated or disappointed with the progress you are making. At such times adopt a positive frame of mind.

REFLECTIVE SKILLS

To develop your TPS you must be able to reflect upon your current abilities and identify your weaknesses as well as your strengths. The development of your reflective skills helps to improve your TPS because only through experimentation and evaluation will you learn. This reflective process requires you to be objective and rational when considering your own skills and this requires a systematic approach.

In order to identify those TPS that you currently use, appraise the activities you enjoy, your interests, the achievements you have attained, the satisfaction you gain from them, and your general temperament. If you do this you can reflect on these TPS to spot where your strengths lie and your weaknesses exist. The clearer the picture you draw of your own characteristics and personality, the easier it will be to assess your TPS.

Begin this reflective process by considering your likes and dislikes as they apply to the activities you pursue.

ACTIVITIES

Some activities you pursue will be obligatory, such as attending college or work, while others will be freely chosen - leisure activities. It is important to recognise from these activities where your TPS strengths lie.

The starting point is for you to list activities you frequently undertake. We give an example of this in the table below. We list activities which are both obligatory and are freely chosen in column one. The TPS that you use in each of these activities are then noted in column two. You can then undertake some simple self-evaluation and enter your assessment in column three. Base this on a rating scale from '1' (not competent in the skill) to '5' (highly competent in the skill).

Column One ACTIVITIES	Column Two TPS	Column Three RATING 1 (low) - 5 (high)
Attend lectures	Note taking	4
	Thinking	3
	Listening	4
Part-time job	Working with others	4
	Conversation skills	2
	Being assertive	1
	Numeracy	1
	Writing letters	5
Scout Leader	Leading others	4
	Planning events	4
	Time management	3
	Oral communication	5

Completing a table like this which covers all the activities you undertake will provide you with a clearer picture of some of the TPS you are currently using, and is a start in identifying where your strengths and weaknesses lie. The table will also give you a view of those TPS that you enjoy using, because these will generally be the ones with the higher scores in which you are competent.

INTERESTS

Like your activities, your interests also give an insight into your TPS. By analysing what you like doing, and the TPS involved, you can shed further light on your capabilities. For example, if you enjoy playing back-gammon it might be because you enjoy competing against other people (an enterprising skill); that you like to study others' approaches and styles of play (requiring the use of intellectual skills); or it gives you a sense of purpose and achievement in trying to improve your performance (personal skills). Your interest may be less in the game itself than in the satisfactions associated with it.

To translate these likes and satisfactions into TPS, you should list the interests you enjoy and then say why you think you like them. The next stage should be to rank these interests in order of enjoyment, and then to state explicitly the TPS that you use successfully in each of the interests, together with an evaluation on the rating scale of 1 - 5 of each of the skills:

RANK ORDER OF INTERESTS	TPS	RATING 1 (low) - 5 (high)
1 Playing back gammon	Intellectual skills	4
	Oral communication skills	2
	Reading body language	5
2 Reading books	Intellectual skills	3
	Reading skills	5
3 Cycling	Dexterity skills	5
	Physical skills	5

Emerging from the analysis is a profile of those interests that you have and the TPS that you most commonly use. The example above portrays an individual with interests that involve little interaction with others. The TPS that have been identified and evaluated are very much intrapersonal skills as opposed to being interpersonal ones. From this you can see that to develop a more balanced portfolio of skills the individual needs to gain interests that involve much more interaction with others, such as team games, or joining clubs and societies.

ACHIEVEMENTS

Just as the activities and interests you enjoy shed light on your TPS, so too can your achievements. Achievements do not have to be headline-making events, simply successes you have enjoyed, or about which you feel pleased.

A useful starting point is to list the achievements you consider are important. These achievements may be connected with work or your social life. For each one, you should write down why that achievement is important to you. Emphasise those achievements that were difficult to attain successfully.

Once you have completed the list, evaluate the TPS revealed. Listing achievements in this way, gives further insight into your TPS. For example:

ACHIEVEMENT	TPS	RATING 1 (low) - 5 (high)
Winning the football competition	Working with others	4
	Leading others	3
	Oral communication skills	4
Attaining top mark in the examinations	Working under pressure	5
	Working to time constraints	4
	Self-motivation skills	4
	Self-discipline skills	4
	Intellectual skills	5
	Written communication skills	3

The achievements listed and their TPS' evaluation will sketch the make-up of your personality. The person profiled above is able to accept pressure and to work well within constraints. To achieve examination success the individual must have been motivated to undertake all the necessary preparation, which has required a self-disciplined approach prioritising examination revision above other interests or activities. You could summarise this individual as being determined and dedicated.

Your personality, though, is made up of many strands, and, importantly, develops over time.

SATISFACTIONS

Your self-awareness will be enhanced by assessing your satisfactions.

Everyone gets satisfaction from some activity or event in which they participate. TPS can be assessed in terms of the satisfaction they give. Listed below are a range of TPS. Against each skill you can indicate whether or not you generally feel satisfaction when using it. The ability to use the skill can be evaluated in the third column.

TPS	GAIN SATISFACTION/DISSATISFACTION	RATING 1 (low)- 5 (high)
Conversing with friends	satisfaction	5
Conversing with strangers	dissatisfaction	2
Making a formal presentation	dissatisfaction	1
Selling	dissatisfaction	2
Negotiating	satisfaction	3
Being interviewed	dissatisfaction	2
Interviewing others	satisfaction	4
Writing reports	satisfaction	5
Writing business letters	satisfaction	4
Using body language	satisfaction	3
Reading body language	satisfaction	4
Solving problems	satisfaction	4
Taking decisions	satisfaction	5
Working with others	dissatisfaction	2
Leading others	satisfaction	4
Chairing meetings	satisfaction	4
Attending meetings	satisfaction	3

The above list of TPS is not exhaustive but it does cover a wide range of activities. By deciding whether or not you get satisfaction from using each of the skills, will give you insight into where your strengths lie, and which weaknesses need to be overcome.

PERSONALITY

Your personality profoundly influences how you behave, react and feel towards other people and towards different situations. In turn, how other people react and respond to you will be determined partly by your personality. Knowing and understanding your own personality is of great importance when evaluating TPS. Such a knowledge and understanding helps you to identify personality characteristics you might have that either support or hinder your ability to interact effectively with other people.

Listed below are a number of adjectives that describe various personal characteristics. Read the list ticking those which you recognise in yourself. Put a cross beside those that you do not think describe you. Leave blank those which are indeterminate:

Adaptable	Aggressive	Amiable
Aloof	Ambitious	Assertive
Assured	Caring	Cheerful
Co-ordinated	Competitive	Confident
Considerate	Creative	Daring
Decisive	Dependable	Determined
Easy-going	Emotional	Enterprising
Extrovert	Fickle	Forceful
Friendly	Gregarious	Hard-working
Honest	Humorous	Introspective
Judicious	Lazy	Mild-mannered
Objective	Obstinate	Open-minded
Orderly	Overcareful	Persistent
Prudent	Reliable	Reticent
Self-conscious	Self-reliant	Shy
Sincere	Systematic	Tactful
Tenacious	Tense	Trustworthy

When you have done this look at the personal traits you have ticked and assess how you come across to others - how do friends think of you, do they see you as being assertive, tactful, or a supportive person, for example? Ask your friends how they see you. Ask colleagues at work. What are their perceptions of you? For instance, do they regard you as ambitious, reliable, decisive?

This analysis will increase your awareness of your 'personal' TPS and give a picture of how you appear to others. To conclude this exercise you should try to summarise your evaluation of your own TPS.

EVALUATING THE PORTFOLIO OF TRANSFERABLE PERSONAL SKILLS

You cannot develop your TPS if you are unaware of your current skills. The exercises you have completed in this chapter will be useful in starting this self-evaluation process by using reflective skills to highlight skills which have already been competently mastered, and those in which you have room for improvement. To draw all the previous sections together, you need to draw up a 'master-list' of TPS, similar to that given below, which you can use to evaluate formally your own levels of competence.

A COMPENDIUM OF TPS

Read each skill statement and use the following rating scale to indicate your level of ability:

> 1 - Not very good, and requiring considerable improvement
> 2 - Acceptable at a basic level but with need for improvement
> 3 - Not bad, but scope for improvement
> 4 - Reasonably competent, slight room for improvement
> 5 - Highly competent, scope for fine-tuning

A   ORAL COMMUNICATION SKILLS: SKILL RATING

I am able to use:

different tones of voice when speaking
different speeds of speech
emphasis in speech, stressing key words
figurative language
clear pronunciation

B   CONVERSATION SKILLS

I am able to:

listen effectively to others
start a conversation with friends
start a conversation with strangers
maintain a conversation
conclude a conversation
use the telephone efficiently
contribute effectively to meetings
chair a meeting
give clear instructions to others

C   BODY LANGUAGE SKILLS

I am able to:

use facial expressions appropriately
use effective eye contact with others
control my posture movements
give appropriate gestures
dress appropriately
read the body language of others

D   WRITTEN COMMUNICATION SKILLS

I am able to:

>   write memos
>   write business letters
>   write business reports
>   present data clearly using graphs
>   present data clearly using bar charts
>   present data clearly using pie charts

E   INTERVIEW SKILLS

I am able to:

>   complete application forms effectively
>   write an effective curriculum vitae
>   create a favourable impression of myself at interviews
>   interview others efficiently

F   PRESENTATION SKILLS

I am able to:

>   prepare for a presentation
>   set explicit presentation objectives
>   design an interesting message
>   structure the presentation
>   deliver the presentation competently
>   evaluate the presentation

G   SELLING AND NEGOTIATION SKILLS

I am able to:

>   present a persuasive message to a group
>   explain the product's benefits
>   establish the needs of a customer
>   handle objections to the sale
>   close the sale
>   negotiate with others
>   make concessions to reach agreement

H   PERSONAL SKILLS

I am able to:

> make a request of others
> cope with the refusal of a request
> refuse a request
> stand up for my rights
> show appreciation to others
> apologise to others
> reflect upon my own TPS

I   GROUP SKILLS

I am able to:

> work in a group with other people
> accept the views of other people
> be sensitive to the views of other people
> plan the work of other people
> motivate other people to work for the group

J   THINKING SKILLS

I am able to:

> analyse a situation
> evaluate a situation critically
> interpret data
> identify weak assumptions
> solve problems systematically
> take decisions

K   INFORMATION GATHERING SKILLS

I am able to:

> use a library
> design a questionnaire
> conduct research interviews
> analyse research findings

The above checklist covers some of the TPS covered in this book. When all the ratings have been given you will have a comprehensive profile of how you rate your own TPS, identifying your strengths and weaknesses. The findings of the checklist can be usefully summarised as follows:

MY STRONGEST TPS ARE:

```
┌──────────────────────────────────────┐
│                                      │
│                                      │
│                                      │
│                                      │
│                                      │
│                                      │
└──────────────────────────────────────┘
```

MY WEAKEST TPS ARE:

```
┌──────────────────────────────────────┐
│                                      │
│                                      │
│                                      │
│                                      │
└──────────────────────────────────────┘
```

THE TPS I NEED TO DEVELOP MOST ARE:

```
┌──────────────────────────────────────┐
│                                      │
│                                      │
│                                      │
│                                      │
└──────────────────────────────────────┘
```

THE WAYS IN WHICH I WILL DEVELOP MY TPS ARE:

```
┌──────────────────────────────────────┐
│                                      │
│                                      │
│                                      │
│                                      │
└──────────────────────────────────────┘
```

By explicitly evaluating your strengths and weaknesses and committing yourself to some form of skills development programme, you will be motivated towards converting weaknesses into strengths, thus developing well-balanced TPS.

You need to develop reflective skills because much of the work involved in developing TPS has to be done by yourself. If you follow no systematic process for reflecting upon your own skill levels then you will be less likely to master new skills and improve existing ones.

In addition to assertive and reflective skills, you must also be aware of your affective skills.

AFFECTIVE SKILLS

The term 'affective skills' is used in this context to refer to your feelings and emotions, your attitudes and values, and how these affect your interpersonal relationships. Very often the success of interpersonal relations with others is determined by how you are feeling at the time of the interaction, and your attitude towards the other party. When trying to establish successful interactions with friends or colleagues at work, bear the following in mind:

* Always treat others with respect. Even though you might be feeling down take care to respect others. For example do not reprimand subordinates in front of their peers; do not release your pent-up frustrations on others ; try to control bouts of moodiness, do not be elated one minute and deflated the next, try for an even balance - working for and with moody colleagues can be difficult.

* Be sensitive to other people's feelings. Always consider the effect of the interaction on the other party - try to avoid offending people by what you say. Do not make personal attacks on others, particularly about their race or religion. Find out what feelings others have and respect them.

* Show concern for the well-being of others; learn to pick-up the signals that are communicated by the other person indicating their concerns. Make time to find out what it is that is causing concern, and provide sympathy and support when it is needed.

* Be polite when interacting with others, do not be rude or expect them to be servile. Treat others the way you would like to be treated.

Your affective skills will be called into use in the TPS training programme. On occasions you may have to provide feedback to your peers on their TPS. When doing so, you should ensure that your comments are offered in a sensitive way, so as not to hurt the feelings of the other people. A number of guidelines need to be followed when offering feedback.

* Offer feedback in a descriptive way rather than as a judgement. For instance a statement such as "I find your tone of voice monotonous to listen to" is a descriptive statement. A judgemental statement would be "Your tone of voice is boring to listen to".

* Offer feedback only on TPS that are controllable. This requires that you first consider why you are offering feedback. Informing a friend that she is thin cannot be helpful as little can be done about it. Many people are self-conscious about their 'natural features' and feel threatened when they are commented upon.

* Offer feedback only to help people. Receiving feedback can be painful. To minimise the pain you may cause another person, give feedback in as

constructive and sensitive a manner as you are able . Think carefully about how the other person is likely to react to your feedback.

Hopefully, the guidelines set out above may assist you in adding a 'human' touch to interpersonal interactions. It is difficult to keep to them all the time but if you make a conscious effort to consider and respect the feelings and attitudes of others then your interpersonal interactions will be warmer and more rewarding as a result. People always have time for considerate human beings, but quickly show their dislike of those who treat others with little respect.

The TPS discussed in this chapter are important. These skills, especially assertive and affective skills, influence how you react towards other people, and how they respond to you. One situation where your personal skills will be crucial for the success of the encounter, is in group situations - working with other people. Chapter Eleven examines group work in more detail.

Chapter Eleven

GROUP WORK SKILLS

Chapter Eleven

GROUP WORK SKILLS

The ability to work effectively with other people is a demand made by everyday life. There will be many times in your life when you will have to work in a group and be responsible for completing certain tasks which will contribute to an overall whole. To establish effective working relationships in a group you will need to develop interactive skills. Such skills are highly transferable and will be useful in many situations at work or college or in your personal life.

Most organisations have some form of management hierarchy with a recognised leader. This is because it is generally accepted that groups work most efficiently with a leader. The leader's task is not simply to administer the tasks which the group will carry out but to lead the members of the group.

This chapter will try to develop your group work skills in three ways. Firstly, we shall consider how to establish good working relationships with others, and secondly how to lead others. Finally we shall consider the group dynamics which exist when you work with others.

ESTABLISHING EFFECTIVE WORKING RELATIONSHIPS WITH OTHERS

If you wish to have good working relationships with other members of a group you will need to develop your interactive skills. This involves a number of factors including:

> a) Presenting yourself to others.
> b) Adopting an open attitude.
> c) Being sensitive to the feelings and needs of others.
> d) Allowing an equal opportunity for all to contribute.
> e) Being able to accept criticisms.
> f) Working with self-confidence.
> g) Working to the best of your ability.
> h) Acknowledging the role of the leader.

a) PRESENTING YOURSELF TO OTHERS

If you wish to work with others you generally have to conform to the norms of the group. Part of this involves how you present yourself to the rest of the group. For example, a new recruit in a bank who arrives for work on his first day with long straggly hair, dressed in faded denim jeans and pop star tee-shirt, may not be accepted by his carefully groomed and neatly dressed colleagues or by the bank's management. The new recruit is not conforming to the dress and appearance requirements of the job. The same individual, however, dressed in the same way would fit in perfectly at a rock concert. Personal presentation plays a part in establishing relationships with others. First impressions are crucial in interpersonal interactions and although your personality and character might be perfect for a career in banking, if your appearance and dress are non-conformist, then you will not be accepted.

b) ADOPTING AN OPEN ATTITUDE

In group situations it is important to be open with colleagues on all matters relating to the group's activities. All information relevant to the group's performance should be freely distributed and consultations between the group members need to take place at regular intervals to discuss what has been done and what will be done in the future.

If communication fails to take place then the group will be acting simply as a series of individuals. Information and communication are the life-blood of groups. Information should be circulated to maximise group cohesion. Some individuals withhold information to provide themselves with a power base, giving them an advantage over their colleagues. This practice leads to the alienation of some members of the group.

You need to build the exchange of information, and consultation processes, into the group's routine activities. One way of doing this in a large organisation is to circulate a 'perusal file' of memos, letters and reports to all members of the group.

c) BEING SENSITIVE TO THE FEELINGS AND NEEDS OF OTHER PEOPLE

When you work closely with other people, you may find that frustrations and tensions build up. To reduce these it is important to gain an understanding of the feelings and needs of your colleagues, for instance whether they are sensitive individuals with strongly held personal views or more easy-going and willing to accommodate views which differ from their own. Tensions can arise between group members because one person is insensitive to the feelings of another. This may become apparent when one person makes a personal remark that is offensive to another. When such tensions arise, people stop talking to each other and this can seriously damage the cohesiveness of the group.

When tensions exist, part of the group's energy will be taken up by the conflict. This energy ought to be used in meeting the objectives of the group. To reduce tensions it is important for all group members to gain a clear picture of the personalities and characteristics of their colleagues and to respect them.

d) ALLOWING AN EQUAL OPPORTUNITY FOR ALL TO CONTRIBUTE

When you work with others you will find that group members feel more committed if they have contributed in some way either to planning the work or deciding how the responsibilities are to be divided. Thus, when a new task is to be undertaken each member of the group should be given the opportunity of contributing to the formulation of the plan of action. It might not be feasible to accept all the ideas that are put forward, but nevertheless the opportunity should be made available to all members of the group.

If members of the group are always simply told what to do then they may become apathetic, or feel resentful and be less committed to the group. By involving all members of the group at the outset you will get a broader range of ideas as to how to plan the work, and this in itself might lead to greater efficiency.

Conflicts might arise as to who should complete certain tasks. This is the time for negotiation. You will need to assess the suitability of each group member for the task, taking into consideration each individual's strengths and weaknesses.

e) ACCEPT CRITICISMS

In all group situations individuals make mistakes or fail to perform as well as they might. To minimise the impact on the group of such imperfections, you must inform the individual concerned of the way in which he went wrong. Your criticisms, however, must be made in a constructive manner, referring to the task that was undertaken rather than specifically to the individual. You should spend time finding out why the error occurred, what if anything can be done to remedy the situation, and what steps could be followed to prevent it occurring in future. You need to be sensitive to the feelings of the individual concerned. If there is a point of contention between members of the group this should be freely expressed. By saying nothing and trying to ignore it greater tension and stress will be created.

When you face criticism, learn to accept that it is not personal, but a criticism of the way in which you undertook the task. It is important to remain calm whether you are giving or receiving criticism and to see this as a positive learning aspect of group work. If you have to criticise individuals try to provide them with help to change their behaviour. This might involve counselling sessions or retraining.

To help in this process of giving and receiving constructive criticisms, it is useful to hold regular appraisal sessions where the members of the group can express their feelings about the way the group is operating. By expressing feelings, including frustrations, the group will be able to dissipate tension.

f) WORKING WITH SELF-CONFIDENCE

Problems will arise if group members doubt their ability to perform as required. To prevent this arising it is important that members of the group are required to complete only tasks which they feel confident about undertaking. By negotiating with each person about what he or she will do you should be able to overcome this. If you simply delegate responsibilities within the group, then you might find that some people will fail to complete their tasks adequately.

Some tasks, however, may be unfamiliar to all members of the group. To cope with this situation it is crucial for the group to maintain a positive attitude. A healthy group welcomes challenges and encourages all members to contribute.

g) WORKING TO THE BEST OF YOUR ABILITY

Group work requires all members to complete their specific tasks to the best of their ability. If you do not complete your tasks, then you will be letting down the rest of the group. To encourage everyone to complete their tasks to the best of their ability, you should agree at the outset the standards of performance for which each person is aiming. If someone performs to a higher than expected standard then he should be congratulated. Conversely, when a person fails to meet the standard set, it is important to establish the reason why.

If a member of the group refuses to co-operate, find out why. Clearly point out the consequences of his actions. If, between you, no positive solution can be found, then you will have to warn the unco-operative person. Eventually, if he still refuses to work as part of the group he will have to be excluded.

Groups achieve their objectives only if all the members work together harmoniously for the benefit of the group. Personal ambitions should never take precedence over the group's objectives. Part of the success of the group will lie with each member's determination to succeed. Each member has to be motivated towards the success of the group. This involves all members accepting responsibility for fulfilling certain tasks to the best of their ability. Each member's responsibilities should be made clear at the outset, with each individual having the right to accept the responsibilities and hence to join the group, or to reject them and so dissociate from the group.

h) ACKNOWLEDGING THE ROLE OF THE LEADER

Some types of group work require one member to work as leader. Most organisations operate in this way. The leader is responsible for over seeing the group's activities and making sure that the group's objectives will be met on time and in the desired manner. This is the traditional, hierarchical view of leadership and groups.

In the traditional model all group members have to accept the need for a leader, and consequently accept the decisions that the leader takes. If the members of the group do not accept the leader and challenge the leader's position, then some of the group's energies are being used in a negative way to destabilise the group. To prevent such a challenge the leader must establish effective working relationships with the others members of the group. In the next section we shall consider the skills you will need if you are to lead others.

LEADING OTHERS

The traditional, hierarchical view of leadership suggests that for the group to be successful a leader has to accept a number of responsibilities. These include:

* Setting group objectives and targets.

* Agreeing mutually acceptable objectives and targets for the individual group members.

* Negotiating responsibilities with group members.

* Consulting with group members on the progress they have made in reaching individual targets and group objectives.

* Motivating the group.

* Encouraging co-operation and communication within and outside the group.

* Coping with the human relationship problems of the group.

* Taking decisions and solving problems.

* Accepting the views, opinions and ideas of the group.

* Encouraging initiative within the group.

* Creating a harmonious atmosphere which encourages others to contribute to the best of their ability.

* Disciplining group members where necessary.

The above list is not exhaustive, but serves to indicate the wide ranging roles of a leader - facilitator, motivator, planner and negotiator, to name but four. To be a successful leader you will need well-developed TPS. As a leader you will have to be a competent communicator. You will need to be assertive to persuade team members to act in the way you consider to be best for the group. You must be aware of your own interpersonal skills and use your own strengths to good effect.

Given the range of TPS required by a leader, one could ask the question 'Are good leaders born, or can they be trained?' We shall now consider the following approaches to this question:

1. The Qualities Approach.
2. The Situational Approach.
3. The Functional Approach.

1. The Qualities Approach

One view of leadership is known as the 'Qualities Approach'. This suggests that certain personal qualities a person may have contribute to an effective leadership style. For example some people might display initiative, courage, intelligence and humour, which when combined create a competent leader. This approach suggests that the potential for leadership varies between individuals and is determined by their particular qualities.

Such personality qualities are seen as inherent rather than developed through training and experience. Furthermore, there is little agreement as to which personal qualities are essential for leadership. The qualities approach, therefore, offers little scope for structured learning. Moreover, this view implies that leaders should be recruited rather than trained.

2. THE SITUATIONAL APPROACH

The 'Situational Approach' proposes that leaders come about in a specific situation. Different leaders come to the fore, depending upon the tasks involved, the organisation and the specific circumstances. This approach sees leadership not just as a series of qualities but as a relationship, in which the leader possesses knowledge appropriate to a given situation.

This approach can be criticised in that it regards leadership skills as relating purely to a specific situation. This is true to a certain extent, however there are obviously some people who are able to lead whatever the situation.

3. THE FUNCTIONAL APPROACH

The 'Functional Approach' sees the group as having a common goal and the group members work together because as individuals they cannot complete the task alone. They must work as a cohesive team. Rules which will promote the unity and cohesiveness of the group are needed. Those who break the rules may be penalised. For the group to work together successfully, certain functions have to be performed. The term 'function' is used here in a very broad sense to include behaviour or areas of leadership responsibility, as well as a particular activity. Some important leadership functions include:

i) PLANNING

The first function of leadership is to define the group's purpose, objectives, or goals. Once this has been done a strategy must be drawn up to allow the group to attain these objectives. The next step is to convert the strategy into a detailed plan of action that can be implemented.

Objectives, strategies and plans provide a sense of direction for the group and form a basis of measuring its success. Leaders, therefore, need to be effective planners, able to distance themselves from short term issues and look to the future. They must evaluate where the group is, where it is heading, and most importantly, where it should be heading.

ii) INITIATING

Once the planning stage is completed, the next function of the leader is to consult the group about the objectives, strategies and plans. The leader needs to discuss and explain the rationale for these with the rest of the group. Negotiations should take place as to who should perform which tasks. Guidelines need to be agreed with the group members for completing their tasks to a certain standard. Encouragement should be provided to motivate the group towards attaining its targets. Assistance and guidance should be given to group members to help them reach their individual goals.

iii) CONTROLLING

When the group members begin work on their individual tasks it will be the leader's role to monitor their progress and to control their activities. The leader has to maintain the group's guidelines and norms, and discipline those who contravene them. The leader has to regulate the pace at which the work is completed to ensure that deadlines will be met and objectives achieved.

When group meetings are held the leader will take the chair and encourage all members to contribute. It is the leader's responsibility to mediate if disputes arise between group members. Part of this function involves the leader maintaining the morale of the group and encouraging good working relationships.

iv) SUPPORTING

If you lead a group you must be supportive to your group members. People tend to be encouraged and motivated if they feel that their contributions are being appreciated and if they are being supported by their leader when they face criticism from others.

If group members have personal problems then, as leader of the group, it is your task to be sympathetic and help them cope with their difficulties. You should try to get to know each member of the team on a personal basis. It helps to know the ambitions, motivations, attitudes, perceptions, capabilities and interests of each group member. You can achieve this by holding individual counselling sessions with all members at regular intervals. If you demonstrate a caring attitude as leader this tends to encourage loyalty from the group.

v) INFORMING

As circumstances change or new information becomes available it will be necessary for the leader to communicate this to the rest of the group. Keeping everyone informed of developments helps to prevent the spread of ill-founded rumours that can damage group cohesiveness and morale.

Just as it is important for the leader of a group to relay news and information to the team, it is important for the group leader to receive news and information from group members. As group leader you should welcome suggestions and comments. Members of the group should feel that their views are important to their leader. This will lead to a stronger commitment to the group.

vi) EVALUATING

Once group members are working together effectively, as leader, you will have to evaluate what is happening to make sure that everything is going according to plan. If it looks like things are not going to plan then you might have to introduce a new initiative, or consider a complete change of strategy.

Once the group has achieved an objective, you should evaluate what has been achieved in order to identify those elements of the plan which were successful and those which were not. Your findings from this evaluation will be helpful when devising future strategies.

The functional approach endorses the view that leaders are multi-talented individuals who have mastered a wide range of TPS. The leadership personality is distinctive: a leader is intelligent, maintains enthusiasm and a positive attitude, and displays personal qualities such as empathy, sympathy, and humour to lead and gain the respect of the group.

Thus, group work skills are vital TPS. Relationships between a leader and a group are apparent in many aspects of life. It is important to recognise, though, that simply being given a leadership position does not make you a competent leader. Nor does simply possessing knowledge. Leadership is more than the sum total of a person's so-called desirable qualities. Group members follow their leader because they are motivated to do so. A leader understands what motivates the members of the group and encourages them to be loyal through a 'human' approach.

GROUP DYNAMICS

If you are going to work with other people or lead them then you need some understanding of group dynamics. We have already noted that groups play an important role in organisations, and the successful attainment of group objectives will be determined partly by how well the members of the group work with each other.

The purpose of this section is to investigate different forms of groups, how groups are developed, and finally different types of groups that can be found in modern organisations.

THE NATURE OF GROUPS

A group is two or more people who form some kind of relationship, whether it be because they have social interests in common, or are colleagues at work, or students at college. Forming groups is a natural process for human beings - individuals seek the companionship and friendship of other people, because being a member of a group offers distinct advantages:

* Groups allow people to pool resources, making the group more effective as a whole than each individual acting independently. Groups frequently accomplish tasks more easily and more efficiently than individuals.

* Groups offer a sense of security. Individuals feel 'protected' when working with other people. Individuals can rely on the expertise of fellow members, and feel more secure if they can share their ideas and views with others before having to make decisions and take action.

* Groups can provide emotional support. When working with other people you can turn to other group members for help and friendship. If you are not a member of a group you might not have such support available to you.

* Groups provide a sense of identity. It is important for people to create an identity for themselves which can increase self-esteem and self-confidence. Being a member of a group in some way gives credibility to the individual. Many groups develop a sense of identity by their dress and appearance - bankers wear pin-stripe suits; soldiers wear army uniforms; punks dye their hair. Other groups might develop a sense of identity through their entry qualifications and requirements.

* When accepted by a group some people feel a sense of pride, of being of value to the other members of the group. For other people joining a particular group may be a question of status. People accept a position of responsibility in the group to gain a sense of importance. If they do something positive for the group and are praised for it, this will increase their self-confidence.

Thus, it can be seen that being a member of a group offers distinct advantages. Most people belong to one form of group or another. We can classify groups into two categories - formal groups and informal groups.

FORMAL GROUPS

Formal groups exist to accomplish specific tasks. Formal groups are usually established with stated goals and objectives. In employment, workers are frequently assigned to departments or sections. At college, students are divided into formal groups to complete assignments. In the public sector, committees are formed to take decisions.

In the world of work it is difficult to identify organisations that do not use formal groups in some way to achieve their objectives. Most employees will belong to at least one formal group and many employees will belong to a number of such groups.

INFORMAL GROUPS

Informal groups tend to be more socially orientated than formal groups. Membership is based upon a common social interest such as a hobby, or arises as a result of family ties or through friendship.

Informal groups do not have to set tasks or objectives, rather they are a means for the group members to meet and relax, and to discuss areas of common concern or interest.

Formal and informal groups can also be classified according to whether they are 'open' or 'closed'.

OPEN GROUPS

An open group is one in which membership is not tightly restricted. Frequent changes of membership may be common as new members join and existing ones leave. Open groups tend to be primarily informal, membership is voluntary, and no entry qualifications have to be obtained to gain membership.

The organisation of open groups tends to be less bureaucratic with positions of authority being granted on a voluntary basis to those who seek them. Members holding positions of authority might remain in post for only a short period of time before another member assumes the responsibility.

Thus, open groups have a certain fluidity - they are not rigid and their organisation and membership change with time. Only a limited amount of formal procedure might need to be followed. Examples of this type of group are:

* Friendship groups formed by a few friends who live near each other, go to the same college, or work for the same organisation.

* Social clubs and societies in which the main criteria for membership is an interest in the activity or hobby common to all members - photographic clubs, badminton clubs, motor sport societies, amateur dramatic societies etc.

The changing membership of open groups makes it more difficult for them to set long term objectives and strategies. They tend primarily to address immediate areas of concern and interest. However, the regular influx of new members brings new ideas and perspectives to the group.

CLOSED GROUPS

Closed groups are characterised by a greater stablity in membership than open groups. Closed groups frequently have some form of constitution (governing regulations) and entry requirements for members. This form of group is more rigid in the sense that members are given positions of responsibility for which they may be accountable. Authority and status may be associated with membership and positions of responsibility.

Closed groups come in many different forms, two examples are given here:

* Professional groups - the Institute of Chartered Accountants; the British Medical Association; the Association of British Travel Agents. Each of these require members formally to join the group either by passing examinations, and (or) complying with specific entry requirements. To become a member of such groups may take a number of years, especially if a series of examinations has to be passed. Once membership has been granted the member will have to follow the 'code of conduct' that has been agreed by the professional group, otherwise membership of the group will be terminated on the grounds of misconduct.

* 'Executive groups' - this term is used to include all those groups which take a management role for their members. Included here are Boards of Directors and Management Committees. Certain responsibilities are bestowed on these groups as laid down by their constitution. Frequently, to become a member of the group the individual has to be elected to a position of responsibility, perhaps for a fixed length of time. Members are elected because of their technical expertise, their standing in society, or for some other reason.

A benefit of the closed group is that it allows stable relationships to develop between the members and the wider community it serves or represents. Such stability enables a long term perspective to be taken by the members who can divorce themselves from day-to-day issues and think about long term objectives and strategies.

Thus, certain types of activity are better performed by each type of group. The closed group is better placed to concern itself with planning issues while open groups might be more appropriate for the management of current activities. This is not to say, however, that the role of each group is mutually exclusive. Some open groups might be quite stable (in terms of changing membership) allowing long term decisions to be taken as well as the addressing of short term issues.

DEVELOPING GROUPS

When thinking about forming and developing groups a number of factors have to be taken into account. Some of the points covered in Chapter Four on Body Language are relevant here.

i) PHYSICAL PROXIMITY

Members of a group will be able to interact more effectively with each other if there are no barriers to communications within the group. We noted in Chapter Four that when people are physically close to each other more intimate relationships can be developed (if all parties wish). When there is a physical distance between people or a physical barrier, then the communication process will be more difficult.

When thinking about developing a group you need to consider the setting in which the group is to operate:

* All group members should be able to communicate easily with each other. You might have to attend to the design of the office or working area. While individual members of the group will need their own work areas these should if possible be in close proximity. Members of a group who are located on different floors of a building or worse still in different buildings often have difficulty in communicating and interacting with each other.

* While the group members will need individual working areas (that they might share with colleagues) if possible there should also be an area set aside for group meetings. This should:

  - be large enough to seat all members of the group in a circle so that they can see one another, and communicate with all members of the group

  - contain all equipment for the group meeting to take place, for example desks and chairs, audio or visual equipment, or technical equipment

  - allow confidential discussions to take place. Some meetings will address confidential topics such as future group plans, or might involve disciplinary proceedings being taken against a group member.

* To encourage the group members to mix socially an area should be set aside for relaxation, such as a small lounge where group members can meet for coffee and lunch. Comfortable chairs, drinks facilities, and small tables should be made available for such rooms.

* All services and equipment that will be required by group members in their activities should be located close to the work area. Secretarial support, photocopying machines and the like need to be close at hand rather than being some distance away.

If you bear in mind the above points then the physical distance between members of the group should be reduced and the cohesion of the group enhanced. Problems will arise for the group if it is located in a setting that has a rigid structure, such as a building that was built in the nineteenth century. These buildings might be divided into small rooms with small interconnecting corridors. Such a setting will cause difficulties for the group. Modern office buildings tend to be designed on an 'open-plan' basis in which the people using them can erect dividing walls and smaller partitions as they think fit. These office buildings enable the group to devise the optimal layout for its needs.

ii) THE INDIVIDUAL CHARACTERISTICS OF THE GROUP MEMBERS

The individual personalities and characteristics of group members will influence the cohesion of the group, and the efficiency with which the group achieves its objectives. People with similar personalities and characteristics tend to work together more harmoniously than opposites.

Group members who find that they have a number of different attitudes to other group members will have difficulty in working with them. Obviously, everybody has their own attitudes, but the more attitudes held in common, the more harmonious the group will be.

In addition to attitudes, the needs and motivations of each group member should be similar in some way. People who are motivated by the desire to earn as much money as possible might find it difficult to work with people who are more interested in working for the 'job-satisfaction' derived from completing a task to a high standard. When people work with others who share similar needs and motivations they can co-ordinate their efforts and energies to ensure that all objectives are met as efficiently as possible.

Apart from individual variables such as attitudes and motivations, the temperament of each group member will influence the success of the group in working together. If the group is dominated by people who easily lose their temper and have little patience, this might have an adverse effect on more timid group members. Less forceful group members will probably feel ill-at-ease working with impatient people, and may therefore contribute less well.

Balancing the personalities and characteristics of group members is a difficult task. Groups work more effectively with a balance of different personality styles. Establishing clearly the characteristic of each member when he wishes to join the group is not always possible, especially if the group is an open, informal one in which no membership procedures, such as an interview, are held. Even if you hold interviews prospective group members might be on 'their best behaviour' and put across an image they think appropriate. It might be only when individuals start working with other group members that their true personality and character become apparent. To help prevent this situation arising you should follow the points discussed in Chapter Seven on Interview Skills.

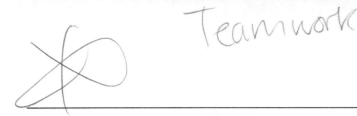

iii) THE PROCESS OF DEVELOPING GROUPS

After considering the physical environment and physical characteristics that can help to improve group cohesiveness, you should attend to the process by which groups are developed. Research undertaken by Tuckman (1965) suggests that groups pass through four stages of development:

> a) Forming.
> b) Storming.
> c) Norming.
> d) Performing.

a) FORMING

The first stage that all groups pass through is that of formation. Here the group members spend time establishing the reactions of other members to themselves and to the tasks and activities to be carried out.

This is a 'testing-the-water' phase during which group members become acquainted with each other and determine what contribution they can make to the group and how they will be expected to behave. They establish the bounds of what is acceptable, and what is unacceptable, by initiating conversations with other members of the group. This is an important stage of the group development process because it helps to set the standards of behaviour to which the group conforms.

When passing through the formation stage each of the group's members tries to create favourable images of themselves:

* Creating a favourable first impression is important. You need to pay particular attention to dress and appearance. Group members who wear clothes that are inappropriate might be treated with suspicion by the other members.

* You need to communicate with the other members of the group. Initiate conversations, ask open questions, and be friendly.

* Listen to what other members of the group are saying. You create a good impression by showing genuine interest and attention.

* It is important to be assertive in this formation stage, for if you do not you may find that decisions are taken with which you disagree. There may not be an opportunity to reverse such decisions at a later stage. Thus, you should assert your influence on the decision making process from the outset.

B.W. Tuckman, 1965, "Developmental Sequence in Small Groups",
Psychological Bulletin 63:384-399.

b) STORMING

The second stage of the group development process is known as 'storming'. After the group has been formed conflicts arise within the group as members argue and disagree as to how power and status will be divided between the group members. Some individuals might want a leader to be appointed with certain responsibilities and authority. Others might seek a more democratic approach, in which decisions are taken by committee as opposed to being taken by one individual. Other group members might feel that a combination of both approaches would be advisable.

At this stage of the process you should use your higher order TPS:

* You will need your negotiation skills to help resolve conflicts that arise. Obviously the group will not be able to achieve its objectives until it is reasonably harmonious. The TPS we discussed in Chapter Nine will be called into use here.

* You will have to use your thinking skills to solve problems that arise and to make decisions. You will need to employ your critical thinking skills when negotiating with others to highlight false assumptions that might have been made, or to offer alternative logical solutions.

* You will have to communicate effectively and be assertive , presenting your views firmly, but not aggressively, to the group.

c) NORMING

Once the initial conflicts have been resolved, a sense of cohesiveness is likely to develop within the group. This is the third stage of the group development process and is called 'norming'. The group now establishes itself in line with the criteria determined in the storming phase. The positions of responsibility agreed in that stage are now adopted, and any procedures that need to be established are implemented. The group is now preparing itself to undertake its tasks and activities.

d) PERFORMING

The final stage of the group development process is that of 'performing'. The 'norming' stage resulted in group establishment of the norms to which, all group members should adhere. Each group member should now be working for the good of the group, rather than for his own benefit, and undertake all responsibilities that are required of him. Conflict between members should have been reduced, if not overcome completely. The group, and its members, can now concentrate on attaining its objectives.

For this final stage in the process to be successful you will need to employ a wide range of TPS. The group work skills discussed in this chapter will naturally be of importance, as well as the personal skills discussed in Chapter Ten.

The process described above is a model. Models simplify reality so that the complex issues and inter-relationships in the real world can be more easily understood. Not all groups will pass through the four stages sequentially. Some stages might be missed out entirely, while additional ones might be added. In formal groups where there might be less scope for debating and negotiating the 'norms' of the group, 'storming' may be ignored completely. Once the group is operational and performing its activities, the stages in the model might be followed through again. For example, when a new leader is appointed the status quo that was arrived at previously might be disturbed. The new leader might wish to alter how the group operates and so temporarily returns to 'storming' or 'norming'.

Understanding how groups develop is important when working with others. Groups are not static entities comprising inanimate objects. They are dynamic, made up of human beings. Each of the group members influence the group by bringing their own personality and characteristics to the group development process.

iv) INFLUENCES ON GROUP PERFORMANCE

Once a group has been established and is operating, a number of factors will influence how successfully it operates:

a) THE INFLUENCE OF OTHER GROUP MEMBERS

If the group members work together cohesively and harmoniously, communicate openly, share problems and difficulties, then the group should be more effective in achieving its goals. Group members who tend to work independently may not contribute efficiently to the efforts of the group as a whole. We have already noted that one of the advantages of group work is that the group members can pool their resources. If members do not do this, then one of the benefits of operating as a group will be lost.

b) GROUP SIZE

The number of people in the group will influence how effectively it operates. There is no specific optimum group size. This depends upon the group's objectives and the skills of those in the group. If the group is performing a relatively straightforward routine task, such as a group of accountants conducting an annual audit for a long standing client, then it might be that a small group will be the optimum size. If a major task is being tackled that requires specific technical skills from different people, for example developing a totally new design of aeroplane, the group will necessarily be larger. Of course as the group grows in size the contribution of each member to the task as a proportion of the whole might be diminished. Each member may contribute only a small part of the work required to achieve the overall objective.

Another important aspect to consider is that the administration and organisation of the group will become more complex as more members join the group. It is likely that more leaders will have to be appointed to monitor and control the work of sub-groups. With increased size some flexibility in decision making and action might be lost. Larger groups can be compared with ocean going tankers - once under way it is difficult to change direction and takes a long time to come to a halt.

Smaller groups, for instance those with fewer than twenty members, are easier to administer, permitting the use of less rigid systems of administration. Decisions can be implemented more quickly and there is more flexibility both in day-to-day operation and in longer term strategy. It is more feasible to have decisions taken by a committee of all the members if the group is smaller and in this way all group members will be able to influence the decisions that are taken. A further benefit of working in smaller groups is that it is easier for the members to identify colleagues who are not working as efficiently as they should be. Such people can be informed that their contributions to the group's objectives are not what they could be, and that improvements are needed. Thus, the productivity of each group member could be higher than for people working in larger groups.

c) THE SKILLS OF THE GROUP

The performance of the group depends upon the skills of its members. We mentioned above that group members will be able to work more harmoniously together if they have similar personalities and characteristics such as common attitudes, motivations, needs and temperaments. This is true. However, if the group members all have similar skills as well as similar personalities and characteristics, this may be counter productive.

Groups which comprise members all of whom have similar skills will probably be unable to look at the task facing the group from different perspectives. They will all see the task in the same way, adopting a 'blinkered approach'. Earlier we noted that one of the benefits of working in groups is that the resources of each group member can be pooled and drawn upon by others. Should all group members have similar skills (a resource), then there might be little to be gained from working as a group. Therefore when a group is established care should be taken to ensure that the membership comprises people who possess a range of skills and experiences. In this way the group should be more creative and innovative. This is not to say that as many different skills and experiences as possible should be included in the group. If the group becomes too large then it may well be more difficult to administer. In addition, the larger the group becomes, the more likely it will be that group members do not share common personalities and characteristics and this may hamper the effectiveness of the group.

d) DELEGATING RESPONSIBILITIES

Another influence on the performance of the group is whether or not the group members have clearly defined responsibilities. Each member of the group should have a specific role to play which will help the group to attain its objectives.

The responsibilities of each group member can be negotiated between the members, delegated by the leader, or arrived at by using a combination of both of these methods. Whichever method is used, it will be important for all members to know what is expected of them. To make sure that there are no misconceptions, the role of each group member should be written down and circulated within the group. It may also be possible at this stage to specify the standard of performance required from each group member.

If group members do not have clearly defined roles and responsibilities, then difficulties might arise. Group members might contribute to the group as they think fit and this may be counter-productive in that the group becomes unco-ordinated. The group members are all working in different directions. Another difficulty is that an overlap of responsibilities could occur. Here, two (or more) members of the group might perform the same task which leads to a duplication of effort.

Clearly, there must be effective communication within the group to keep the group members informed of their responsibilities. Each person's responsibilities should be specified:

i) In writing. The responsibilities of each group member should be clearly stated in writing, following the TPS discussed in Chapter Five.

ii) Verbally. Responsibilities should also be verbally explained to each group member to ensure that they are understood.

iii) Regularly. Regular meetings should be held to review the work of each individual and make sure that they are performing satisfactorily and that they are not encountering difficulties. If problems are identified then action can be taken to overcome them.

It is important to follow these communication guidelines. Groups sometimes fail simply because the group members do not know what it is they are trying to achieve. Group members may operate in isolation from each other and have no clear idea of their roles within the group. All new members to the group should have explained to them not only their own roles, but also the responsibilities of their colleagues.

If these guidelines are ignored you might find that role conflict develops. Role conflict refers to the situation where different people have different perceptions of what each individual group member should be doing. This arises because the communication within the group is inadequate and there is ambiguity about the responsibilities of each individual.

e) STATUS

Status can be defined as the individual's standing in the group. It may also refer to people's social standing and how they are socially placed against the other group members. Status can be signified in the following ways:

* Job title - manager, supervisor, clerk etc.

* Salary - the monthly earnings of the individual.

* Tangible rewards - the type of car that the person is given by the organisation, the size and location of a person's office (is it on the top floor, for example).

* Tangible awards - receiving a prize as the 'top salesperson of the month' such as a free holiday.

* Authority - what the individuals can do as part of their responsibilities and their right to use power.

Status symbols are designed to differentiate between the members of the group. In certain circumstances the performance of the group could be influenced by the presence of such status symbols. Some people find that they are motivated to work more effectively if, as a result of their efforts, they gain status, either through an increase in salary, promotion, a reward or an award, or increased authority. Some group members also appreciate the stability that status can offer the group. Some individuals like to feel that there is someone in authority, in a higher position, who receives a higher salary, and takes the major decisions. This makes those group members feel more secure, especially if they are individuals who lack self-confidence.

Status symbols also help to create an identity for individual group members. Individuals in positions of authority frequently like their status to be displayed to others by tangible signs such as more prestigious offices, cars and job titles. This helps to satisfy their need for self-esteem and self-gratification.

Thus, status can influence the group's performance. Clearly defined status symbols that are acknowledged as being appropriate by all group members may increase motivation. This is particularly true if all group members gain status as a result of the group's success.

However, a status symbol for one group might be inappropriate for another. Some people will be motivated to work harder if they are promised an increase in salary. Other people might be motivated to work harder by being offered a change in job title. Before introducing such status symbols to the group it is important to recognise the factors that motivate each group member, and the reward and award system be built around these.

f) GROUP REGULATIONS

Group regulations are the guidelines or rules of the group used to ensure that group members behave consistently when working together. Group regulations are either formally written and circulated among the group, or informally agreed verbally.

Group regulations help members to conform to certain patterns of behaviour. This is important if a consistent image is to be portrayed to the wider environment. The Association of British Travel Agents (ABTA) has its own Code of Conduct that all ABTA members (travel agents and tour operators) must follow. The Code of Conduct covers all areas of a travel agent or tour operator's business activities and inter-relationships with customers. ABTA members contravening the Code of Conduct can be expelled from the Association.

When a group operates without regulations, especially a large group, its members can lack a sense of purpose or direction, and feel uncertain about how to behave in particular situations. Guidelines help to reduce uncertainty.

If regulations are to be accepted by group members, however, they should not be imposed on the group, but should be negotiated by as many group members as possible. People find it difficult to commit themselves to regulations imposed on them without negotiation by other people. It is easier to accept regulations, and therefore to conform to them, when the regulations have been agreed by those group members who are expected to respect them. It is important that all regulations help the activities of the group, rather than restrict the group's productivity or output. For this reason, rules and regulations should be regularly reviewed.

g) THE GROUP'S COHESIVENESS

Cohesiveness is the ability of the group to work together harmoniously and effectively. For the group to be cohesive the group members must want to work together and they must be attracted to the group. When the group is cohesive, a number of benefits arise:

* Each individual's personal satisfaction gained from working in the group is improved. When all group members work together harmoniously, free from conflict and tension, it is more enjoyable and less stressful.

* The performance of the group is improved. Communication within the group is more effective.

* Commitment to the group is increased. Individual group members will feel more loyal to the group when it is cohesive and will have a greater commitment to contribute to the best of their ability.

Given the advantages outlined above, how can the group ensure that it is cohesive? The answer lies in adopting the points we raised earlier in this section. For group members to work together harmoniously:

* They should have similar personalities and characteristics.

* The group size should not be so large that problems of administration arise.

* The skills of each individual should be complementary to the skills of other group members.

* The responsibilities of each individual should be explicit and unambiguous.

* Rewards and awards should be used to motivate the group members.

* Regulations should be accepted by all.

DIFFERENT TYPES OF GROUPS

We have considered already the different forms of group, for example whether they are informal or formal, closed or open. This chapter concludes with discussion about different types of groups to be found in organisations.

COMMITTEES

A committee is a group of people who meet to further a shared concern, with a view to steering action by themselves or by other people. Committees may operate over a period of time or until a problem has been solved. They are found in many different types of organisation in the public, private, and voluntary sectors. Below we give a few examples:

* In colleges, committees are formed to discuss and evaluate the progress of courses. Teaching staff and students will be represented on the committee.

* In business organisations, committees are formed to manage day-to-day activities (such as the spending of a particular budget) and to develop long-term strategies.

* In local government, committees enable councillors to determine policies, for instance on the Housing Committee.

Committees generally meet at regular intervals to discuss their business. They are managed in a formal sense, with a Chairperson and a Secretary. Minutes are recorded and agendas produced. The more formal the committee, the greater the likelihood that members are elected to it. Elections follow procedures laid down in the committee's constitution.

Should the area of interest to the committee require further research, investigation, or action, a sub-committee could be formed. This comprises fewer members than the main committee and has certain set objectives. For example a committee formed in a college to look after the Outdoor Activities Programme, might set up a smaller committee to raise funds so that the programme can be implemented.

Committees are primarily vehicles for discussion and decision making. When a decision has been made, the committee may ask an individual or group of individuals to carry out the specified task. Committees and sub-committees are disbanded when they have met their objectives.

PROJECT GROUPS

A project group is normally established to handle a specific problem. In this way it is similar to a sub-committee. A project group differs from a sub-committee in that it does not have to be related to another committee. The project group could be an entity in its own right.

Project groups have many different uses. In business a project group might be established to investigate organisations that could be suitable for take-over. In a college a project group could be set up to plan an overseas field trip. In a local authority a project group could be used to monitor the success of changing the road system in the town centre, drawing members from a number of different departments, for example the Highways Department, the Department of Environment and the Housing Department.

One of the benefits of a project group is that, if it includes members from different departments, it may be able to cut across the normal structure of the organisation. Such groups often improve communication and co-operation throughout the organisation. The project group will be dissolved when it has completed its task.

EXECUTIVE OR COMMAND GROUPS

Executive or command groups are usually composed of managers and their staff who are elected or appointed to serve on the group because of their technical expertise. Such groups have wide responsibilities and tasks which may include:

> * Planning future developments for the organisation.
>
> * Organising the implementation of plans.
>
> * Motivating other group members.
>
> * Co-ordinating the different groupings within the organisation.

It is likely that each executive or command group will have its own specialism, for example the New Product Development Group, or the Production Planning Group.

Within an organisation there might be a number of these groups, each with a different purpose. To ensure against duplication of roles, however, effective communication between groups is necessary. Good communications between the groups will also prevent each group from operating in isolation, so that they are all co-ordinating their efforts.

Administration of a group will usually be handled by the manager responsible for the group's performance, for instance, the New Product Development Manager, or the Production Manager. The manager of such a group will normally have authority to implement decisions taken by the group.

QUALITY CIRCLES

Quality circles originated in the early 1960s in Japan and are an increasingly popular way of encouraging group work. Quality circles generally consist of 8 - 10 workers engaged in associated work. They meet as a committee on a frequent and regular basis, usually once a week, to discuss problems or concerns associated with their work. The purpose of the meeting is to discover solutions to these problems or concerns, which are then implemented after managerial approval.

Quality circles have specific features:

> * Membership of the quality circle is voluntary and open to all workers in the section.
>
> * One purpose of the quality circle is to solve work-related problems. To help the members do this, training may have to be provided in problem-solving (see Chapter Twelve).

* Once a potential solution to a given problem has been identified, management must be informed (requiring presentation skills as discussed in Chapter Eight).

* When approval is given to implement the solution the members implement it and monitor how successful the solution has been.

The use of quality circles is growing because this approach to group work offers five distinct benefits:

i) SOCIAL BENEFITS

People make friends when they are working in a group. Group members can share problems which in itself helps to reduce anxiety and stress. By offering solutions to problems, workers feel that they have more influence and control over their working activities.

ii) TECHNICAL BENEFITS

Group members have a good knowledge and understanding of the processes involved in their work. They are well placed, therefore, to be able to propose solutions to problems that arise. Quality cirlcles enable such solutions to be proposed and implemented.

iii) MANAGERIAL BENEFITS

Quality circles are popular with workers as they allow them to take more of an active role in the operational side of their work. This leads to increased motivation at work, improved quality of work, and a source of suggestions for improving the way in which the work is completed. These benefits free the managers to concentrate on other elements of their work.

iv) OPERATIONAL BENEFITS

Workers are more willing to accept changes in their methods of working if they have recommended such changes themselves. There is less uneasiness than when changes are imposed by those in authority without discussions or negotiations with the work force.

v) FINANCIAL BENEFITS

Quality circles in effect act as a consultant for the organisation. No additional direct payments are made to quality circles, however, as the group members are volunteers. Compare this to the costs the organisation would incur if a firm of external consultants was to be employed.

For the quality circle approach to be successful, all concerned must be committed. Senior managers must endorse the quality circles and implement any feasible solutions that are proposed. Middle managers have to allow time during the working day for the quality circles to meet, and need to provide a room that is conducive to a group discussion.

It might be the middle manager's role to see that a senior member of the quality circle is trained in group management skills. The individuals forming the quality circle must be aware of how to organise and run meetings.

Group members in a quality circle must be confident that they will not suffer through contributing to it, especially when their proposals appear to criticise the organisation. Instead, the group should be rewarded for any suggestions that are implemented, for example by cash bonuses or a special gift.

Quality circles offer benefits to organisations that use them, but there are also some cautionary aspects that need to be borne in mind:

* Quality circles should not be seen as a solution to all the problems faced by the organisation. The problems best tackled by such groups are problems related to the immediate working methods and surroundings of the group members.

* Workers who do not volunteer to participate in the quality circle might be unwilling to accept proposals made by the quality circle, especially if such proposals lead to an increase in the pace of the work, or to cut backs in the labour force.

* Some people may volunteer for the quality circle simply to receive time-off from their normal working activities. Their value to the group is questionable. Other volunteers might see the quality circle as a vehicle for venting their frustrations, rather than as a means of solving problems.

If the organisation using quality circles is aware of these potential difficulties, however, then steps can be taken to reduce the likelihood of them arising.

Group work skills are important. When working with other friends or colleagues, much thought must be given to knowing and understanding their personalities, interests and skills. Thinking skills are a TPS in their own right, and will be considered in the next chapter.

Chapter Twelve

THINKING SKILLS

Chapter Twelve

THINKING SKILLS

If you want to be a manager you must be able to communicate, to work with others, be assertive, and be able to negotiate. Yet these skills by themselves will not be sufficient to take you to the higher levels of management. You also require the abilities to think critically, to solve problems and to take decisions. If you work in a rapidly changing environment, you cannot depend on routine behaviour or tradition when making decisions, you must be capable of intelligent and independent thought. Perhaps these skills are the key to how far up the managerial ladder you will progress.

But what are thinking skills? A dictionary definition would include the following:

> **"to summarise; to believe; to consider; to esteem; to reason; to form judgement; to imagine."**

Clearly, thinking involves a series of high level intellectual skills. In fact a hierarchy of intellectual skills can be identified.

THE HIERARCHY OF INTELLECTUAL SKILLS

There is a hierarchy of intellectual skills that you need to be aware of when considering the thinking process. Each of these levels plays a part in critical thinking. These are:

(i)   Gaining knowledge.
(ii) Understanding.
(iii) Applying knowledge and understanding.
(iv) Analysing.
(v)   Synthesising.
(vi) Evaluating.

We shall now consider what each of these involves.

(i) GAINING KNOWLEDGE

The lowest level intellectual skill is that of knowing something, by remembering, or recalling, facts, ideas, or phenomena. Nevertheless acquiring knowledge underpins critical thinking as it is the reference source from which facts or ideas are drawn to start the reasoning process.

The knowledge you acquire helps to provide you with a picture of the situation which you are considering.

Knowledge helps to answer questions such as:

"Who? What? Where? When?"

When individuals have a store of knowledge they are able to recall facts, make observations or arrive at definitions:

"What does marketing mean?"

"Who is Peter Drucker?"

Some individuals have a hunger for knowledge, and assume that the greater their store of knowledge the better equipped they are to make the optimum decision. The key, though, is to ensure that the knowledge which you gain is relevant to your needs. You must therefore, always be discriminating in the knowledge you seek. Indeed, with the wealth of knowledge available to managers it is now, more than ever, important for them to have skills to interpret knowledge rather than simply to retain it.

(ii) UNDERSTANDING

The second level of the hierarchy of your intellectual skills involves understanding facts, ideas or concepts. By understanding these you can transfer such knowledge to new, unfamiliar situations. Understanding is part of the critical thinking process and enables you to

"describe, compare, contrast, and explain"

For example, when you have understood facts, ideas, or concepts you will be able to:

"Explain in your own words the problems faced by the economy as a result of inflation".

"Compare the duties of a cost accountant with those of a tax accountant".

A good test of your understanding is the ability to explain to other people the situation or concept being considered.

(iii) APPLYING KNOWLEDGE AND UNDERSTANDING

The application of facts or ideas to predict consequences or to solve problems is the next level in your intellectual hierarchy. This process involves first of all understanding the fact (or idea), then restructuring it or reorganising it, so that you can use it to draw meaningful conclusions about the new situation.

The key verbs here are:

"apply, solve, classify, select, employ, use"

For example when you are able to apply facts or ideas you can answer questions such as:

"What is the latitude of London?"

"If you wanted to telephone New York at 10.00am local time, what time would it be in London?"

and to undertake tasks such as:

"Classify these customers according to their contributions to our profitability."

(iv) ANALYSING

Analysis involves breaking down a given situation into its constituent parts. This intellectual skill is of value to you as a critical thinker because it allows you to separate and to categorise data. When you have done this you can probe behind the surface and look for unseen or abstract principles that give you a greater understanding of the problem you are considering. If you are skilled at analysing material you will be able to answer 'Why?' questions, for example:

"Why do you think increasing advertising expenditure leads to an increase in sales?"

You will then be able to draw inferences, identify motives, or causes, and be skilled at finding evidence to support generalisations. Once you have completed the analysis you should be able to undertake synthesis.

(v) SYNTHESISING

This is the penultimate intellectual skill in the hierarchy and is the one which draws together individual components after they have been analysed. Synthesis involves recreating the whole once it has been dissected, and learning from this process. When you have completed the synthesis you will be able to plan, predict, propose, or develop. The questions that you will be able to answer will be ones similar to:

"What action could our organisation take to improve the loyalty of our work force?"

"What do you predict would happen if we were to increase the size of our work force by 20%?"

In addition you will be able to:

"Write a report detailing company progress over the last 20 years."

When you have mastered this skill of synthesis you will be capable of original thought.

(vi) Evaluating

When the whole has been created again you can then evaluate the situation, judging it in order to reach an opinion, or conclusion. To be evaluative you must look at all the evidence surrounding a given situation and consider the arguments supporting it, as well as those against it, to look at "both sides of the coin".

If you can evaluate a situation you will be able to:

"judge, decide, and appraise".

You will be able to give opinions on issues, determine the validity of ideas, or judge the merit of a solution to a problem. You will need evaluation skills to answer the following questions:

"Do you think it is true that increased advertising expenditure leads to increased sales of the product?"

"Should our work force be given a 10% pay rise?"

"Which product would you drop from our product portfolio?"

Being able to arrive at a reasoned and objective judgement on a particular issue is considered to be the highest level of intellectual skill that you can develop. To reach a judgement involves all the skills listed above. You must have knowledge which you understand and can apply to the situation under consideration. You must be able to break the situation down and consider each element independently, before putting the whole back together again. The final evaluation will involve looking at all the evidence in favour, and all the evidence against, before arriving at the judgement.

The intellectual skills discussed here help to constitute your thinking process. Referring back to the definition of thinking we gave at the beginning of this chapter it is clear that in order to summarise, believe, consider, or reason you must be able to use all the skills discussed in the hierarchy.

Critical thinking skills, though, warrant further analysis.

CRITICAL THINKING SKILLS

Critical thinking could be thought of as independent thought where you use all the intellectual skills in the hierarchy in order to arrive at your own judgement of a situation or issue. Another term to use instead of critical thinking might be reflective thinking, implying that you divorce yourself from your immediate surroundings, take a step backwards, and then judge the issue in an objective and rational manner. We can divide critical thinking into a number of steps:

(i) Interpreting data.
(ii) Applying facts and principles.
(iii) Logical reasoning.

(i) Interpreting data

To be a critical thinker you must be able to interpret data of various sorts and to generalise from them. The term 'data' is used here in a broad context to include statistics, the written word, diagrams, formulae, and even cartoons. As a critical thinker you should be able to digest the data and derive meaning from them. The process of interpretation will involve singling out important facts or ideas, relating them to each other, and deriving generalisations from them.

Interpretation in its lowest form might simply involve reading points off a graph or looking for trends. At a higher degree of complexity, interpretation will consist of inferring causes or consequences from a situation. Let us use an example to illustrate this:

CINEMA ADMISSIONS 1982 - 1988

YEAR	MILLIONS	INDEX
1982	60	100
1983	64	107
1984	54	90
1985	71	118
1986	73	121
1987*	75	125
1988*	78	130

Source: Mintel Leisure Intelligence, Vol 3, Aug 1987
*: Author's estimate

From the table it can be seen that cinema admissions have risen by 18 million since 1982, although a fall in attendances was experienced in 1984. A critical thinker might deduce that this could have been a result of a steep rise in admission prices in 1984 and the wider availability of videos for home viewing. The critical thinker might continue by reflecting that since 1984, however, cinemas have been refurbished and a stream of higher quality films been released, which could account for the increase in cinema admissions.

Evaluating the dependability of data and recognising their limits is also involved in critical thinking. Certain data are rendered academically unsound, or ideological, because of the way in which they are written:

* Ambiguous terms or statements make data unsound. If the meaning of the sentence, phrase, or word appears to have more than one interpretation, then the quality of the data should be questioned.

* Vacuous terms, terms which are hollow and lacking in content make data academically unsound. For example, 'good', 'bad', 'many', 'few', or 'heavy', are vacuous as each individual could interpret the term differently.

* Inconsistent statements - ones which contain contradictory terms or arguments, should not be accepted.

* Selective use of evidence makes data ideological e.g. if consideration is given only to one side of the argument, where there are reasons for and against a view, or not all relevant considerations are made, then the data will be unsound.

* Inaccurate account of evidence. If evidence is used to support an argument, and the evidence is inaccurately reported or inaccurately used then the validity of the data will be questionable.

* Over-generalisations make arguments invalid. Here a person argues a case by showing that all situations will follow a similar pattern, but uses an unrepresentative sample, or a sample whose size is not large enough, in order to make the generalisation.

* Appeals to consensus, where the person arguing a case makes a suggestion which she thinks will be accepted by the majority, but which in fact is not, means the soundness of the data can be questioned. Even if there is consensus about some view it does not make that view correct. Only when independent authorities or individuals can provide evidence supporting such data should it be accepted - this indicates the importance of fully referencing reports and other types of communication to show the source of data that has been used to compile the report.

* Appeals to authority - just because an expert supports a view does not mean that it is correct. Like appeals to consensus, appeals to authorities are only valid when the expert has evidence to support her view; however, different experts might have different views and the real test of their validity will be the way in which the research was conducted.

* Appeals to self-evidence - when an individual supplies the data herself, great care should be taken to evaluate the reliability of the data collection method, and the interpretation of the data.

* Appeals to common sense - when data indicate that the conclusions drawn are based on common sense, care needs to be taken as common sense to one individual might not be common sense to another.

* Emotive language - when data use certain words such as 'lively', 'challenging' or 'interesting', the writer is being complementary, or commendatory, towards the issue or course of action. The use of such a writing style makes the data unsound.

If you identify the above points in data it makes them academically unsound, and their validity and value can be questioned. Indeed, when you produce your own data you need to ensure that your writing does not include any of the above.

When interpreting data, if you are a critical thinker, you will be able to identify the relevant facts and ideas in each and draw appropriate inferences.

(ii) APPLYING FACTS AND PRINCIPLES

Applying facts and principles in order to solve problems, or to predict, or to explain new phenomena are other aspects of critical thinking. This process involves you first understanding the relevant fact or principle, then understanding the problem, and finally seeing the relationship between the two.

Some facts and principles are highly transferable, whereas others are not. For example, the law of gravity applies in the United Kingdom, the United States of America, and the United Arab Emirates. Other generalisations are less universal, for example generalisations which account for the causes of inflation. If you are a critical thinker, you will be able to distinguish between hypotheses and universally dependable principles.

As a critical thinker, you will also be able to determine when a value judgement is being made. A value judgement is what an individual believes and feels about an issue without having any empirical evidence to support that view - an opinion. Value judgements may interfere with an individual's clarity of thought and result in her reasoning being subjective, biased or irrational.

Part of the critical thinking process is to be able to apply facts and principles logically without reference to or at least acknowledging value judgements.

(iii) LOGICAL REASONING

Being able to reason logically and critically are the final component parts of critical thinking. To be able to reason logically and critically sometimes requires you to identify faulty assumptions that others propose, and formulating adequate ones yourself. In this situation logical reasoning is not accepting assumptions, or evidence, at face value, but analysing their underlying rationale.

As a critical thinker, you will judge where facts end and opinions begin, and you will be able to recognise conclusions based on faulty logic or reasoning. For example, when listening to a discussion on the causes of inflation, you should be able to determine what is taken for granted in the discussion, whether all relevant facts and arguments have been considered, and how relevant they are to the conclusions drawn. Thus, you, as a critical thinker are using your knowledge, understanding, application, analysis, synthesis, and evaluation skills in order to judge the arguments of others. You will be looking for ideological statements using the points raised above - for example, identifying emotionally charged words, or vacuous terms.

The use of:
"What if..." and "if then...."

statements will form part of your portfolio of reasoning skills as a critical thinker. It has to be stated, though, that being able to evaluate critically other people's arguments does not necessarily improve your own reasoning. You must practise this in a variety of contexts.

Critical thinking skills, like the other TPS discussed in this book are not developed overnight. Whereas it is relatively straightforward to demonstrate most of the other TPS in action it is less easy to demonstrate critical thinking skills as they are to some extent intangible. Developing these high order intellectual skills will also be determined by your capacity for abstract thought, as without this ability you will find it difficult to evaluate the assumptions and arguments of others.

Your ability to judge critically the arguments of others (in other words to be a critical thinker) will determine your ability to reach the upper levels of management. Senior managers have to be able to evaluate the arguments of others and decide whether they are logical and feasible. Without this skill as a senior manager you will not be fulfilling all the functions of your role.

There are other intellectual skills that managers need to master, namely those of being able to solve problems, and to take decisions. We shall now break these down into their constituent elements and examine them.

PROBLEM SOLVING SKILLS

One of the main aspects of managerial work is solving problems of one degree of complexity or another. Your success as a manager can partly be gauged by how effective you are at producing feasible solutions to difficult situations.

Problems can be regarded as open-ended in that a number of potential solutions will probably be apparent. The key is to select the solution which is the most feasible. When solving problems, however, it is frequently the case that not all the information that is required to reach the best solution is available, and you have to reach a solution on imperfect knowledge of the situation.

You can follow a series of steps when solving problems that should lead you to identify the most feasible solution to the problem.

THE PROBLEM SOLVING PROCESS

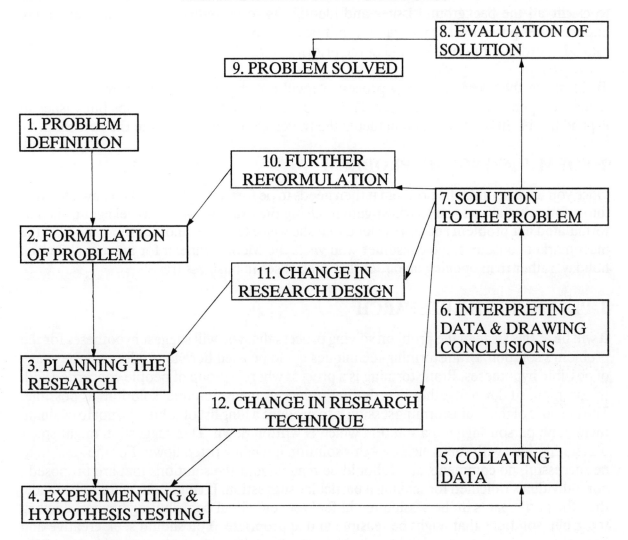

We can simplify this model into the main eight steps which are:

1. Defining the problem
2. Formulating the problem
3. Planning the research
4. Experimenting
5. Collating the data
6. Selecting a preferred solution
7. Implementing the solution
8. Evaluating the solution

We shall now look at each of these in turn.

1. DEFINING THE PROBLEM

The first stage in being able to solve a problem is to be able to define it. The important thing is to identify the difficulty clearly, defining precisely its characteristics. You must collect relevant information about the problem and consider it from various perspectives. You need to clarify all the background issues and identify its scale and constraints, as well as the opportunities posed by it. If you have identified a number of problems, they may need to be ranked in order of importance and in the priority in which you will try to solve them.

To illustrate the problem solving process we will use the problem of a travel agent who wishes to open a new travel agency. The travel agent currently has 5 shops but wishes to expand her business. The problem facing the travel agent is where to site the new shop.

2. FORMULATING THE PROBLEM

Once you have defined the problem it then needs to be formulated, or broken down further, into a form that allows you to investigate it. Using the example of the travel agent, she has formulated her problem and has decided that she wishes to open another shop aimed at the mass market consumer, the consumer who visits the Mediterranean for an annual 2 week holiday, rather than opening an outlet that specialises in business travel.

3. PLANNING THE RESEARCH

It will be at this stage in the problem solving process that you will suggest hypotheses for the problem's solution. Brainstorming techniques could be used here to produce a wide range of possible hypotheses. Brainstorming is a process where a group of people concerned with the problem sit down together in order to produce as many potential solutions as possible. The purpose of the brainstorming session is to produce a long list of solutions, not to evaluate them. One person suggests a solution which is written down. This suggestion might spark off another idea with someone else - this solution is again written down. For the session to be successful, no comments at all should be made about the solutions that are proposed , nor individuals ridiculed for making a particular suggestion. If comments were to be made, then the participants in the session might feel reticent about contributing further, denying the group solutions that might be feasible and appropriate. You should seek creative and imaginative solutions, especially for problems that you have not encountered before. This is known as divergent thinking. If you are a divergent thinker you consider as many aspects as possible and try to choose the best solution from these alternatives.

For example, consider the travel agent's problem. The divergent thinker might consider a wide range of possible towns to site the new agency, and within those towns believe that there are several viable locations. She might think about locating in Birmingham, Manchester, or Glasgow, and possible sites might be in shopping centres, in high streets, or in residential suburbs.

An alternative type of thinker is known as the convergent thinker. This is a person who converges straight away on an answer. This approach can be used to solve problems for which there is a known or generally accepted answer. So, in the example of the travel agent the convergent thinker assumes that the best location is in the new shopping centre that has just been built on the outskirts of the town where she currently operates. Her decision is based on the fact that the shopping centre will attract large numbers of the type of customer in whom she is interested, it is close to her existing operations enabling control to be maintained over the day-to-day running of the agency, and that there will be no other travel agency in the shopping centre.

The thinking process adopted, therefore, is to some extent dependent on the problem. With some problems there are no alternative solutions - just one. Many managerial problems, however, will involve more than one solution and you will probably have to use divergent thinking in your approach. Where there is no one right solution it is important not to arrive at an answer too quickly - you must spend time on hypothesis testing.

4. EXPERIMENTING

When you have formulated hypotheses (or possible alternative courses of action) the next step is to devise experiments that will show whether, or not, the hypothesis holds true. Experiments in the world of science can be carefully designed, implemented and controlled, and clear results obtained. In the world of business and commerce, however, experiments might sometimes be influenced by external uncontrollable factors which affect the results. Alternatively, the research methods you use for collecting the data might be prone to error and bias, restricting the validity and reliability of the data collected. Market research questionnaire surveys fall into this category and need to be rigorously designed, implemented and monitored.

5. COLLATING THE DATA

The experimentation stage of your problem solving process will produce data that need to be recorded and translated into meaningful forms for analysis, such as tables, graphs, pie charts and histograms. You should follow the conventions discussed in Chapter Six to ensure that you make correct representations of the data.

Once you have represented the data in this way you can then interpret them, looking for trends that have occurred and identifying relationships that allow you to draw conclusions. Your critical thinking skills will be called into use here, and you must ensure that an objective and rational view is taken of the findings from the research.

6. SELECTING A PREFERRED SOLUTION

The next stage in the problem solving process requires you to use the highest order intellectual skill in the hierarchy - evaluation. When all your hypotheses have been tested, when you have analysed and synthesised your findings you should now evaluate them in order to select a preferred solution.

In this stage you evaluate the results of the experiments, looking at the conclusions drawn from each of the hypotheses that was tested and arrive at a judgement as to which solution to the problem, or which hypothesis, should be accepted. You should devise criteria which you can use to judge each possible solution. You need to evaluate each solution to see how close it comes to meeting your preferred criteria. You have to adopt a balanced view that considers the strengths of each solution as well as its weaknesses. Reject those solutions or hypotheses that do not meet your criteria. When you have completed this process you will then have either one or two solutions that do meet the criteria.

Referring again to the travel agent, if a number of possible locations for the new retail agency have been identified then each one should be evaluated against a number of criteria, for example:

CRITERIA FOR EVALUATING THE SITE OF A NEW RETAIL TRAVEL AGENCY

CRITERIA	OPTIMAL SITE CHARACTERISTICS	SITE 1	SITE 2	SITE 3
1 Proximity to bus stops	100 metres			
2 Proximity to car parks	200 metres			
3 Average pedestrian flow	50 per minute			
4 Number of competitors close by	fewer than 3			
5 Demographic profile of the catchment area	C1 & C2 socio-economic groups			
6 Cost of rent & rates	£400 per month			
7 Size of the unit, sq metres	1000 sq metres			

If after the evaluation stage, however, you reject all the hypotheses or potential solutions you have three further options:

    a. You can return to the problem formulation stage and consider whether the problem was initially defined correctly. If it was not then you should reformulate the problem.

    b. Failing (a) above, you should examine the investigation stage of the research process - were appropriate hypotheses formulated or do new ones need to be proposed?

    c. The final area to consider is that of the implementation of the experiment, did error or bias creep into the research process causing incorrect results to be obtained.

By evaluating these stages in the problem solving process you will gain insight as to why you have not found a solution to the problem, and you may gain ideas for modifying your research.

7. IMPLEMENTING THE SOLUTION

Now that you have identified a solution to the problem you need to implement it. You will need to have the necessary resources required for implementation such as finance, personnel, computer or production facilities, and a plan drawn up allocating responsibilities to those involved in the implementation process. As well as considering resources, your plan will also provide a time scale that prioritises the actions to be taken and allocates responsibilities to all those concerned in the implementation process. This enables the close co-ordination of all activities and provides you with a logical pattern for sequencing the implementation stages.

In the implementation stage you should consider contingency plans to provide alternative courses of action if problems arise while implementing the original plan.

8. EVALUATING THE SOLUTION

The final stage in the problem solving process requires you to carry out an evaluation once your plan has been implemented. The purpose of this is to determine how successfully the problem has been overcome. You will have to collate information that can be used to judge the results achieved from the implementation process. Actual outcomes are compared with expected outcomes, and if the former do not equal the latter, or under-perform, then the problem solving process has not been fully completed, and you might have to follow the cycle again. If the actual outcome is the same as the expected outcome, or surpasses it, then you have solved the problem.

The travel agent before opening her new shop will have set a target sales turnover figure that she would expect to achieve, for example a sales turnover of £250,000 in the first six months of operation. If this figure is attained, then she will have chosen a feasible site for the new agency and her problem solving process will have been successful.

Problems can be regarded as obstacles. These obstacles can be overcome by following a logical methodology, that takes you step by step towards the solution. If any of the steps are missed out then it is likely that you will come up with an incorrect solution. Each problem that you face, however, will be different and will involve different factors. You must not become complacent and treat all problems alike, but must use your critical thinking skills to ensure that the most feasible solution to the problem is found and successfully implemented.

DECISION MAKING SKILLS

Problem solving, when required, normally precedes decision making. The purpose of problem solving is to discover what caused a particular situation, so that you may use this knowledge to decide how to handle it. A key element of the decision making process is that of balancing risk. You must try to be aware of all the risks that may arise when a particular decision is taken, and take only those decisions for which the risk is acceptable.

There are overlaps between problem solving and decision making skills in terms of the methodologies you will use to solve problems and those to arrive at optimal decisions, but there are also differences. The steps in the decision making process are as follows:

1. Specifying aims
2. Reviewing the factors
3. Determining the possible courses open
4. Making the decision
5. Implementing the decision.

1. SPECIFYING AIMS

Your first stage in the decision making process is to ensure that the aim of your decision is clearly understood - What is the task under consideration? What is the purpose of the decision? What is to be achieved? What is the expected outcome likely to be?

Synthesis is important here to pull together the various strands of the situation and to look beyond its constituent parts. You need to take a broad perspective, thinking laterally and divergently.

2. REVIEWING THE FACTORS

Having confirmed the aim or purpose of the decision, you then need to consider the factors surrounding the decision. These should be analysed, synthesised and evaluated. You should list all the factors which are important in the decision, and you should determine the impact on the decision of each one, giving weightings to indicate their relative importance. This process should highlight the critical factor(s), the one upon which the success of the decision really hinges.

Returning to the example of the travel agent, the most critical factor she has determined for the success of the new agency might be the pedestrian flow on the pavement outside, followed by the proximity of bus stops and then car parks. These factors are given higher weightings than the size of the shop or the rent and rates, when arriving at a decision regarding the most feasible site.

You then need to establish the combined impact of all the factors to create a clear picture of the situation. This is a critical step in the decision making process and you should carry it out with great accuracy.

3. DETERMINING THE POSSIBLE COURSES OPEN

Having considered all the relevant factors you may be able to recognise a number of courses of action that may be feasible. These need to be listed. Indeed, you need to keep an open and creative mind at this stage to produce a broad range of possibilities, before narrowing them down. At this stage in the decision making process you should be concerned simply to produce as long a list as possible of potential actions, without attempting to evaluate them.

4. MAKING THE DECISION

When you have proposed a broad range of possible courses of action each one then has to be analysed, synthesised and evaluated against the critical factors identified above. You must take as wide a view as possible of each alternative, considering its advantages against its disadvantages. In addition, you have also to bear in mind what risks are associated with each possible course of action, particularly if it were not to be successful when implemented. You must decide what is an acceptable level of risk and that should be an important factor in the evaluation process.

Your most important intellectual activity at this point is critical thinking - questioning all the assumptions you have made, evaluating the arguments of others, appraising the data to make sure they are academically sound and not ideological.

You will then either reject or retain possible courses of action. You should reach a decision when only one course of action remains, after all the other possibilities have been shown to be less feasible or impractical.

This should be a logical decision if you have followed all the steps mentioned above.

5. IMPLEMENTING THE DECISION

To complete the decision making process you need to implement the decision. When the consequences of taking the decision become apparent it is then possible for you to determine whether the decision that was taken and implemented was the most appropriate, or whether you need to reconsider another of the possibilities.

This will test your leadership skills, treading the line between rigidity or flexibility of decisiveness. In such circumstances you will have to decide the point of no return: the last stage at which you can change a course of action without impeding the achievement of your goal. Your responsibility for taking a decision includes the responsibility for changing it up to the point of no return.

If you follow this decision making process, it will lead you through a logical sequence of steps that will allow you to make a feasible decision. As with problem solving, you will need to use your intellectual skills to ensure that a rational decision is reached, based upon critical thinking.

This chapter has considered the high order TPS of thinking. In Chapter Thirteen we go on to consider information gathering skills.

Chapter Thirteen

INFORMATION GATHERING SKILLS

Chapter Thirteen

INFORMATION GATHERING SKILLS

Many different situations which you will face require the gathering of information. Prior to attending for an interview you have to research the organisation to which you are applying for background information in order to show the interviewer that you are knowledgeable about the organisation and its operations. In negotiation sessions you have to research the background issues that will affect the discussions you are involved in. If you are a salesperson selling a product to a customer you must be knowledgeable about competing products, and how they differ from your own. As a consultant undertaking a project for a client you would be frequently involved in some form of research - finding information in order to support your conclusions.

Information gathering skills, therefore, are personal skills that are highly transferable to different situations. You need to be aware of different types of information gathering, and the steps involved in the research process.

THE NATURE OF INFORMATION GATHERING

Information gathering can be thought of as being the systematic collection and recording of data (data is used here in a wide sense, and refers to any type of information). Information gathering is not an end in itself, however, as the data must be analysed and evaluated. When you have completed this stage you can use the data for problem solving and decision making. This chapter is primarily concerned with the data collection process. Other skills which are mentioned are covered elsewhere in this book.

Before considering information gathering techniques, we should first try to identify situations in which the collection of data will be useful.

THE ROLE OF INFORMATION

The primary objective of gathering information is to answer questions. These questions will be diverse, and will depend on the situation with which you are faced. But by answering questions, you will be better placed to understand an issue, to make a decision or to solve a problem.

The collection of information, its analysis and its evaluation will help to reduce the uncertainty and inherent risk in decision making and problem solving. Very few people can make decisions or solve problems without a store of knowledge to draw upon. A lack of appropriate information can be responsible for you making an incorrect decision which in turn causes grave difficulty for you and your organisation.

While the overall objective of gathering information is to answer questions, we can identify a number of other situations in which information gathering would be useful:

* General background data can be collated that helps you to put into perspective a situation you are faced with. For example, you can follow trends in the market place, study competitor activity, identify new opportunities or highlight threats.

* When you are planning a course of action information is useful to help you to decide which course of action you should implement. Consider the possible outcomes from your decisions by posing questions which begin with "what if ..."?

* When you have taken the decision and implemented the plan, information can be collected to help you to evaluate the success of the decision. Did you reach the expected outcome by following a particular course of action?

From our discussion here it is apparent that three types of information can be collected - firstly, general information about the situation under consideration; secondly, information that is useful in forecasting likely occurrences in the future; and thirdly, information that can be used to evaluate the success of having followed a particular course of action.

Information that is gathered can be quite specific, relating to one discrete area, for example the effect of spending an extra 10% on advertising as opposed to spending that cash on sales promotions. Or the information can be of a general nature - the different types of political systems that can be found in the world today.

In all organisations, information gathering should be part of a continuous process, and be conducted in a systematic manner. As we have already seen, you should gather information when you are faced with a situation for which you do not know the answer. Rather than making an irrational decision with little information, you should gather data that sheds light on the situation and which allows you to arrive at a rational and informed decision.

THE CHARACTERISTICS OF INFORMATION

As part of the process of understanding information gathering, it is clearly appropriate to consider the characteristics of information itself:

* Information covers all forms of knowledge from hard facts such as a set of monthly sales data to abstract ideas, for example the product life cycle concept that is considered in marketing courses.

* Information is exchangeable - many different exchange techniques can be used ranging from high technology communications systems that use satellites to transmit messages from one part of the world to another, to the simple use of speech.

* The medium in which information is expressed is closely related to its content, its purpose and its intended audience. For example, the evening news bulletin on television uses speech, graphics and visual images to inform the viewer.

* Information may be transmitted erratically and in an unplanned way, such as a person's response to an unexpected telephone call, or it can be communicated in accordance with an overall plan or structure, such as the information system operating within an organisation.

Different types of information are available to you, ranging from the personal types such as anecdotal information received in conversations, to the more formal types of information obtained by rigorous survey techniques. Determining your information requirements when faced with a given task or problem is a personal skill, and in a broader sense is part of a research process.

THE INFORMATION GATHERING PROCESS

The quality of information available to you can vary from an uninformed opinion to thoroughly researched facts. The aim of the information gathering process is to provide you with the most accurate and reliable data possible within the limits imposed by time, cost, and your research ability. If you are a skilful information gatherer you will be able to use the most sophisticated techniques and methods available to you within these limits. You should always strive to collect the most reliable and accurate information within the constraints we have just noted. If you collect unreliable, or inaccurate data then you are likely to make faulty judgements and decisions.

To ensure that you collect accurate and reliable information you need to adopt a systematic and orderly approach. If you use a systematic approach then whatever may be your particular reason for collecting the data, your approach to collecting them will be uniform and hence highly transferable.

Your research process should:

1. Define the research problem and set research objectives.

2. Determine the information required to solve the problem.

3. Determine the sources of information to fulfil the research objectives.

4. Gather the relevant data from primary and/or secondary sources.

5. Analyse, interpret, and present the findings.

Your task is to execute each of these stages with objectivity and accuracy. The stages are the same for all situations you will face. Let us now consider each stage in more detail.

1. DEFINING THE PROBLEM AND ESTABLISHING OBJECTIVES

The first stage in the information gathering process is to define clearly the problem that needs information to solve it, and then to set specific research objectives. This is quite a difficult stage in the information gathering process as you might not be fully aware of the nature of the problem, or may not have clearly defined it, and so collect the wrong type of information. You can waste much time and effort, as well as cost, if you have defined the problem inappropriately.

Put yourself in the position of Lord Teasdale who opens his Historic House in the summer months to tourists. In recent years the number of tourists visiting each year has been declining. This decline in visitors has resulted in your sales revenue falling, and hence the profitability of your business. You are unsure of the reason why visitor numbers have been decreasing. Thus, the problem that needs investigating is the factors which are responsible for the reduced numbers of visitors at Teasdale House.

Once you have defined the problem the next step is to set research objectives. The purpose of setting objectives is to give a focus for the research to ensure that all your energies and activities are relevant to the problem that you have identified. By stating explicit research objectives, you can take measures to gauge whether they have been met. As with all objectives, research objectives can be either quantitative or qualitative, or a combination of both. In Lord Teasdale's case you might set the following objectives:

* To determine which factors have had greatest effect on causing visitor numbers to the house to decrease.

* To produce a profile of the existing visitors to the house - (so that strategies can be devised to encourage more of these consumers to visit the house in the future.)

* To establish the existing visitors' satisfaction with their visit (in order to determine whether any modifications or improvements have to be made to the house to attract more visitors).

The objectives that are set should enable you to proceed towards a solution of the problem.

The next stage is to identify the types of information that you will require to help solve the problem and attain the objectives.

2. DETERMINE TYPES OF INFORMATION REQUIRED

You can use a number of different approaches to help determine the type of information you need to gather. You should ask yourself a number of questions to help you to gain a clear idea of your information needs. You will require creative and divergent thinking here.

Your aim should be to produce as long a list as possible of different questions. In Lord Teasdale's case your questions might include the following:

* Who are the competitors and what selling points do they offer visitors, that Teasdale House does not?

* What are the visitors' views with regard to the house opening hours?

* Is the house open on sufficient days per week?

* Are the entrance fees too high?

* Are the staff friendly to the visitors?

* Are the rooms open to the public interesting?

* Is the food on sale appealing to visitors?

* Are the souvenirs on sale tempting to visitors?

* Is the advertising that is undertaken effective?

* Do tourists enjoy visiting historic houses, or will some other attraction be more appealing?

* What trends are occurring in tourism and leisure?

* Can any new features be added to Teasdale House that will make it more attractive to visitors?

It is useful at this stage for other people to review the questions to see if they can add a new perspective. As a result some additional questions might be forthcoming, for example:

* Do tourists only visit when the weather is wet?

* Does the house only interest a certain type of person?

* Can the sign at the entrance to the house be seen easily by passing motorists?

By asking other people to consider the problem, you get further objectivity, and additional causes of the problem may be identified.

As well as simply posing questions, a brain storming session is sometimes of value. Brain storming involves a group of people considering the issue together. The purpose of the session is to suggest as many different causes for the decline in visitors as possible. Each person listens carefully to what the others are suggesting and tries to think of additional causes. All the suggestions are accepted without any discussion as to their validity. The aim is to produce as many different causes as possible.

When a lengthy list of questions and possible causes of the problem have been produced, the next step is to think about the types of information that will have to be gathered in order to answer the questions and to shed further light on the problem.

Your intellectual skills will be called into use here, with you having to decide the information requirements based upon your evaluation of the situation. As Lord Teasdale you might conclude that you have a number of different information needs:

* Information concerning competing tourist attractions, both local ones and national ones - to indicate trends that are occurring in the tourism industry.

* Information describing who your current visitors are, why they visit the house, what they enjoy about their visit and what they dislike.

* Information showing how your visitors heard about the house and what motivates them to visit.

When all the different types of information that you require have been listed, you can then decide the sources you should refer to in order to collect the appropriate data.

3. DETERMINE THE SOURCES OF INFORMATION

Your starting place is to determine what information is readily available to you either internally within your organisation, or externally in some other published form. Information collated in this way is known as secondary data, since it is obtained from secondary research, that is research carried out by others for another purpose. If no information has been collated and published internally or externally, you will have to devise ways of collecting the necessary information yourself. This is known as primary research.

4. GATHERING THE DATA

The diversity of secondary data available to you may be considerable. Your main constraint will be that you are unaware of all the possible sources of secondary data available. The starting place for the search process should be with data that are already collected and published by your own organisation:

* Most organisations collate data referring to their level of activity i.e. sales achieved, number of units sold. This information, when compared with that of competing firms or industry trends will show whether the organisation is performing at the same level, or better or worse than its competitors.

* Data referring to costs. All organisations keep accounts detailing the costs involved with their operations. If you analyse these they may indicate if a particular cost centre has over spent its budget, thus having a negative effect on profitability.

* Geographic data. The organisation may well collate information on the source of its business by region. If certain regions are increasing their contribution to the organisation's business, and others are declining, then this is a trend that you need to explain.

* Customer feedback. Many organisations use customer satisfaction questionnaires to find out whether their clients are satisfied with the products or services provided for them. If the number of customer complaints has increased then this might provide further insights into the problem.

* In addition to the above there might be a variety of other information that has already been collated, for instance market research surveys which have been conducted and have findings which are still valid. Special reports might have been purchased from other organisations, or produced by consultants.

You should undertake an extensive trawl of possible sources of information that might be available internally. Indeed, the organisation might maintain its own library or data index, which you should investigate thoroughly before you consider external sources.

If the information that you require has not been collated by your organisation then your next step should be to consider external sources of published data. There are many sources of published data, the most widespread of which are libraries. Different types of library are designed to meet different needs. All towns have a general public library primarily containing fiction sections but also holding non-fiction reference books. Universities, polytechnics and colleges have academic libraries housing journals, reports, professional magazines, as well as academic texts. The sections in these libraries will be classified according to subject.

Specialist libraries also exist. These tend to be located in the larger cities such as London, Edinburgh and Manchester. Examples include the Westminster Central Reference Library, and the City Business Library in London. Government departments collate material that can be accessed by members of the public. For example the Department of Trade and Industry in London has a library containing information that will be of use to British exporters wanting information about overseas markets.

Irrespective of the type of library that is used, a diverse range of information will be available:

* Government statistics. Some libraries have extensive sections devoted to collating data published by the government. Indeed, the government is one of the largest research organisations in the UK and it makes available much of this information to the public. All the government departments publish reports and statistics, and you should become familiar with what is available. Two major government research bodies are the Government Statistics Office and the Office of Population Censuses.The former collates

data on all businesses incorporated in the UK, while the latter conducts the Census of Population every ten years.

* Special reports. Various private sector organisations specialise in collecting information and publishing it in report form. Libraries will stock a selection of these. Examples include the Mintel organisation that publishes monthly market research reports investigating different products or services. The Jordan Reports analyse the financial performance of organisations. Euromonitor Reports adopt a similar approach.

* Consumer publications. The 'Which' publications investigate a variety of different products and services each month, informing the reader about potential faults or problems that might arise. Specialist interest magazines cover every hobby or interest that might be of concern to the researcher. They provide up to date information on new products and developments, and assess existing ones.

* Professional publications. Each Professional body will have its own publication, for example the British Medical Association journal, 'The Lancet'. These document recent developments in the sphere of interest of the members, for example new drugs that have been developed and launched onto the market.

* Reference Journals. These are academic journals such as the 'Cambridge Law Journal', which allow authors to consider theoretical issues relating to their subject, or to present research findings. Each article includes a list of references to enable the reader to investigate further the topic being considered.

* Directories. Large reference directories contain factual information. The Kompass Register lists companies situated in the different regions and counties of the UK. Publications such as this give you an idea of potential competitors, or a list of possible suppliers for the product.

* Extel. Extel collates information from company reports and publishes it. These data are useful for discovering financial trends that are occurring within an industry, or for finding out how competing firms are prospering.

* Dictionaries, Glossaries and Encyclopedias. These do not simply cover the meaning of and pronunciations of words, but also provide technical and factual information or data.

* Audio & visual data. In addition to books, magazines, and journals, libraries also contain video tapes and audio tapes. These will be of an educational nature and might contain the information you are looking for. The Ceefax and Prestel information services contain up to date information. Most libraries will have television sets able to receive Ceefax and Prestel data.

It is clear from the above that libraries contain a great wealth of secondary data. Your task will be to become fully familiar with your local library, to know what information sources are available, and just as importantly how to find them. Each library will have its own referencing system, the more modern using the Microfiche System. You should fully understand how the referencing and index system works so that information can be obtained quickly, without wasting time. If the source of information is not available at the local library then it can be obtained under the Inter-Library Loan System.

The Inter-Library Loan System requires you to provide your local librarian with full details of the text or article you wish to see: the author, publication title, article title (if applicable), the publisher, date of publication, page numbers (if applicable) and ISBN number if known. These details are then sent to the British Library Document Supply Centre which is able to obtain copies of all texts and journal articles published in the UK.

If you are unsure what texts or journal articles have been published on a subject and cannot find any suitable references or texts using the local library's index system, then two further sources of information are available - the Abstracts, and the On-Line Search System. Abstracts are published reference sources that provide synopses of all articles published in a given time period, on a particular subject. For example, the Anbar Abstract lists journal articles published on the subject of 'marketing', giving brief details of the content of each article, along with the author's name, the journal where it was published, and the publication date.

The On-Line Search System involves the librarian punching key words into a personal computer linked to a journal and subject data base. Details of any articles that are found which contain the key words are then printed out. For example, Lord Teasdale might wish to see if any articles have been published on the subject of the 'Marketing of a Historic House'. Thus, the librarian would key in the words 'Historic House' into the personal computer, and the details of all articles on this subject held in the data base would be printed out.

As well as visiting the local library to discover what information is available, you should be aware of the following further information sources:

* Local authorities. Local councils are involved in collecting data on the local environment and have information that might be of interest to you.

* Public bodies. A number of different public bodies exist. National and Regional Tourist Boards operate in the UK and collate tourism statistics. The Civil Aviation Authority publishes data on air-traffic into and out of the UK.

* Professional associations. Organisations such as trade unions and professional associations like ABTA (the Association of British Travel Agents) collect information that is pertinent to their members and sometimes publish special reports.

* Banks. Domestic banks, in particular the National Westminster, the Midland, Barclays, and Lloyds, publish reports and special journals that are available to members of the public.

* Commercial research organisations. Private sector research agencies conduct research and publish the results, selling their findings to interested parties. These publications, though, tend to be expensive. The British Market Research Bureau (BMRB) conducts an annual survey of 24,000 respondents in the UK, known as the Target Group Index (TGI). The survey involves respondents completing a 70 page questionnaire that details their purchasing habits of some 4500 brands, as well as their media buying habits. Information produced by the TGI will inform an organisation who their customers are, and which media methods should be used to communicate with them.

The above list is not exhaustive, as the sources of information available to you are continually changing. Apart from being aware of these 'formal' sources of information there are also 'informal' ones that you can refer to. The 'Yellow Pages' can be used to analyse the number of companies competing in a given area. Local newspapers are a valuable source of up to date information on local environmental trends, such as new roads being built, new employers locating in the vicinity, or details of competitive activity. National newspapers and magazines, as well as television and radio programmes are useful sources of up to date information. Leaflets and brochures from competitors can be analysed to see how their products differ from yours. Indeed, you can attend exhibitions and conferences to meet competitors and to see their products.

Thus, there are many potential sources of secondary data that you can use to obtain the information you require. However, you must be discriminating in your use of such data, otherwise you will suffer from 'information overload'.

THE LIMITATIONS OF SECONDARY DATA

Before you use secondary data to solve your problem you must evaluate its validity and reliability. This requires you to screen the data; to do so you should ask yourself the following questions:

* Who collected the data? Have they been collected by a reputable organisation? Would there be any reason for them to deliberately misrepresent the facts (e.g. to present a product in a favourable manner)?

* For what purpose were the data collected? Was it for a similar purpose to your needs? If not are the data still valid?

* How were the data collected? Was the sample size (if a questionnaire survey was conducted) large enough to enable generalisations to be made?

* Are the data internally consistent and logical in the light of known data sources or other factors?

You should look very carefully at the source of the data and not use them if you are in doubt as to their accuracy. Some organisations when obtaining data do not adopt reliable methods of data collection, and publish findings that are too optimistic. However, much valuable information can be obtained from secondary sources and all researchers should start their information gathering by referring to data that have already been published. Not only is it less expensive than primary research, but it is also less time consuming.

If the information that is required has not been published then you will have to undertake primary research. Lord Teasdale will be able to obtain some of his information requirements from published sources, for example about trends in the tourism industry, but will need to instigate primary research to determine the attitudes, perceptions and motivations of the visitors to the house.

PRIMARY RESEARCH

When there are no adequate sources of secondary data, you must collect primary data - undertake your own research in order to obtain the information you need. There are three approaches to collecting primary data:

(i)   By Observation.
(ii) By Experimentation.
(iii) By Questionnaire.

(i) BY OBSERVATION

A relatively simple way of collecting primary data is by observing a given situation and noting down what is happening. Data collected in this way will help to describe what is happening. For example, if you were Lord Teasdale you might observe visitors when they are touring the house, recording how they react to the different rooms, or recording how long they spend in each room before moving on to the next. To give an idea of the level of demand achieved at different times of the day you might ask the cashier to record how many visitors enter the house at the different times it is open, and on the various days that it is open.

When you carry out observations yourself it is vital that you concentrate fully on the situation being observed and do not lose concentration, or undertake any other activities. If you lose concentration, especially if you have to note down every single occurrence, then you will make inaccurate observations and the research data obtained become biased. If other people are acting as your observers, specially designed observation record forms need to be used that explain what is to be observed, how it is to be observed, and the way in which the record form is to be completed.

You must ensure that you do not distract the person being observed. If this person feels that he or she is being watched then he or she might not act in a normal way, which again will cause inaccurate recordings to be made. Thus, you need to be discrete when observing the actions of others. To overcome problems created by human observation you can use a variety of mechanical aids, such as tape recorders and video-cameras.

In other situations it can be appropriate to ask respondents to keep a record in a diary of all the times, on what occasions, and for what purposes a particular activity was undertaken.

For example, the users of a product might be asked to keep a diary. In this the respondent will be asked to record all the occasions that the product was used, the time it was used, the circumstances of its use, and how satisfactorily it performed.

It is generally believed that data obtained from observations is more objective than that derived from questioning techniques, as purely factual information is being recorded. In addition, the data collected has not been influenced by questioning, nor by the respondents' ability to answer. Care has to be taken, though, to ensure that any measuring or recording equipment that is used is reliable and accurate. Attention has also to be paid to the particular respondents used to ensure that they are representative of the population at large.

Some inferences might be made from the results of the observational study, but your main purpose in using such a technique is to become better acquainted with what is happening in the situation under observation. Data collected by this method should be used to confirm data gained from the other two approaches.

(ii) BY EXPERIMENTATION

A more sophisticated approach than simple observation is that of experimentation. Here you propose a hypothesis which is then tested in a controlled way, before you draw conclusions.

If conditions permit you could conduct a rigorously designed and implemented laboratory experiment. This type of experiment will allow you to control the experimentation process in order to prevent error or bias creeping into the research. Special equipment may be needed for this, as well as a specially controlled environment. For example, when new cars are designed they are tested in a wind-tunnel to determine their aerodynamic qualities; models of new ships to be built are tested in special water tanks to establish their sea-worthiness before the actual ship is built. With these 'lab experiments' the findings of the research will be unambiguous. However, a problem that sometimes arises is that the experiment is not a true simulation of what occurs in reality, and the results of the experiment may not be totally transferable to the real setting.

An alternative is to conduct experiments 'in the field'. Here the experiment takes place in circumstances as close as possible to reality. A difficulty that will arise will be that of controlling a number of external influences that might affect the recorded results. However, if you identify possible sources of error and bias and endeavour to minimise their effect, then the results which you produce should be valid.

Experiments can be used in many different situations. Using Teasdale House as an example, Lord Teasdale might experiment by opening the house for more hours in the day, and for more days in the week, in order to see what effect this has on the demand by visitors. Another approach would be to see whether the visitors are price conscious. Thus, on certain days of the week the entrance fees might be reduced, and the effect on the demand measured. The advertising that is used to inform tourists of the house could be modified to see whether this attracts more visitors. Observations are made to evaluate the results of the experiments.

To record the data obtained from experiments special forms need to be devised that can be used in the analysis process. Experiments like those discussed here can provide you with much valuable information.

(iii) BY QUESTIONNAIRE

A questionnaire is a prepared document used to obtain information from respondents by asking questions. Questionnaires can serve a variety of purposes.

Market researchers use them to obtain information about consumer needs, attitudes, beliefs, perceptions and motivations towards a company or its products, advertising, or pricing strategy, and so on. Organisations in the public sector use them to find out whether their 'consumers' or clients are satisfied with the services provided for them. Employers use questionnaires to investigate the motivations of their employees. Students use questionnaires to discover information to assist with their project work.

The benefits provided by using questionnaires for obtaining information are that they:

* Allow you to ask questions, the answers to which will meet your information needs.

* Enable information to be collected in a standard form, which ensures the information obtained from one respondent can be analysed in conjunction with that obtained from others.

* Provide a way of obtaining the information relatively quickly, and if the questionnaire is correctly designed permit data collection and analysis to be achieved efficiently.

* Allow for a large number of people to be questioned, all in the same way, thus improving the validity of the data that are collected.

The questionnaire approach offers considerable flexibility. Questionnaires can be completed by an interviewer or by the respondent. Interviews can be conducted at the respondents' home, in the street, at work, in social situations, over the telephone, or the questionnaire can be mailed to the respondent.

PERSONAL INTERVIEWS

You should use personal interviews where the questionnaire is quite long, or complex. It is best to train interviewers to conduct the interviews, otherwise error and bias will undoubtedly creep into the research process. This type of questioning allows props, samples, or other aids to be shown to the respondent. A successful interviewer will be able to sustain the respondents' interest throughout the interview.

With this type of interviewing you will probably have little direct control over the interviewers. To confirm that the interviews were conducted in a professional way you should make sure the name, address, and telephone number of each respondent is obtained.

From this list you could later contact 10% of the respondents to ask them whether they were interviewed and if they felt satisfied with the approach adopted by the interviewer.

BY TELEPHONE

With telephone interviews you are unable to use any visual aids when talking to the respondent. Thus you have to ask straightforward questions. However, an advantage of the telephone survey is that certain types of respondent can be more easily reached than by the personal interview, for example business people at work in different parts of the country.

This method of obtaining information is rapid, and it enables the interviewers to work safely at unsociable hours. You have direct control over the interviewers (if they are working from the research office) and thus you are able to monitor the way in which the questions are being asked and recorded.

Both personal interviewing and telephone interviewing require you to brief the interviewers fully as to the purpose of the survey and the ways in which the questions on the questionnaire are to be asked. Each question should be discussed in turn, with you drawing the interviewers' attention to the wording and any special props or aids that are to be used. The method of completing the questionnaire also needs to be addressed.

BY POST

Personal interviewing and telephone interviewing do tend to be expensive. In addition to the costs of producing the questionnaire, you have to recruit, train and employ a team of interviewers. Postal questionnaires, however, are not so costly, as a team of interviewers is not required - the questionnaires are mailed direct to the respondent.

Postal questionnaires, though, tend to suffer from low response rates. To overcome this problem you will have to draft a polite introductory letter informing the respondent of the purpose of the survey, and giving a deadline for the return of the completed questionnaire. In addition it is useful to offer the respondent an incentive to encourage him or her to complete and return the questionnaire. Such an incentive might be free entry into a prize draw - the respondent whose name is drawn out receives a free gift.

Another limitation of the postal questionnaire is that the respondent can read all the questions before answering them. If he or she decides that the questions being asked are too confidential, too complex, or too 'uninteresting' then they might discard the questionnaire.

From the discussion here, it is evident that the way in which the questionnaire is to be used will to some extent determine its design. If the survey is to be conducted using trained interviewers then more complex questions can be included in the questionnaire. However, if a postal survey is to be used you will have to take care to ensure that all questions can be easily understood by the respondent.

No matter which method of implementing the survey is chosen, adopt a systematic approach to its design.

QUESTIONS TO BE ASKED

The questions to be included in the questionnaire will be determined by the research objectives, and the way in which the questions are asked will be influenced by the method you are using to undertake the survey. A number of general guidelines, though, need to be borne in mind when actually writing the questions:

* You should only ask questions that the respondent will be able to answer. Hypothetical questions should be avoided. Questions that concern an occurrence too long ago should not be used - the respondent's memory might not be reliable, and he may give an incorrect answer.

* The use of words on the questionnaire is critical. Use words and phrases that are unambiguous and familiar to the respondent. For example, 'dinner' has a number of different interpretations - an alternative would be to use 'evening meal'.

* Vacuous words/terms should be avoided. 'Generally', 'usually', or 'normally' are imprecise terms with various meanings. You should replace them with quantitative statements e.g. 'at least once a week', 'at least once a month' etc.

* Questions should only address a single issue. For example, questions like: "Do you take annual holidays to Spain?" should be broken down into two discrete stages, firstly find out if the respondent takes an annual holiday, and then secondly find out if they go to Spain.

* The wording of the questions should avoid all unnecessary words - keep them simple and to the point. Make sure that the respondent will be able to express an answer in words. If the respondent finds it difficult to respond he might simply end the interview.

* If you are providing additional information for the respondent, or the respondent is required to make a choice from a set of answers, then provide this information on a 'show card' that the respondent can read. Show cards can act as 'memory joggers' for the respondent.

* Ensure that the questions asked do not test the respondent's intellect. For example, asking the respondents whether they know a particular fact will probably result in all of them answering in the affirmative. This is because the respondents will not wish to appear ignorant or foolish to the interviewer.

* Give careful thought to the wording of questions concerning a respondent's behaviour. Respondents might answer in a way that shows they conform to what they believe is the norm, rather than answering in a way that suggests that their behaviour is somehow abnormal.

* Avoid leading questions. Such questions encourage the respondent to answer the question in a certain way because of the way the question is asked. For example if you were to ask someone "You believe in God, don't you?", this indicates that you expect the answer to be yes.

It is evident that designing the wording of the questions to be asked is an intellectually challenging task. If you give insufficient attention to this part of the research process then you will possibly face a great number of potential sources of error and bias, which could invalidate the survey. You should prepare draft questions before polishing them into a final form for inclusion in the questionnaire. In addition to thinking about the wording of the questions, pay attention to the type of questions that are used.

You can include a number of different types of question on the questionnaire:

(i) Closed questions.
(ii) Open questions.
(iii) Direct questions.
(iv) Indirect questions.
(v) Attitude questions.

(i) CLOSED QUESTIONS

Here a question is asked, and then a number of possible answers are provided for the respondent. The respondent selects the answer which is appropriate to him or her:

How have you travelled to Teasdale House? Tick the mode of transport that is applicable:

By car   ----------
mini-bus   ----------
coach   ----------
motor bike   ----------
public transport ----------
walk   ----------
other means   ----------
please specify:

You should always include an 'other' response category because not all possible responses might have been included in the list of possible answers. Sometimes the respondent can indicate that more than one answer is applicable. These are called multiple-choice questions:

Why have you visited Teasdale House? Tick the relevant answer(s) - (you may tick more than one) :

a) I enjoy visiting historic houses.   ----------

b) The weather was bad and I could
not enjoy outdoor activities.   ----------

c) I have visited Teasdale House
before and wished to return.   ----------

d) Other reason, please specify: ----------

(ii) OPEN QUESTIONS

With these, respondents are free to answer the question as they wish, in their own words. The interviewer has to write down the exact words that are used:

What new features would you like to see introduced at Teasdale House?

Sometimes analysing the answers to open-questions is quite time consuming as you can get many different responses. Therefore, take this into account when deciding the number of open questions to be included in the questionnaire.

(iii) DIRECT QUESTIONS

These seek to obtain direct information from the respondent about behaviour, attitudes, beliefs, motivations or perceptions:

What have you most enjoyed about your visit to Teasdale House?

These questions are useful in that they help you to gain an understanding of how respondents' behave, and why they do so.

(iv) INDIRECT QUESTIONS

If the topic under consideration is sensitive, so that the respondents might feel embarrassed by giving their own answer, you can use indirect questions:

What do you think people least enjoy about their visit to Teasdale House?

Posing the question in this way might be less threatening to the respondent and so you might get a more honest answer.

(v) ATTITUDE QUESTIONS

It is frequently important for you to understand the respondents' attitudes towards a given situation, and also to be able to quantify the number of respondents holding a given attitude. To do this you can follow two approaches. Firstly, you could provide a battery of attitude statements and then ask respondents to say how much they agree or disagree with each one, using what is referred to as a 'Likert Scale':

Listed below are five statements. Read each statement carefully and then indicate by a tick, whether you strongly agree, agree, disagree, or strongly disagree with it:

STATEMENT	STRONGLY AGREE	AGREE	DISAGREE	STRONGLY DISAGREE
1 My visit to Teasdale House has been good value for money.				
2 The opening hours from 1.00pm to 4.00pm are adequate.				
3 The staff on duty have been friendly.				
4 The souvenirs on sale are varied.				
5 The rooms I have seen are interesting.				

In addition to the four categories of agreement detailed above, you could include an additional one - 'neither agree or disagree' - to ensure that all possible answers have been catered for. When analysing this type of question it will be possible for you to say how many people agree or disagree with each statement. An alternative is to ask the respondent to rank the various attitude statements, so that the most important one is ranked first and the least important, last.

To see how strongly an attitude is held by the respondent, a 'semantic differential scale' can be used. This is the second approach that can be used for determining the respondents' attitudes.

With semantic differential scales double-ended terms are put to the respondents who are asked to indicate where their attitude lies on the scale between the terms:

Place a tick on the following scales to indicate what your attitude towards Teasdale House as venue for a family day out has been:

Very interesting + + + + + + Uninteresting

Excellent value for money + + + + + + Poor value for money

Educational + + + + + + Not educational

To assist with the analysis of this type of question, you could use a nominal scale between the two semantic differentials, and respondents are asked to circle the value that indicates where their attitude lies:

Very interesting   1 2 3 4 5 6   Uninteresting

DESIGNING THE QUESTIONNAIRE

Questionnaires can be either:

(i) Structured.
(ii) Unstructured.

(i) STRUCTURED QUESTIONNAIRES

Here, the questions are asked in a pre-determined order, and a pre-determined manner. The interviewer must not alter or explain questions, or deviate from the order. Many of the questions used will be closed questions.

When designing a structured questionnaire a number of points have to be borne in mind:

* Confirm the objective of the research. Ensure that both its purpose and the information required are clearly understood.

* List the topics that need to be covered in the questionnaire. Then sequence the topics so that their order is logical and will come across coherently to the respondent without causing confusion.

* Include an introduction to the questionnaire that explains its purpose, what the findings will be used for, and who is undertaking the research.

* Start the questionnaire with easy, non-threatening questions and topics. Explore the respondents' present behaviour, rather than ask for future actions or attitudes.

* Place threatening, embarrassing, or personal topics towards the end of the questionnaire. These are best asked when the respondent trusts the interviewer i.e. details about the respondents' age, occupation, name, income etc.

* Use a variety of different types of question. Too many of one particular type will not motivate or interest the respondent.

* Check and double-check the questionnaire for questions that will lead to error and bias invalidating the findings e.g. leading questions, ambiguous

questions, questions that might be seen as a test of the respondents' intellect etc.

We have already noted that planning a questionnaire is an intellectually challenging task. It is likely that you will need a number of attempts to achieve an appropriate design. To test out your design, conduct a test survey (pilot survey) which not only provides you with feedback on the success of the design, but also the wording of the questions.

In addition to thinking about the design and wording of the questionnaire, pay attention to its layout:

* Each questionnaire should have an identification code/number. This helps to locate individual questionnaires when they have been completed and stored.

* Each question should, wherever possible, be pre-coded for computer analysis. Each questionnaire will be allocated a separate 'card' for inputting the responses onto the computer programme. Each question should be allocated a separate column number (there are 80 in total on the card), and each question be coded (up to 10 different responses can be coded for each question asked).

* Provide instructions informing the respondent or the interviewer how to answer the questions, for example should answers be ticked or circled.

* Provide sufficient space so that all questions can be answered legibly. Give some thought to the space allowed for the answering of open-questions.

Designing questionnaires is a TPS, and like all skills your ability to design effective questionnaires improves with practise. The true test of a questionnaire will be whether it collects the information that is required in order to solve the problem. Shown below is the first page of Lord Teasdale's Visitor Questionnaire,

TEASDALE HOUSE VISITOR QUESTIONNAIRE

INTRODUCTION

(Interviewer to read out)

"Good morning/afternoon. Have you enjoyed your visit of Teasdale House?

Lord Teasdale is concerned to make sure that visitors have been satisfied with their visit to his home and would be extremely grateful if you could spare 10 minutes to answer a few questions about your visit. Analysing the views of visitors to the house, enables us to make modifications to the facilities available to visitors and increase the enjoyment of future visitors.

Can you spare me 10 minutes of your time to answer a few short questions?" (If the response is 'yes' ask the questions. If 'no' thank the visitor for visiting the house, and wish him or her a safe journey home).

	Column	Code
Questionnaire Number	1	
	2	
	3	
Interviewer reference	4	
Date of interview	5	
	6	

1. YOUR JOURNEY

a) How have you travelled to Teasdale House?   7
Please tick the appropriate mode of transport:

By Car	------
Mini-bus	------
Coach	------
Motor bike	------
Public transport	------
On foot	------
Other means	------

please specify:

b) Have you travelled from your home, or from holiday accommodation? Please tick the appropriate answer:

From home	------	
From holiday accommodation	------	8

If you are on holiday what is the name of the camp site, hostel, guest house or hotel at which you are staying?
Write your answer in the space below:

9
10

(ii) UNSTRUCTURED QUESTIONNAIRES

This form of questionnaire uses a number of open-ended questions, and allows the interviewer to modify the order of the questions, depending on how the interview is developing. This approach allows for 'in-depth' interviews to be held with the respondent. Structured interviews do not always permit this, but allow for many more respondents to be questioned in the time available.

In addition to thinking about the questionnaire's design, you must also consider the sample of respondents to interview.

Sampling

There are many different ways of choosing respondents to be included in a survey. We shall examine the main ones:
(i)   Probability sampling (or Random sampling).
(ii) Purposive sampling.
(iii) Stratified sampling.
(iv) Proportionate sampling.
(v)   Quota sampling.

(i) PROBABILITY SAMPLING (OR RANDOM SAMPLING)

In this type of sample each member of the population has the same known chance of being selected for the survey. You need to have a list of all members of the target population, for example all the members of a club or society. The sample is then drawn from the list in a random way - each name is given a number and respondents are then selected using random number tables.

(ii) PURPOSIVE SAMPLING

The selection of respondents is based purely on human judgement. Here, the interviewer decides who to interview.

(iii) STRATIFIED SAMPLING

In this type of sample the population in question is divided into groups with similar characteristics (known as strata) whose relative size is known, for example age groups, or socio-economic groups. Each strata used must be separate and self-contained. A random sample is then taken of each strata.

(iv) PROPORTIONATE SAMPLING

The strata sampling approach is used, but instead of a random number of respondents being chosen from each strata, a fixed proportion of respondents is drawn e.g. 10% of the population from each strata will be interviewed.

(v) QUOTA SAMPLING

Here, strata are identified, for example different age groups, and the interviewer is given a number of respondents to interview who fall into each of the different strata. For example, the interviewer might have to interview 50 people aged 25 - 44 years, and 40 people aged 45 - 64 years. The number of people to be interviewed in each strata will be proportionate to the relative size of the strata to the population as a whole.

Probability, or random, sampling is the approach that is most commonly used. This is because random sampling offers two distinct advantages to the researcher:

* Random drawing of respondents from the population allows statistical relationships to be established between the sample and the population from which it was drawn.

* When respondents are drawn randomly there is less chance that the sample will be affected by the researcher's judgement.

Irrespective of the sampling method used the objective is to draw respondents from the population in such a way that the sample chosen provides a good representation of the population being surveyed. If you achieve this, and the sample you interview is large enough, then you can make generalisations about that population based on the results of the survey.

There is no definitive answer to the question - 'how large should the sample be?' This depends on the population being surveyed and the resources available to the researcher. What is important is that the sample is large enough to pick up variations in the behaviour and attitudes of the respondents, and that these variations apply to the total population. Some surveys of the national population of the UK might interview 5000 respondents, while surveys in one region might interview 1000 people. When surveys are conducted of specialised populations that have a total population size of 100, for example, then a sample size of 50 would be sufficient for you to draw generalisations from the survey.

Not only is it important to consider the size of the sample, it is also important to consider where the interviews will be conducted (if the survey is based on personal interviewing)? Again no definitive answer can be provided for this question. What you should ensure is that the interviews do not all take place at the same location. This in itself could lead to error and bias. Try to include a number of different locations for the interviews to take place, locations that will enable a broad section of the population to be included in the survey.

When the sample of respondents has been selected you can then contemplate how to manage the interviewing process.

THE RESEARCH INTERVIEW

You should apply the TPS discussed in Chapter Seven on interviewing when conducting interviews to obtain information. In addition, you have to bear further considerations in mind:

* Respondents frequently resent being interviewed and often erect barriers to the interviewer. To overcome these barriers you need to appear non-threatening and sensitive. You can achieve this by:
  – dressing smartly and appearing well-groomed

- smiling
- explaining the purpose of the survey and its rationale
- stressing the confidentiality of the information that is given
- sympathising with respondents who say they are pushed for time, while still being assertive, 'it will only take 10 minutes of your time'
- speaking in a soft, yet audible tone of voice
- speaking slowly and deliberately, pronouncing each word carefully so that its meaning can be clearly understood
- controlling the body language signals that you give - try not to show your reaction to the respondent's answers, for example don't raise your eyebrows to unexpected answers
- being polite and courteous at all times.

* Always carry some form of identification to indicate that you are a bona-fide interviewer undertaking a legitimate survey.

* If you are holding interviews on private property, for example in a shopping centre, obtain the permission of the owners or management before starting to interview.

* If you are interviewing outdoors, use interview points that will not be affected by bad weather.

* Try to avoid outdoor interview sites that are too noisy.

* During the interview ask all the questions on the questionnaire. Try not to deviate from the structure of the questionnaire.

* Ask all the questions in the same way to each respondent. Do not give signs of encouragement to the respondents to answer the questions in a particular way, for example by nodding or shaking your head.

* Never suggest answers for the respondent. If the respondent cannot answer a question then note this on the questionnaire.

* Be familiar with all the questions on the questionnaire, practise using any aids, show cards, or other items before starting to interview respondents. You will lose credibility if you appear to be disorganised.

* Complete each questionnaire neatly and legibly. Untidy and difficult to read questionnaires might lead to errors occurring at the data analysis stage.

* Remain calm at all times during the interview. Do not become ruffled by the attitude, or any of the responses given by the respondent.

* When all the questions have been asked, thank the respondent for taking part in the survey.

If you follow the above guidelines then the likelihood of error and bias creeping into the information gathering process will be reduced.

When all the questionnaires have been completed, the final stage in the research process is to analyse the results of the survey and to draw conclusions.

ANALYSING THE DATA

You need to translate the data produced from the survey into a form that is meaningful. You should use the data handling and presentation skills discussed in Chapter Six.

When drawing inferences and conclusions from the data, you will use your thinking skills, especially the critical thinking skills as discussed in Chapter Twelve. This part of the research process will call for great objectivity to ensure that you make no false assumptions, or ignore findings produced from the survey, especially if they contradict your personal view.

Returning to the questionnaire implemented by Lord Teasdale, it might be that the following findings are produced by analysing the questionnaires:

The Age Structure of Visitors to Teasdale House

Age Groups	Percentage of Visitors %
0 - 15 years	19
16 - 24 years	5
25 - 34 years	11
35 - 44 years	20
45 - 54 years	15
55 - 64 years	18
65 years plus	12
Total	100%

From this table it can be seen that the 16-24 years age group is the least likely to visit Teasdale House. An explanation could be that people within this age group are not as interested in history, and/or have other leisure activities that are more adventurous and active than visiting a historic house. There is a strong incidence of children visiting the house. Given the house's rural location it is likely that these children are visiting on a family outing. A visit to a historical house is probably seen as an educational occasion by the family.

Turning to the socio-economic group of the respondent to the questionnaire, the following data were produced from the survey:

The Respondent's Socio-economic Group

Socio-economic Group	Percentage of Respondents
A	5
B	38
C1	27
C2	2
D	0
E	28
Total	100%

When a socio-economic group is used for classifying a population, the respondent is classified according to the occupation of the head of the household, in which he or she lives. Six broad socio-economic group classifications are identified:

Socio-economic Group	Occupation of the Head of the Household
A	Higher Managerial, administrative or professional.
B	Intermediate managerial, administrative, or professional.
C1	Supervisory or clerical, and junior managerial, administrative or professional.
C2	Skilled manual workers.
D	Semi and unskilled manual workers.
E	State pensioners or widows, casual or lowest grade workers.

The data displayed above indicates that the visitors to the house are primarily from the B and C1 socio-economic groups. Indeed, virtually no visitors are drawn from the C2 or D groups. The high incidence of visitors in group E reflects the house's appeal to retired individuals, who probably appreciate the nostalgic side of a visit to such a tourist attraction. Taking all of these points into account it could be stated that Teasdale House appeals to quite a distinct type of visitor.

When the responses to the attitude statements were analysed it was found that:

> 96% of respondents felt their visit represented good value for money.
> 33% of respondents felt the opening hours/days were inadequate.
> 100% of respondents felt the staff on duty were friendly.
> 42% of respondents felt the souvenirs being sold were of insufficient variety.
> 100% of respondents felt the rooms on view were interesting.
> 69% of respondents had no complaints about their visit to Teasdale House.

The findings from these attitude statements are now providing useful information about the satisfaction visitors gain from their visit. The fact that 96% of respondents felt their visit to be good value for money might be seen as implying that the prices charged could be increased, especially as visitors found the rooms on view interesting and the staff friendly.

Clearly no major changes need to be made to Teasdale House to make it more attractive to visitors. It could be concluded that a reason why visitor numbers have not been increasing is that very few tourists know about it. Now that Lord Teasdale is developing a profile of his existing visitors it will be possible for him to devise communication strategies that will reach more of these people.

The above discussion has been an example of how you can gain information from a questionnaire survey. By having such information available you are in a much better position to evaluate alternatives and make sensible and well reasoned decisions.

Information gathering skills are highly transferable. At some stage in your career you will inevitably need information to help you with your work. The skills discussed in this chapter will ensure that the information you collect will be valid and reliable.

Chapter Fourteen

CONSULTANCY SKILLS

Chapter Fourteen

CONSULTANCY SKILLS

We have decided to include consultancy skills as part of the TPS programme because managers at work, and students at college, are increasingly being required to act as consultants to colleagues within their own organisations, or to other organisations as part of special projects.

To be a successful consultant you must master the full range of TPS discussed in this book, from verbal and non-verbal communication skills right through to critical thinking and information gathering skills. The purpose of this chapter is to highlight the stages in the consultancy process, developing further special applications of TPS already mentioned and providing guidelines for additional ones that need to be developed.

THE STAGES OF THE CONSULTANCY PROCESS

Consultants are recruited by organisations to carry out a wide range of functions such as:

* Solving specific problems.

* Providing specialist advice.

* Providing special skills that are not available 'in house'.

* Carrying out ad hoc studies and research.

* Assisting with the selection and recruitment of staff.

* Providing training courses.

* Implementing specific courses of action.

The range of skills and functions that consultants offer clients is increasing and so too are the number of consultants available. To act as a consultant you must be aware of the distinct stages of the consultancy process.

(i) Pitching for the account.
(ii) The administrative arrangements.
(iii) Maintaining a good relationship with the client.

(iv) Undertaking the work.
(v) Presenting the work.
(vi) Follow-up procedures.

(i) PITCHING FOR THE ACCOUNT

The first stage in the consultancy process is gaining the client's account. Frequently this will involve competing against other consultants. The client will probably require each consultant to make a brief presentation covering how each intends tackling the work involved. This is known as 'pitching for the account'. When pitching for the account you need to bear in mind all the points raised in Chapter Eight on Presentation Skills, and in Chapter Nine on Selling and Negotiating Skills. In particular you need to stress to the client the benefits that will be gained from awarding you the contract. The presentation should be viewed as a means of establishing your credibility - a major factor when the client decides who will be awarded the contract. Following the guidelines below will help to establish your credibility:

* Research the clients, their business, their needs, problems and expectations.

* Prepare thoroughly for the first meeting with a client.

* Look smart and efficient - dress in a proper business-like manner.

* Be honest, and avoid exaggeration and claims that you cannot substantiate, do not make promises that you cannot keep.

* Listen attentively to what they say.

(ii) THE ADMINISTRATIVE ARRANGEMENTS

If you win the account it is important clearly to specify at the outset all administrative arrangements of the consultancy:

* A formal, legal agreement should be drawn up that specifies:
  - who the client is
  - a full description of the nature of the work and what achievements (reports, training, recommendations, etc.) by the consultant for the client will constitute fulfillment of the contract
  - the timescale involved in completing the work
  - the fee to be charged, plus expenses, plus VAT, and when fee payments are to be paid
  - the liability of both parties
  - how the contract can be terminated if either party wishes to do so.

* Your terms of reference.

* Where the work is to be carried out e.g. the physical working conditions.

* Reporting procedures if you have to work off-site.

(iii) MAINTAINING A GOOD RELATIONSHIP WITH THE CLIENT

At all stages during the consultancy process it will be important for you to maintain an impeccable relationship with all members of the client's organisation. To do this :

* Keep the client fully informed of the progress you make, the successes you achieve and difficulties you encounter. Be totally honest about these. Never make false claims.

* Arrange for regular de-briefing sessions with the client to discuss the progress you make.

* Ensure that all work that you give to the client is meticulously presented - the client will be judging your ability to complete the contract at all stages of the process.

* Establish an informal relationship with clients, getting to know their interests, hobbies, likes, and family relationships. This gives you conversation topics other than the work, and will be helpful for developing a long-term association.

The relationship that you establish with the client is clearly an essential ingredient of the consultancy process and every effort should be made to nurture it into a friendly, yet business-like one.

(iv) UNDERTAKING THE WORK

You will have been recruited because of your specialised skills. The client will naturally have certain expectations that you will wish to meet. To achieve a successful outcome you need to bear in mind those points raised in Chapter Twelve - Thinking Skills, as this really is why you have been recruited:

* Clearly define the problem or nature of the consultancy at the outset, and establish mutually agreed objectives.

* Use divergent thinking skills to develop creative solutions to the problem - the client will be looking for new ideas, ones perhaps which have not already been considered.

* Adopt professional standards when collecting data e.g. follow the Market Research Society's Code of Conduct when undertaking questionnaire research.

* Follow logical problem solving and decision making steps.

* Critically evaluate all possible solutions to the problem.

* Draw reasoned conclusions, and produce data that are academically sound and free from ideological statements.

In undertaking the work you will have to manage your own time effectively to ensure that all deadlines are met.

TIME MANAGEMENT SKILLS

In consultancy work time is of the essence. You should have worked out beforehand how long you expect to be involved with the client, and your fee will have been based on this. If you overrun, then you are unlikely to be able to charge a higher fee. The client will be wanting to see the results of your labours as soon as possible - profitability might depend upon it. Thus, you must be able to plan your working schedule effectively. This involves the following:

* Arrange the work into order of priority. You must decide at the outset what are the most important tasks that need to be carried out, and the least important. The tasks should be listed, and ranked in order of priority.

* In arranging the order of priority for the work you should take a long term view. You must think and plan ahead. For example if certain information is required in two weeks time, and that information has to be collected, then the research process to obtain the information needs to be instigated immediately.

* If interviews are to be conducted with colleagues of the client, or other people, these should be arranged well in advance to allow all concerned to prepare for them.

* On a daily basis, a plan of action should be drawn up - 'things to do today', once again in order of priority. Time should be set aside each day for making telephone calls, for dealing with unplanned events, and for writing up the progress made to date.

* Ensure that all working time is constructively used.

In thinking about managing your time, you must work out what you have to achieve in the time available, then consider how much can be achieved day by day, and translate this into a diary of activities. During the course of the consultancy you can check with this diary to see whether you are on schedule. The key to successful time management is to have a realistic plan of action that sets out all the steps involved in completing the consultancy work. Set targets that have to be met if the work is to completed on time. You should ensure that each of these 'incremental' targets is attained.

When such an approach is adopted, you know precisely what has to be achieved each day and each week.

(v) PRESENTING THE WORK

If you manage your time efficiently then the work will normally be completed to schedule. Your presentation of the final work needs to be meticulous. If you produce a written report then follow all the guidelines given in Chapter Five - Written Communication Skills. In particular, though, you must remember to:

* Be concise, clear and to the point. Follow all the conventions in writing academically sound data discussed in Chapter Twelve.

* Structure the report as in Chapter Five, and make sure that there is an 'Executive Summary' at the beginning - this provides an overview of the key points raised and is useful in giving the reader a picture of the report's content.

* Pay careful attention to the front cover - remember this will be the first thing the client sees and so it must create a favourable impression.

* Provide a title page that indicates the title of the project, who has completed it, their qualifications, and the date.

* Check to make sure that there are no grammatical errors. Have the report word-processed and printed using a daisy-wheel or laser printer. Use a desk-top publishing programme to produce diagrams/tables/pie charts/histograms etc.

* Thoroughly proof read the report to ensure that all typing errors have been corrected.

* Find out how many copies of the report the client requires, and arrange for these to be printed or photocopied.

* Check to make sure that all the pages are in the correct order and then have the report bound.

* Retain a personal copy as a permanent record of the work.

* Present the report personally and discuss the main findings with the client.

In addition to the report the client may also require you to make a formal oral presentation. It is likely that the presentation will involve communicating data, and their interpretation, to the audience. Remember the points raised in Chapters Six and Eight. In particular you should:

* Produce a handout of the key data being referred to and distribute this to the audience prior to the presentation, giving them the opportunity to digest the information.

* Prepare effective visual aids for communicating the main points that are raised - use 35mm photographic slides for maximum impact.

* Do not spend too much time describing the data, concentrate on their interpretation - what do they mean for the client?

If you follow the above points then you will have completed a successful piece of work and hopefully created a good impression with the client.

The true test of your ability is how far you met the objectives that were initially set. This, plus the ability to deliver on time, every time, are the hallmarks of a competent consultant.

(vi) FOLLOW-UP PROCEDURES

To foster a continuing relationship with the client, you should maintain regular contact, commencing with the 'CSQ', the client satisfaction questionnaire. Soon after work has been completed questionnaires should be sent to clients asking them to formally evaluate you and the work that you completed. Not only will this provide valuable feedback to you about the client's satisfaction with your work, but will show the client that you do care about your customers.

Thereafter, visit the client from time to time to see what progress is being made, and to further the personal relationship that will have developed. Indeed, the client might have further consultancy work, or may refer you to other business associates.

Consultancy skills, therefore, draw upon all the TPS mentioned in this book. In the discussion above it has been implied that you are working by yourself, but on many occasions you might be leading a team, or working as a group member requiring you to use your group work skills. The consultancy might involve implementing decisions for the client. Your full range of personal skills, assertive and affective, will be required here, as well as selling and negotiating skills to convince others to change their behaviour. Following all the guidelines detailed in this book will strengthen your skills and increase your chances of confirming success as a consultant.

CONCLUSION

The purpose of the preceding chapters in this book has been to highlight some of the TPS that individuals need to develop. This book will act as a reference text, informing you what a competent TPS comprises. After reading it, you need to practise each of the skills discussed, in order to improve your level of competence. As mentioned in the Introduction, however, TPS are not developed overnight. Their development is a life-long process, with each new business and social encounter providing you with the opportunity to try out new behaviours. It is this experimentation-experience process, followed by a time of reflection, which leads to successful TPS development.

... Good Luck ...

INDEX